PEACE WITH JUSTICE

PEACE WITH JUSTICE

NOAM CHOMSKY IN AUSTRALIA

Edited by Clinton Fernandes

© Copyright 2012

All rights reserved. Apart from any uses permitted by Australia's Copyright Act 1968, no part of this book may be reproduced by any process without prior written permission from the copyright owners. Inquiries should be directed to the publisher.

Monash University Publishing
Building 4, Monash University
Clayton, Victoria 3800, Australia
www.publishing.monash.edu

Monash University Publishing brings to the world publications which advance the best traditions of humane and enlightened thought.

Monash University Publishing titles pass through a rigorous process of independent peer review.

National Library of Australia Cataloguing-in-Publication entry:

Title: Peace with justice : Noam Chomsky in Australia / editor, Clinton Fernandes.

ISBN: 9781921867361 (pbk.)

Series: Investigating Power Series.

Notes: Includes index.

Subjects: Chomsky, Noam--Political and social views; Chomsky, Noam--Interviews; Sydney Peace Prize; Award winners--Sydney.

Other Authors/Contributors: Fernandes, Clinton.

Dewey Number: 320

www.publishing.monash.edu/books/pwj-9781921867361.html

Design: Les Thomas

Printed in Australia by Griffin Press an Accredited ISO AS/NZS 14001:2004 Environmental Management System printer.

Foreword

It should be no secret that Noam Chomsky was nominated several times for Australia's only international award for peace, the Sydney Peace Prize. During that time, Professor Chomsky's wife Carol, his lifelong companion in struggles for justice, suffered a terminal illness and for several years, in order to be with his wife and look after her, Noam Chomsky refused invitations to travel far beyond their Massachusetts home. In this loving, caring role he obviously found a sense of inner peace, another measure of the man.

Eighteen months after Carol's death Noam Chomsky was again nominated and after the usual three months of deliberations over that year's twenty-two candidates, Chomsky became the Peace Prize jury's unanimous, enthusiastic choice. Even among a diverse jury of eight men and women, there was a sigh of relief that Chomsky had been chosen and on this occasion would be likely to accept. At last Australians would have a chance to hear and see him and to express their gratitude for his lifetime's work for freedom of speech, for challenges to authoritarianism, for peace with justice.

Chomsky has been described as one of the West's most influential intellectuals in the cause of peace, as the most significant challenger of unjust power and as an individual who is not only brilliant but also heroic. Members of the Peace Prize jury agreed with such judgments. Their citation for the award of the 2011 Sydney Peace Prize read:

> For inspiring the convictions of millions about a common humanity and for unfailing moral courage. For critical analysis of democracy and power, for challenging secrecy, censorship and violence and for creating hope through scholarship and activism to promote the attainment of universal human rights.

In a press release issued a week before Noam Chomsky arrived in Australia, I elaborated the reasons for the jury's choice by insisting that Professor Chomsky gives hope to millions because he articulates alternatives in countries' domestic and foreign policies. Chomsky himself admits to being inspired by the British mathematician, philosopher and nuclear disarmament campaigner Bertrand Russell, who insisted that a primary goal of any education is to elicit and fortify whatever creative impulse a person possesses, 'through literature, laughter and creative discourse'. Chomsky also allies himself with his great friend the Palestinian social scientist and musician Edward Said who wrote, 'The intellectual must be unwilling to accept easy formulas or ready-made clichés or the smooth, ever-accommodating confirmations of what the powerful or conventional have to say.'

On 2 November 2011, in a crowded Sydney Town Hall, Chomsky delivered the City of Sydney Peace Prize Lecture, titled 'Revolutionary Pacifism: Choices and Prospects'. Nearly seventeen years before, at the invitation of that courageous campaigner for his people, Jose Ramos-Horta, Chomsky had come to the same platform in the Sydney Town Hall. On that occasion he warned his Australian audience of the massive human rights abuses that were occurring in East Timor and that this was a genocide comparable in terms of deaths per head of population to the genocide in Cambodia. On 3 November, at a gala dinner ceremony in Sydney University's elegant, nineteenth-century MacLaurin Hall, Professor Chomsky received the 2011 Peace Prize from a previous recipient, the legendary Indigenous leader and 'Father of Reconciliation', Patrick Dodson.

The following morning in a welcome entitled 'Voices Inspiring Peace', Chomsky appeared in the Cabramatta High School as the guest of 2000 high school students representing twelve different schools. Against a background of an imaginative, informative collage of his life and work, their festival welcome in Cabramatta's gymnasium included a choir, drummers, dancers and student poets. Questions to Chomsky about human rights and international affairs followed these performers.

From the gymnasium the guests proceeded to the school's playground and peace garden where Chomsky and other guests engaged in conversation with students from all over the world, dressed in their eye-catching national costumes. After Professor Chomsky planted a tree of remembrance in the peace garden, the morning finished with the release of peace doves who first circled the garden then disappeared into the sky. Joy across Noam Chomsky's face and laugher in the eyes of the students who joined him in releasing the doves provided a great opportunity for photographers and an unforgettable end to Noam Chomsky's time in Sydney. After those demanding four days you could be forgiven for thinking that he had ended his commitments to Australia. Instead, a few hours later he flew to Melbourne to address a crowd of over 4000 in that city's convention centre and the following morning he flew to Adelaide to give the Edward Said oration.

As he has done throughout his life, Noam Chomsky did not spare himself in the service of others. With the close attention of his good friend Dr Clinton Fernandes – some might refer to Clinton as Noam's minder – he proceeded without complaint from one appointment to another, many of them not planned such as his meeting on the steps of the Sydney Town Hall with the 'Women in Black' who stand each week in silent vigil against the occupation of Palestine. Minutes before delivering his Peace Prize lecture he also found time to address members of the Occupy Movement, the Sydney group who are supporting the original Wall Street protesters against corporate greed, massive inequalities, deeply entrenched poverty and the concentration of wealth in the hands of only a tiny proportion of the US population.

Chomsky's support for the Occupy Movement conveys why he meets the 'peace with justice' criteria for the award of the Sydney Peace Prize. In an Occupy Movement blog, Chomsky wrote, 'The courageous and honorable protests underway in Wall Street should serve to bring this calamity to public attention and to lead to dedicated efforts to overcome it and set the society on a more healthy course.'

Perhaps the most fitting end to this foreword for a book signifying 'Noam Chomsky in Australia' comes from another of his great friends, the Indian novelist, writer, human rights campaigner and herself a former recipient of the Sydney Peace Prize, Arundhati Roy. Arundhati wrote, 'He is a man beyond prizes. He is somebody who has helped the world to deepen its understanding of what peace means, of what war means and to expose the subterfuge that lies under the easy deployment of those words.'

Professor Stuart Rees, 3 April 2012

Professor Rees is Director of the Sydney Peace Foundation and Professor Emeritus of the University of Sydney.

Contents

Foreword v

Acknowledgements. x

Introduction
Peace with justice : Noam Chomsky in Australia. xi
Clinton Fernandes

Revolutionary pacifism: choices and prospects
2011 City of Sydney Peace Prize Lecture 1

Sydney Peace Prize acceptance speech
2011 City of Sydney Peace Gala Dinner. 17

2011 Edward Said Memorial Lecture 23

Changing contours of global order
Deakin University lecture 57

Interview with Phillip Adams 89

Problems of knowledge and freedom
In conversation with Mary Kostakidis. 109

Interview with Richard Glover 129

Selections from additional interviews 137

Index 153

Acknowledgements

For the swift completion of this book, I acknowledge the generous support of Professor David Lovell, Head of the School of Humanities and Social Sciences, University of New South Wales (Canberra). I also thank Jo Muggleton, Lydia Randall, Kate Hatch, Nathan Hollier, Debra Salvagno and Noam Chomsky.

Introduction

Peace with justice: Noam Chomsky in Australia

Clinton Fernandes

'Not by might, nor by power, but by my spirit ...' (Zechariah 4-6)

In November 2011, the cognitive scientist, philosopher and political activist Noam Chomsky arrived in Australia to receive the Sydney Peace Prize, which is awarded for 'peace with justice'. He delivered lectures and answered questions about economics, history, international relations, linguistics, philosophy, justice and much more. This book is an edited reconstruction of talks, informal notes, interviews and transcripts of lectures delivered during his few days in Sydney, Melbourne and Adelaide.[1]

It is no accident that Noam concluded his Sydney Peace Prize Lecture with a call for justice for East Timor – for the perpetrators to be brought to justice and the whereabouts of the disappeared to be clarified. On his last visit to Australia, in January 1995, he had spoken extensively in support of East Timor's right to self-determination. He was not adopting an eclectic, scattergun approach. Rather, he followed a basic moral principle: we have a special obligation to terminate those atrocities for which we (through our governments) bear responsibility. He spoke up for East Timor because the US, the UK and Australia aided Indonesia's genocidal operations in that territory, where thirty per cent of the population died between 1975 and 1999.[2] This was perhaps the worst death toll relative to total population since the Holocaust.

From 1975 to 1979, there was mass murder of comparable proportions in East Timor and in Cambodia. The slaughter in East Timor could have been terminated by withdrawing Western support to the Indonesian military. But many self-described 'public intellectuals' in Australia and the US

---

1   I have rephrased some of the material from his oral responses in order to make it more readable, added footnotes throughout, and expanded on some replies in order to provide relevant details and evidence. Noam approved the text before I sent it to the publisher.
2   C. Fernandes, *The Independence of East Timor*, Sussex Academic Press, Eastbourne, 2011, especially chapters 1, 2, 3 and 9.

said little about it, preferring instead to denounce Pol Pot in Cambodia, where they had no prospect of terminating the atrocities of the Khmer Rouge. Other intellectuals repeatedly ignored opportunities to highlight the atrocities in East Timor, or their connection to Australian foreign policy. Robert Manne, for instance, was the editor of *Quadrant* magazine between 1989 and 1997. I read through every issue of *Quadrant* during the eight years of his term as editor, and the paucity of East Timorese voices is remarkable.[3] Instead, he gave space to writers like Peter Ryan, who complained about 'these left-wing lunatics' in the 'Timor claque' who 'resemble the English prigs of the left in the 1930s'.[4] Under Manne's editorship, *Quadrant* also carried a long article by John Hirst that blamed the Australian media ('perhaps the press should be more careful about what it publishes') and attacked refugees who campaigned for their country ('we should impose some limits on Asian refugees in their campaigning against the governments they have fled').[5] Manne railed against crimes that he had no ability to stop (Cambodia), while ignoring a privileged opportunity to struggle against crimes in which his government was complicit (Australia's support for Indonesia's occupation of East Timor). This is why Noam says that 'the intellectual tradition is one of servility to power and if I didn't betray it I'd be ashamed of myself'.[6]

Noam had taken action in support of East Timor as far back as the 1970s, testifying before the UN Decolonisation Committee and writing and speaking at every opportunity.

According to expert evidence tendered to East Timor's Truth Commission, 'Chomsky's words on this matter had a real influence, sometimes indirect, and history should record it, because it was of vital importance in helping to alter the state of widespread ignorance about East Timor that then existed in the United States and elsewhere'.[7] I well remember my late friend, the heroic activist Andrew McNaughtan, telling me how Noam's 1979 analysis helped clarify his outlook on world affairs.[8]

---

3   For more, see C. Fernandes, 'The Wild Man in the Wings', *Overland*, vol. 180, 2005. For a rare exception, see D. Glover 1995, 'East Timor: A challenge to conservatives', *Quadrant*, December 1995, pp.30–36.
4   P. Ryan, 'Indonesia and Me', *Quadrant*, July–August 1995, p.120.
5   J. Hirst, 'In defence of appeasement', *Quadrant*, April 1996, pp.10–16.
6   N. Chomsky, *Interview*, BBC2, 25 November 1992.
7   A. Kohen, Testimony before East Timor's Commission for Reception, Truth and Reconciliation, 16 March 2004.
8   N. Chomsky and E. Herman, *The Political Economy of Human Rights*, vols I and II, South End Press, Boston, 1979.

His words may be well known but his financial support of the cause is largely unknown. When the US media were refusing to interview Timorese refugees, claiming that they had no access to them, an impoverished activist who felt that Congress needed to hear their testimony decided to ask Noam for help. He obliged immediately. The activist says, 'I intended to pay him back but there never was enough money. I never did pay him back, and he never asked for it'.[9] The money paid for the airfares of several refugees, bringing them to the US, where lobbying efforts eventually had an effect. An East Timorese activist later wrote, 'we learnt that the Chomsky factor and East Timor were a deadly combination' and 'proved to be too powerful for those who tried to defeat us'.[10] When the East Timor Action Network was formed in the US after the 1991 Santa Cruz massacre, the first donation it received was from Noam Chomsky. Similarly, activists who worked on the Philippines Information Bulletin in the 1970s always received their first subscription renewal in the mail every year from Noam Chomsky. Activists in numerous other causes have also received his unflagging, discreet support. The Noam Chomsky I know is unaffected by academic snobbery: he treats the questions of people from less prestigious institutions than his, or from no institution at all, with at least as much attention as the questions of Nobel Prize winners.

Noam's moral calculus places him at the very core of the Jewish tradition into which he was born in 1928. His mother was a widely respected teacher and his father was a renowned Hebrew scholar who once described the major objective of his life as 'the education of individuals who are well integrated, free and independent in their thinking, concerned about improving and enhancing the world, and eager to participate in making life more meaningful and worthwhile for all'.[11] His study of Hebrew culture converged with his political concerns, and he became a Zionist youth leader in the cultural Zionist movement. This movement supported a Jewish cultural home in Palestine and Arab-Jewish cooperation within a socialist framework. It opposed 'the deeply antidemocratic concept of a Jewish state', which would inevitably discriminate against non-Jews.[12] In his late teens, Noam helped his mother write and direct a play, *Hevele Mashiah*, about Jewish refugees

---

9   C. Fernandes, *The Independence of East Timor*, p. 59.
10 A. Pereira, Preface to N. Chomsky, *Perspectives on Power*, Black Rose, Montreal, 1997, p.viii.
11 C.P. Otero, 'Chomsky and the Libertarian Tradition: A Renewed Egalitarian Vision, a Coherent Social Theory and Incisive, Up-to-Date Analysis', vol.3, p.5 of C.P. Otero, ed., *Noam Chomsky: Critical Assessments*, four volumes, Routledge, London, 1994.
12 J. Peck, ed., *The Chomsky Reader*, Serpents Tail, London, 1987, p.7.

yearning to go to Palestine.¹³ It showed the horror of the Holocaust being followed by the formation of Israel. Noam continued to argue against the partition of Palestine, arguing 'that the socialist institutions of the Yishuv – the pre-state Jewish settlement in Palestine – would not survive the state system'.¹⁴

Noam 'reacted with virtually uncritical support for Israel' during the June 1967 war.¹⁵ He later realised that the threat to Israel had been exaggerated, and then the ongoing belligerent occupation of Palestinian land led him to speak out against the US government's support that is a crucial enabler of it. Often attacked as 'anti-American' or a 'self-hating Jew', Noam's actions are derived from his place at the very core of the Jewish prophetic tradition. Rabbi Abraham Joshua Heschel's study of the biblical prophets demonstrated that the prophets were not fortune-tellers who predicted the future. Rather, they were concerned 'about widows and orphans, about the corruption of judges and affairs of the market place'. Their moral sense was aroused not by 'the spiritual realities of the Beyond, but the life of the people; not the glories of eternity, but the blights of society'.¹⁶ Unsurprisingly, they were hated by those who were committed to an unjust status quo. In the first book of Kings, for instance, the militaristic King Ahab and his elite supporters despised the prophet Elijah, describing him as 'ocher yisrael' or 'hater of Israel'. Noam is attacked in almost identical terms. One wonders how future generations will view his detractors. He has no shortage of detractors of course, and misinformation and outright falsehoods about him are in wide circulation – all the more so because Noam does not sue for defamation on principle.¹⁷

Although he is known for his political activism, his professional reputation derives from his achievements in the field of linguistics and from his philosophy of science, both of which have been revolutionary. His conversations with Mary Kostakidis in this volume touch on these specialised fields. Since there is a lot of curiosity about Noam's linguistics

---

13 H. Feinberg, *Elsie Chomsky: A life in Jewish Education*, Hadassah International Research Institute on Jewish Women, Waltham, 1999, pp.20–21.
14 *The Chomsky Reader*, p.9.
15 N. Chomsky, *Middle East Illusions*, Rowman & Littlefield, Lanham, p.99.
16 A.J. Heschel, *The Prophets*, two volumes, Harper & Row, New York, 1962, vol.1, p.3 and vol.2, p.144.
17 For a detailed discussion of two major falsehoods, with full documentation and evidence, see http://hass.unsw.adfa.edu.au/timor_companion/politics_of_starvation/cambodia.php and http://hass.unsw.adfa.edu.au/timor_companion/politics_of_starvation/chomsky_and_free_speech.php.

project, I provide a basic, non-technical outline of just one aspect of his method: his abstraction and idealisation of complex phenomena in a manner similar to Galileo's cosmological innovations.

Galileo made considerable use of abstraction in his scientific work as he overturned the Aristotelian view of the universe. According to this view, the earth was the centre of the universe. The sun, the moon and the planets rotated round the earth. As a consequence, there were two kinds of motion – circular and linear. The sun and the moon appeared to move in a circle around the earth; they (and other 'heavenly bodies') possessed circular motion. Their motion contrasted with motion on the earth, which was linear; an object dropped on the earth fell in a straight line. Terrestrial motion therefore occurs in straight lines: plants grow vertically, human vision follows straight lines (we cannot see around corners), and so on. For Aristotelians, heavenly motion and terrestrial motion were two quite different things. Galileo's theory defied this commonsense observation. His abstract, counter-intuitive approach did not directly reflect the way we perceive reality, but started with an imaginative leap that postulated the rotation of the earth around its axis and involved an inferential chain that later made contact successfully with the real world.

After Galileo, Newton also employed abstractions in his idea of gravity. He suggested that heavenly and terrestrial motion could be unified with the idea of a gravitational force that operated in perfectly straight lines. But by conceiving of linear movement, Newton's account was abstract; it did not precisely reflect terrestrial motion. After all, a ball thrown in the air does not move in a straight line but in an arc, and an object dropped on to a flat surface does not move in a perfectly straight line in real life. But Newton's abstraction explained the observed motions of the planets and their moons, and was also confirmed from other phenomena such as the tides and orbits of comets.

Noam too used abstraction and idealisation in order to achieve an explanatory theory of language. The classic statement is in his *Aspects of the Theory of Syntax*:

> Linguistic theory is concerned primarily with an ideal speaker-listener, in a completely homogeneous speech-community, who knows its language perfectly and is unaffected by such grammatically irrelevant conditions as memory limitations, distractions, shifts of attention and interest, and errors (random or characteristic) in applying his knowledge of the language in actual performance … We thus make a fundamental

distinction between competence (the speaker-hearer's knowledge of his language) and performance (the actual use of language in concrete situations).[18]

In focusing on an ideal speaker-listener, Noam made an abstraction whose character he explains when he writes that such a speaker-listener 'knows its language perfectly and is unaffected by performance problems'. By 'ideal' he means 'idealised', not 'best'. He sets aside aspects of language that do not illuminate the underlying system of knowledge, or the way this system is acquired. Of course, the issue is which idealisations should be made, not whether one ought to idealise in the first place. This is because all descriptions of a language make idealisations even if they do not acknowledge them. A grammar book of Tetum (one of East Timor's languages) contains numerous grammatical rules, but it (obviously) says nothing about the actual speech of a native Tetum speaker-listener. Such speech would certainly contain 'grammatically irrelevant conditions [such] as memory limitations, distractions, shifts of attention and interest, and errors …' but no grammar book would be expected to deal with them. The Tetum described in the book therefore makes an idealisation of the performance of native speakers. This is a most useful idealisation because it tells the reader what all native speakers of the language have in common by virtue of being native speakers of the language. In this sense, any description of Tetum or any other language focuses on knowledge rather than behaviour.

Noam's mention of a 'completely homogenous speech community' is another abstraction. It ignores the wide variation in pronunciation, grammar, vocabulary and usage in favour of an idealised version in which there is only one kind of English. There is a good reason for this idealisation. Although real speech communities are not homogenous, the idealisation 'open[s] the possibility for discovering fundamental properties of the language faculty'.[19] Regardless of one's ability to perform the variations in pronunciation and the rest, one's own variety and the other varieties must still conform to the underlying principles of knowledge of language. So the linguist loses nothing by ignoring variation, which is not a relevant factor in obtaining deep insights into the 'system of knowledge' present in the human language faculty.

---

18 N. Chomsky, *Aspects of the Theory of Syntax*, MIT Press, Cambridge, MA, 1965.
19 N. Chomsky, *Rules and Representations*, Columbia University Press, New York, 1980, pp. 25–6.

Noam's abstraction of instantaneous language acquisition means that he conducts his research as though it did not take years to become a native speaker. In real life, of course, native speakers acquire their knowledge of language until just before puberty. But Noam hypothesises that nothing in real language acquisition affects the process in such a way that the outcome would be different had the process been instantaneous. Finally, Noam is interested in 'the physical mechanisms' involved in the system of knowledge and in the use of this knowledge. In this final question, still on the horizon, it is clear that Noam sees linguistics as a theoretical psychology. It is worth recalling a previous example from the history of science to help clarify what is at stake. In the nineteenth century, chemistry developed abstract representations of complex molecules long before the physicists were able to show, in the early part of the twentieth century, that such things existed. It was much later that physicists began to discover the physical entities that had the properties corresponding to the chemists' abstract computational ideas. These computational ideas told physicists what to look for. They could not have developed the structure of the atom and the molecule if nineteenth-century chemistry hadn't provided the abstract theories. Those theories of the chemist are similar to a linguist's theory of computations of the brain. Cognitive linguistics is to the future brain sciences what nineteenth-century chemistry was to quantum physics. Developments in related disciplines such as neuro-linguistics, which looks for the neurological mechanisms underlying different components of linguistics theory, and advances in technology, particularly in brain imaging techniques, will continue to contribute to this area of inquiry.

When reading Noam Chomsky on linguistics, one reviewer wrote, one repeatedly has the impression of attending to one of the more powerful thinkers that ever lived. That's true, but few of us can aspire to emulate those towering achievements. His decency, humility, doggedness and willingness to deploy his analytical skills in the service of activists are in a different category; we can all try to do that. Now in his eighty-third year, one only hopes Noam keeps going for many more years – and that he visits Australia again.

Revolutionary pacifism: choices and prospects

2011 City of Sydney Peace Prize Lecture

Sydney Town Hall, 2 November 2011

As we all know, the United Nations was founded 'to save succeeding generations from the scourge of war'. The words can only elicit deep regret when we consider how we have acted to fulfill that aspiration, though there have been a few significant successes, notably in Europe.

For centuries, Europe had been the most violent place on earth, with murderous and destructive internal conflicts and the forging of a culture of war that enabled Europe to conquer most of the world, shocking the victims, who were hardly pacifists, but were 'appalled by the all-destructive fury of European warfare', in the words of British military historian Geoffrey Parker.[1] The culture of war enabled Europe to impose on its conquests what Adam Smith called 'the savage injustice of the Europeans', England in the lead, as he did not fail to emphasise.[2] The global conquest took a particularly horrifying form in what is sometimes called the 'Anglosphere', England and its offshoots, settler-colonial societies in which the indigenous societies were devastated and their people dispersed or exterminated. But since 1945

---

1   Geoffrey Parker, *The Military Revolution: Military innovation and the rise of the West, 1500–1800*, Cambridge University Press, Cambridge, 1996, p. 118: 'Different as these regions [Central and Northeast America, Siberia, some coastal areas of sub-Saharan Africa and the islands of Southeast Asia] and their inhabitants undoubtedly were, their experience of the European invaders was, in one crucial respect, identical: the white men, they found, fought dirty and (what was worse) fought to kill. Thus the Narragansett Indians of New England strongly disapproved of the colonists' way of making war. "It was too furious," one brave told an English captain in 1638, "and [it] slays too many men." The captain did not deny it. The Indians, he speculated, "might fight seven years and not kill seven men." Roger Williams, a colonial governor, likewise admitted that the Indians' fighting "was farre less bloudy and devouring than the cruel wars of Europe." Meanwhile, on the other side of the world, the peoples of Indonesia were equally appalled by the all-destructive fury of European warfare.'
2   Adam Smith, *The Wealth of Nations*, University of Chicago Press, Chicago, 1976 (original 1776), Book IV, Chapter I: 'The savage injustice of the Europeans rendered an event, which ought to have been beneficial to all, ruinous and destructive to several of those unfortunate countries.'

Europe has become internally the most peaceful and in many ways most humane region of the earth – which is the source of some its current travail, an important topic that I will have to put aside.

In scholarship, this dramatic transition is often attributed to the thesis of the 'democratic peace': democracies do not go to war with one another. Not to be overlooked, however, is that Europeans came to realise that the next time they indulge in their favorite pastime of slaughtering one another, the game will be over: civilisation has developed means of destruction that can only be used against those too weak to retaliate in kind, a large part of the appalling history of the post-World War II years. It is not that the threat has ended. US-Soviet confrontations came painfully close to virtually terminal nuclear war in ways that are shattering to contemplate, when we inspect them closely. One might argue, in fact, that it is a miracle that the catastrophe has not yet occurred. From November 1946 to October 1973 there were nineteen incidents in which US strategic nuclear forces were involved. We do not have the record since, nor the record for the USSR and other powers.[3] And the threat of nuclear war remains all too ominously alive, a matter to which I will briefly return.

Can we proceed to at least limit the scourge of war? One answer is given by absolute pacifists, including people I respect though I have never felt able to go beyond that. A somewhat more persuasive stand, I think, is that of the pacifist thinker and social activist A.J. Muste, one of the great figures of twentieth-century America, in my opinion: what he called 'revolutionary pacifism'. Muste disdained the search for peace without justice. He urged that 'one must be a revolutionary before one can be a pacifist' – by which he meant that we must cease to 'acquiesce [so] easily in evil conditions', and must deal 'honestly and adequately with this ninety percent of our problem' – 'the violence on which the present system is based, and all the evil – material and spiritual – this entails for the masses of men throughout the world'. Unless we do so, he argued, 'there is something ludicrous, and perhaps hypocritical, about our concern over the ten per cent of the violence employed by the rebels against oppression' – no matter how hideous they may be.[4] He was confronting the hardest problem of the day for a pacifist, the question whether to take part in the anti-fascist war.

---

3   Barry M. Blechman and Stephen S. Kaplan, *Force Without War: U.S. Armed Forces as a Political Instrument*, Brookings Institute Press, 1978, Table 2–8, p. 48.
4   A.J. Muste, 'Pacifism and Class War', in Nat Hentoff, ed., *The Essays of A.J. Muste*, Bobbs-Merrill, Indianapolis, 1967, pp. 179–185.

In writing about Muste's stand forty-five years ago, I quoted his warning that 'The problem after a war is with the victor. He thinks he has just proved that war and violence pay. Who will teach him a lesson?'[5] His observation was all too apt at the time, while the Indochina wars were raging, and on all too many other occasions since.

The allies did not fight 'the good war', as it is commonly called, because of the awful crimes of fascism. Before their attacks on Western powers, fascists were treated rather sympathetically, particularly 'that admirable Italian gentleman', as FDR called Mussolini.[6] Even Hitler was regarded by the US State Department as a 'moderate' holding off the extremists of right and left.[7] The British were even more sympathetic, particularly the business world. Roosevelt's close confidant Sumner Welles reported to the president that the Munich settlement that dismembered Czechoslovakia 'presented the opportunity for the establishment by the nations of the world of a new world order based upon justice and upon law', in which the Nazi moderates would play a leading role.[8] As late as April 1941, the influential statesman George Kennan, at the dovish extreme of the postwar planning spectrum, wrote from his consular post in Berlin that German leaders have no wish to 'see other people suffer under German rule', are 'most anxious that their new subjects should be happy in their care', and are making 'important compromises' to assure this benign outcome.[9]

Though by then the horrendous facts of the Holocaust were well known, they scarcely entered the Nuremberg trials, which focused on aggression, 'the supreme international crime differing only from other war crimes in that it contains within itself the accumulated evil of the whole': in Indochina, Iraq, and all too many other places where we have much to

---

5 N. Chomsky, 'The Revolutionary Pacifism of A.J. Muste: On the Backgrounds of the Pacific War', in *American Power And The New Mandarins: Historical and Political Essays*, Pantheon, New York, 1967, pp. 159–220.
6 David F. Schmitz, *Thank God They're On Our Side: The United States and Right-Wing Dictatorships, 1921–1965*, Chapel Hill: University of North Carolina Press, 1999, p. 139.
7 David F. Schmitz, *The United States and Fascist Italy, 1922–1940*, pp. 133, 140, 174 and chapter 9; *Foreign Relations of the United States, 1933*, vol. II, US Government Printing Office, 1949.
8 *New York Times*, 4 October 1938.
9 Christopher Simpson, *The Splendid Blond Beast: Money, Law, and Genocide in the Twentieth Century*, Common Courage Press, Monroe, 1995: 'It cannot be said that German policy is motivated by any sadistic desire to see other people suffer under German rule ... Germans are most anxious that their new subjects should be happy in their care; they are willing to make what seems to them important compromises to achieve this result, and they are unable to understand why these measures should not be successful.'

contemplate.[10] The horrifying crimes of Japanese fascism were virtually ignored in the postwar peace settlements. Japan's aggression began exactly eighty years ago, with the staged Mukden incident,[11] but for the West, it began ten years later, with the attack on military bases in two US possessions. India and other major Asian countries refused even to attend the 1951 San Francisco Peace Treaty conference because of the exclusion of Japan's crimes in Asia – and also because of Washington's establishment of a major military base in conquered Okinawa, still there despite the energetic protests of the population.

It is useful to reflect on several aspects of the Pearl Harbor attack. One is the reaction of historian and Kennedy advisor Arthur Schlesinger to the bombing of Baghdad in March 2003. He recalled FDR's words when Japan bombed Pearl Harbor on 'a date which will live in infamy'. 'Today it is we Americans who live in infamy', Schlesinger wrote,[12] as our government adopts the policies of imperial Japan – thoughts that were barely articulated elsewhere in the mainstream, and quickly suppressed: I could find no mention of this principled stand in the praise for Schlesinger's accomplishments when he died a few years later.

We can also learn a lot about ourselves by carrying Schlesinger's lament a few steps further. By today's standards, Japan's attack was justified, indeed meritorious. Japan, after all, was exercising the much lauded doctrine of anticipatory self-defense when it bombed military bases in Hawaii and the Philippines, two virtual US colonies, with reasons far more compelling than anything that Bush and Blair could conjure up when they adopted the policies of imperial Japan in 2003. Japanese leaders were well aware that B-17 Flying Fortresses were coming off the Boeing production lines, and they could read in the American press that these killing machines would be able to burn down Tokyo, a 'city of rice-paper and wood houses'. A November 1940 plan to 'bomb Tokyo and other big cities' was enthusiastically received by Secretary of State Cordell Hull. President Roosevelt was 'simply delighted'

---

10 Tribunal opinion 30 September 1946: 'The charges in the indictment that the defendants planned and waged aggressive war are charges of the utmost gravity. War is essentially an evil thing. Its consequences are not confined to the belligerent states alone, but affect the whole world. To initiate a war of aggression, therefore, is not only an international crime; it is the supreme international crime, differing only from other crimes in that it contains within itself the accumulated evil of the whole.' http://avalon.law.yale.edu/imt/09-30-46.asp.
11 18–19 September 1931.
12 Arthur Schlesinger Jr., 'Good Foreign Policy a Casualty of War', *Los Angeles Times*, Sunday, 23 March 2003, sec. M, p. 1.

at the plans 'to burn out the industrial heart of the Empire with fire-bomb attacks on the teeming bamboo ant heaps of Honshu and Kyushu', outlined by their author, Air Force General Chennault. By July 1941, the Air Corps was ferrying B-17s to the Far East for this purpose, assigning half of all the big bombers to this region, taking them from the Atlantic sea-lanes. They were to be used if needed 'to set the paper cities of Japan on fire', according to General George Marshall, Roosevelt's main military adviser, in a press briefing three weeks before Pearl Harbor. Four days later, *New York Times* senior correspondent Arthur Krock reported US plans to bomb Japan from Siberian and Philippine bases, to which the Air Force was rushing incendiary bombs intended for civilian targets. The US knew from decoded messages that Japan was aware of these plans.[13]

History provides ample evidence to support Muste's conclusion that 'The problem after a war is with the victor, [who] thinks he has just proved that war and violence pay.' And the real answer to Muste's question, 'Who will teach him a lesson?', can only be, 'Domestic populations, if they can adopt elementary moral principles.'

Even the most uncontroversial of these principles could have a major impact on ending injustice and war. Consider the principle of universality, perhaps the most elementary of moral principles: we apply to ourselves the standards we apply to others, if not more stringent ones. The principle is universal, or nearly so, in three further respects: it is found in some form in every moral code; it is universally applauded in words, and consistently rejected in practice. The facts are plain, and should be troublesome.

The principle has a simple corollary, which suffers the same fate: we should distribute finite energies to the extent that we can influence outcomes, typically on cases for which we share responsibility. We take that for granted with regard to enemies. No one cares whether Iranian intellectuals join the ruling clerics in condemnation of the crimes of Israel or the United States. Rather, we ask what they say about their own state. We honored Soviet dissidents on the same grounds. Of course, that is not the reaction within their own societies. Their dissidents are condemned as 'anti-Soviet' or supporters of the Great Satan, much as their counterparts here are condemned as 'anti-American' or supporters of today's official enemy. And of course, punishment of those who adhere to elementary moral principles can be severe, depending on the nature of the society. In Soviet-run Czechoslovakia, for example, Vaclav Havel was imprisoned. At the same

---

13   Michael Sherry, *The Rise of American Airpower*, Yale University Press, New Haven, 1987.

time, in US-run El Salvador his counterparts had their brains blown out by an elite battalion fresh from renewed training at the John F. Kennedy School of Special Warfare in North Carolina, acting on explicit orders of the High Command, which had intimate relations with Washington.[14] We all know and respect Havel for his courageous resistance, but who can even name the leading Latin American intellectuals, Jesuit priests, who were added to the long bloody trail of the Atlacatl brigade shortly after the fall of the Berlin Wall – along with their housekeeper and daughter, since the orders were to leave no witnesses?[15]

Before we hear that these are exceptions, we might recall a truism of Latin American scholarship, reiterated by historian John Coatsworth in the recently published Cambridge University *History of the Cold War*: from 1960 to 'the Soviet collapse in 1990, the numbers of political prisoners, torture victims, and executions of nonviolent political dissenters in Latin America vastly exceeded those in the Soviet Union and its East European satellites'.[16] Among the executed were many religious martyrs, and there were mass slaughters as well, consistently supported or initiated by Washington. And the date 1960 is highly significant, for reasons we should all know, but I cannot go into here.[17]

In the West all of this is 'disappeared', to borrow the terminology of our Latin American victims. Regrettably, these are persistent features

---

14 There is now even better evidence than what was available to America's Watch in 1991. The Spanish press published a copy of the actual orders of the high command: Antonio Rubio, 'El Estado Mayor de El Salvador ordenó 'eliminar' a Ignacio Ellacuría', *El Mundo*, 21 November 2009. http://www.elmundo.es/elmundo/2009/11/21/espana/1258830475. html Also, America's Watch, *El Salvador's Decade of Terror: Human Rights Since the Assassination of Archbishop Romero*, Yale University Press, New Haven, 1991: 'The Jesuit murders were carried out by officers and troops from the elite Atlacatl Battalion, created, trained, and armed by the United States ... It is almost certain that the murder of Father Ignacio Ellacuria and the others was engineered at the highest level of the army, and it is absolutely certain that the high command acted repeatedly to cover up its involvement, sometimes with the collusion of US Embassy officials.'
15 The six Jesuit priests were Ignacio Ellacuria, Segundo Montes, Ignacio Martin-Baro, Joaquin Lopez y Lopez, Juan Ramon Moreno, and Amado Lopez. Their housekeeper was Mrs Elba Ramos. Her daughter was Celia Marisela Ramos. They were murdered on the campus of the University of Central America in San Salvador, El Salvador on 16 November 1989.
16 John H. Coatsworth, 'The Cold War in Central America, 1975–1991', *The Cambridge History of the Cold War*, vol. III, Cambridge University Press, Cambridge, 2010, p. 221: 'In other words, from 1960 to 1990, the Soviet Bloc as a whole was less repressive, measured in terms of human victims, than many individual Latin American countries.'
17 'A Program of Covert Action against the Castro Regime', 16 March 1960, declassified 9 April 1998. Society for Historians of American Foreign Relations, *SHAFR Newsletter* vol. 33, no. 3, September 2002.

of intellectual and moral culture, which we can trace back to the earliest recorded history. I think they richly underscore Muste's injunction.

If we ever hope to live up to the high ideals we passionately proclaim, and to bring the initial dream of the United Nations closer to fulfillment, we should think carefully about crucial choices that have been made, and continue to be made every day – not forgetting 'the violence on which the present system is based, and all the evil – material and spiritual – this entails for the masses of men throughout the world'. Among these masses are six million children who die every year because of lack of simple medical procedures that the rich countries could make available within statistical error in their budgets.[18] And a billion people on the edge of starvation or worse, but not beyond reach by any means.

We should also never forget that our wealth derives in no small measure from the tragedy of others. That is dramatically clear in the Anglosphere. I live in a comfortable suburb of Boston. Those who once lived there were victims of 'the utter extirpation of all the Indians in most populous parts of the Union' by means 'more destructive to the Indian natives than the conduct of the conquerors of Mexico and Peru' – the verdict of the first Secretary of War of the newly liberated colonies, General Henry Knox.[19] They suffered the fate of 'that hapless race of native Americans, which we are exterminating with such merciless and perfidious cruelty ... among the heinous sins of this nation, for which I believe God will one day bring [it] to judgment' – the words of the great grand strategist John Quincy Adams,

---

18 'US$5.1 billion in new resources is needed annually to save 6 million child lives in the 42 countries responsible for 90% of child deaths in 2000. This cost represents $1.23 per head in these countries, or an average cost per child life saved of $887.' Jennifer Bryce, Robert E Black, Neff Walker, Zulfiqar A Bhutta, Joy E Lawn, Richard W Steketee, 'Can the world afford to save the lives of 6 million children each year?', *Lancet* 2005; 365: 2193–2200; 'UNICEF, *The State of the World's Children; 1997–2011; The Progress of Nations 1996; Progress for Children: Achieving the MDGs with Equity, Number 9, September 2010*. 'In 2007, an estimated 9.2 million children worldwide under the age of five died from largely preventable causes. Some are directly caused by illness such as pneumonia, diarrhoea and malaria. Others are caused by indirect causes including conflict and HIV/AIDS. Malnutrition, poor hygiene and lack of access to safe water and adequate sanitation contribute to more than half of these deaths. Two thirds of both neonatal and young child deaths – over six million deaths every year – are preventable.' http://www.unicef.org/childsurvival/index.html.
19 Henry Knox, 29 December 1794, cited by Reginald Horsman, *Expansion and American Indian Policy, 1983–1812*, University of Oklahoma Press, 1992: 'It is a melancholy reflection, that our modes of population have been more destructive to the Indian natives than the conduct of the conquerors of Mexico and Peru. The evidence of this is the utter extirpation of nearly all the Indians in most populous parts of the Union. A future historian may mark the causes of this destruction of the human race in sable colore.'

intellectual author of Manifest Destiny and the Monroe Doctrine, long after his own substantial contributions to these heinous sins.[20] Australians should have no trouble adding illustrations.

Whatever the ultimate judgment of God may be, the judgment of man is far from Adams's expectations. To mention a few recent cases, consider what I suppose are the two most highly regarded left-liberal intellectual journals in the Anglosphere, the New York and London Reviews of Books. In the former, a prominent commentator recently reported what he learned from the work of the 'heroic historian' Edmund Morgan: namely, that when Columbus and the early explorers arrived they 'found a continental vastness sparsely populated by farming and hunting people … In the limitless and unspoiled world stretching from tropical jungle to the frozen north, there may have been scarcely more than a million inhabitants.'[21] The calculation is off by tens of millions, and the 'vastness' included advanced civilisations, facts well known to those who choose to know decades ago.[22] No letters appeared reacting to this truly colossal case of genocide denial. In the companion London journal a noted historian casually mentioned the 'mistreatment of the Native Americans', again eliciting no comment.[23] We would hardly accept the word 'mistreatment' for comparable or even much lesser crimes committed by enemies.

Recognition of heinous crimes from which we benefit enormously would be a good start after centuries of denial, but we can go on from there. One of the main tribes where I live was the Wampanoag, who still have a small reservation not too far away. Their language has long ago disappeared. But in a remarkable feat of scholarship and dedication to elementary human rights,

---

20 William Earl Weeks, *John Quincy Adams and American Global Empire*, University Press of Kentucky, Lexington, 1992.
21 Russell Baker, 'A Heroic Historian on Heroes', *New York Review of Books*, 11 July 2009. No letters appeared in reaction, though the editors later published a 'clarification' (8 October): Baker, it reads, 'wrote that in North America at the time of Columbus, "there may have been scarcely more than a million inhabitants." However, archaeological evidence and demographic research in recent decades suggest that the number was much larger, with estimates ranging up to 18 million.' The calculation is off by many tens of millions, and the 'vastness' included advanced civilisations, in the United States too. Baker was not referring to North America – rather, 'from tropical jungle to the frozen north …' The research is decades old.
22 Charles Mann, *1491: New Revelations of the Americas Before Columbus*, Knopf, 2005; David E. Stannard, *American Holocaust: Columbus and the Conquest of the New World*, Oxford University Press, New York, 1992, Appendix I. Stannard cites population estimates of as high as 145 million. Even low estimates are that there were at least seventy-five million, with seven or eight million people in what is today known as the United States and Canada.
23 Mark Mazower, 'Short Cuts', *London Review of Books*, vol. 32, no. 7, 8 April 2010.

the language has been reconstructed from missionary texts and comparative evidence, and now has its first native speaker in 100 years, the daughter of Jennie Little Doe, who has become a fluent speaker of the language herself. She is a former graduate student at MIT, who worked with my late friend and colleague Kenneth Hale, one of the most outstanding linguists of the modern period. Among his many accomplishments was his leading role in founding the study of aboriginal languages of Australia. He was also very effective in defense of the rights of indigenous people, also a dedicated peace and justice activist. He was able to turn our department at MIT into a center for the study of indigenous languages and active defense of indigenous rights in the Americas and beyond.

Revival of the Wampanoag language has revitalised the tribe. A language is more than just sounds and words. It is the repository of culture, history, traditions, the entire rich texture of human life and society. Loss of a language is a serious blow not only to the community itself but to all of those who hope to understand something of the nature of human beings, their capacities and achievements, and of course a loss of particular severity to those concerned with the variety and uniformity of human languages, a core component of human higher mental faculties. Similar achievements can be carried forward, a very partial but significant gesture towards repentance for heinous sins on which our wealth and power rests.

Since we commemorate anniversaries, such as the Japanese attacks seventy years ago, there are several significant ones that fall right about now, with lessons that can serve for both enlightenment and action. I will mention just a few.

The West has just commemorated the tenth anniversary of the 9/11 terrorist attacks and what was called at the time, but no longer, 'the glorious invasion' of Afghanistan that followed, soon to be followed by the even more glorious invasion of Iraq. Partial closure for 9/11 was reached with the assassination of the prime suspect, Osama bin Laden, by US commandos who invaded Pakistan, apprehended him and then murdered him, disposing of the corpse without autopsy.

I said 'prime suspect', recalling the ancient though long-abandoned doctrine of 'presumption of innocence'. The current issue of the major US scholarly journal of international relations features several discussions of the Nuremberg trials of some of history's worst criminals. There we read that the 'US decision to prosecute, rather than seek brutal vengeance was a victory for the American tradition of rights and a particularly American brand of legalism: punishment only for those who could be proved to be guilty through a fair trial with a panoply of procedural protections'.[24] The journal appeared right at the time of the celebration of the abandonment of this principle in a dramatic way, while the global campaign of assassination of suspects, and inevitable 'collateral damage', continues to be expanded, to much acclaim.

Not to be sure universal acclaim. Pakistan's leading daily recently published a study of the effect of drone attacks and other US terror. It found that 'about 80 per cent [of] residents of [the tribal regions] South and North Waziristan agencies have been affected mentally while sixty per cent people of Peshawar are nearing to become psychological patients if these problems are not addressed immediately', and warned that the 'survival of our young generation' is at stake.[25] In part for these reasons, hatred of America had already risen to phenomenal heights, and after the bin Laden assassination increased still more. One consequence was firing across the border at the bases of the US occupying army in Afghanistan – which provoked sharp condemnation of Pakistan for its failure to cooperate in an American war that Pakistanis overwhelmingly oppose, taking the same stand they did when the Russians occupied Afghanistan. A stand then lauded, now condemned.

The specialist literature and even the US Embassy in Islamabad warn that the pressures on Pakistan to take part in the US invasion, as well as US attacks in Pakistan, are 'destabilising and radicalising Pakistan, risking a geopolitical catastrophe for the United States – and the world – which would dwarf anything that could possibly occur in Afghanistan' – quoting British military/Pakistan analyst Anatol Lieven.[26] The assassination of bin Laden greatly heightened this risk in ways that were ignored in the general enthusiasm for assassination of suspects. The US commandos were under orders to fight their way out if necessary. They would surely have had air cover, maybe more, in which case there might have been a major confrontation with the Pakistani army, the only stable institution in Pakistan, and deeply committed to defending Pakistan's sovereignty. Pakistan has a large, rapidly expanding nuclear arsenal, and the whole system is laced with radical Islamists, products of the strong US-Saudi support for the worst of Pakistan's dictators, Zia ul-Haq, and his program of radical Islamisation. This program, along with Pakistan's nuclear weapons, are among Ronald

---

24 Margaret E. McGuinness, 'Peace v. Justice: The Universal Declaration of Human Rights and the Modern Origins of the Debate', *Diplomatic History*, vol. 35, no. 5 (November 2011).
25 '80pc people suffer from mental illness in Waziristan', *Dawn*, 21 June 2011.
26 Anatol Lieven, 'A Mutiny grows in Punjab', *The National Interest*, 23 February 2011.

Reagan's legacies. Obama has now added the risk of nuclear explosions in London and New York, if the confrontation had led to leakage of nuclear materials to jihadis, as was plausibly feared – one of the many examples of the constant threat of nuclear weapons.

The assassination of bin Laden had a name: 'Operation Geronimo'. That caused an uproar in Mexico, and was protested by the remnants of the indigenous population in the US. But elsewhere few seemed to comprehend the significance of identifying bin Laden with the heroic Apache Indian chief who led the resistance to the invaders, seeking to protect his people from the fate of 'that hapless race' that John Quincy Adams eloquently described. The imperial mentality is so profound that such matters cannot even be perceived.

There were a few criticisms of Operation Geronimo – the name, the manner of its execution, and the implications. These elicited the usual furious condemnations, most unworthy of comment, though some were instructive. The most interesting was by the respected left-liberal commentator Matthew Yglesias. He patiently explained that 'one of the main functions of the international institutional order is precisely to *legitimate* the use of deadly military force by western powers', so it is 'amazingly naïve' to suggest that the US should obey international law or other conditions that we impose on the powerless.[27] The words are not criticism, but applause; hence one can raise only tactical objections if the US invades other countries, murders and destroys with abandon, assassinates suspects at will, and otherwise fulfills its obligations in the service of mankind. If the traditional victims see matters somewhat differently, that merely reveals their moral and intellectual backwardness. And the occasional Western critic who fails to comprehend these fundamental truths can be dismissed as 'silly', Yglesias explains – incidentally, referring specifically to me, and I cheerfully confess my guilt.

Going back a decade to 2001, from the first moment it was clear that the 'glorious invasion' was anything but that. It was undertaken with the

---

27 Matthew Yglesias, 'International Law is made by powerful states', *ThinkProgress*, 13 May 2011: 'International law is made by states, powerful states have a disproportionate role in shaping it, and powerful states have obvious reasons to not be super-interested in the due process of suspected international terrorists or the sensibilities of mid-sized countries. Many people are pacifists and/or strong critics of western military power, and that's fine. But it's simply not the case that international law is identical with these policy preferences. On the contrary, one of the main functions of the international institutional order is precisely to *legitimate* the use of deadly military force by western powers.' http://thinkprogress.org/yglesias/2011/05/13/200961/international-law-is-made-by-powerful-states/.

understanding that it might drive several million Afghans over the edge of starvation, which is why the bombing was bitterly condemned by the aid agencies[28] that were forced to end the operations on which five million Afghans depended for survival. Fortunately the worst did not happen, but only the most morally obtuse can fail to comprehend that actions are evaluated in terms of likely consequences, not actual ones. The invasion of Afghanistan was not aimed at overthrowing the brutal Taliban regime, as later claimed. That was an afterthought, brought up three weeks after the bombing began. Its explicit reason was that the Taliban were unwilling to extradite bin Laden without evidence,[29] which the US refused to provide – as later learned, because it had virtually none,[30] and in fact still has little that could stand up in an independent court of law, though his responsibility is hardly in doubt. The Taliban did in fact make some gestures towards

---

28 The press reported that the number of Afghans at risk of death from starvation, disease and exposure was expected to increase by fifty per cent, to about 7.5 million: an additional 2.5 million people. No comment was elicited by the report that Washington had 'demanded [from Pakistan] the elimination of truck convoys that provide much of the food and other supplies to Afghanistan's civilian population', millions of them already on the brink of starvation. Pleas to stop the bombing to allow delivery of food and other aid were rebuffed without comment, mostly without even report. These came from high UN officials, major relief and aid agencies, and others in a good position to know. Afghan specialists concurred, warning that the withdrawal of aid workers and severe reduction in food supplies left 'millions of Afghans ... at grave risk of starvation'. By late September, the Food and Agricultural Organization (FAO) had warned that more than seven million people would face starvation if the threatened military action were undertaken, and after the bombing began, advised that the threat of 'humanitarian catastrophe' was 'grave', and that the bombing had disrupted the planting of eighty per cent of the grain supplies, so that the effects next year could be even more severe. John F. Burns, 'Pakistan Antiterror Support Avoids Vow of Military Aid', *New York Times*, 16 September 2001; Samina Ahmed, 'The United States and Terrorism in Southwest Asia: September 11 and Beyond', *International Security* vol. 26, no. 3 (winter 2001–02); 'UN Food Agency Warns of Mass Starvation in Afghanistan', AFP, 28 September 2001; Edith Lederer, 'US Bombing Disrupting Planting which Provides 80 percent of Annual Grain Harvest', Associated Press, 18 October 2001.

29 Patrick Tyler and Elisabeth Bumiller, 'Bush Offers Taliban "2nd Chance" to Yield', *New York Times*, 12 October 2001: 'Mr. Bush tonight gave the Taliban another chance to halt America's military action by handing over Mr. bin Laden. "If you cough him up and his people today, then we'll reconsider what we are doing to your country," he said. "You still have a second chance. Just bring him in," he added. "And bring his leaders and lieutenants and other thugs and criminals with him."'

30 In June 2002, eight months after the bombing, FBI director Robert Mueller said that 'investigators *believe* the idea of the September 11 attacks on the World Trade Center and Pentagon came from al-Qaeda leaders in Afghanistan', though the plotting and financing may trace to Germany and the United Arab Emirates. He said, 'We *think* the masterminds of it were in Afghanistan, high in the al Qaeda leadership.' (Walter Pincus, 'Mueller Outlines Origin, Funding of Sept. 11 Plot', *Washington Post*, 6 June 2002. Italics added).

extradition, and we since have learned that there were other such options,[31] but they were all dismissed in favor of violence, which has since torn the country to shreds. It has reached its highest level in a decade this year according to the UN,[32] with no diminution in sight.

A very serious question, rarely asked then or since, is whether there was an alternative to violence. There is strong evidence that there was. The 9/11 attack was sharply condemned within the jihadi movement, and there were good opportunities to split it and isolate al-Qaeda.[33] Instead, Washington and London chose to follow the script provided by bin Laden, helping to establish his claim that the West is attacking Islam, and thus provoking new waves of terror. The senior CIA analyst responsible for tracking Osama bin Laden from 1996, Michael Scheuer, warned right away and has repeated since that 'the United States of America remains bin Laden's only indispensable ally'.[34]

These are among the natural consequences of rejecting Muste's warning, and the main thrust of his revolutionary pacifism, which should direct us to investigating the grievances that lead to violence, and when they are legitimate, as they often are, to address them. When that advice is taken, it can succeed very well. Britain's recent experience in Northern Ireland is a good illustration. For years, London responded to IRA terror with greater violence, escalating the cycle, which reached a bitter peak. When the government began instead to attend to the grievances, violence subsided and terror has effectively disappeared. I was in Belfast in 1993, when it was a war zone, and returned a year ago to a city with tensions, but hardly beyond the norm.

There is a great deal more to say about what we call 9/11 and its consequences, but I do not want to end without at least mentioning a few more anniversaries. Right now happens to be the fiftieth anniversary of President Kennedy's decision to escalate the conflict in South Vietnam from vicious repression, which had already killed tens of thousands of people and finally elicited a reaction that the client regime in Saigon could not control, to

---

31 Karen DeYoung, 'Allies Are Cautious On "Bush Doctrine,"' *Washington Post*, 16 October 2001: 'On Sunday, Bush rejected a Taliban offer to turn over bin Laden to a third country.'
32 Alissa J. Rubin, 'Record Number of Afghan Civilians Died in 2011, Mostly in Insurgent Attacks, U.N. Says', *New York Times*, 4 February 2012; Afghanistan Annual Report 2011, *Protection of Civilians in Armed Conflict*, UN Assistance Mission in Afghanistan – UN Office of the High Commissioner for Human Rights, Kabul, February 2012.
33 Fawaz Gerges, *The Far Enemy* Cambridge University Press, Cambridge, 2005; *Journey of the Jihadist*, Harcourt Books, New York, 2006.
34 M. Scheuer (Anonymous), *Imperial Hubris: Why the West is losing the war on terror*, Brasseys, Inc., Dulles, 2004, p xv.

outright US invasion: bombing by the US Air Force, use of napalm, chemical warfare soon including crop destruction to deprive the resistance of food, and programs to send millions of South Vietnamese to virtual concentration camps where they could be 'protected' from the guerrillas who, admittedly, they were supporting.[35] There is no time to review the grim aftermath, and there should be no need to do so. The wars left three countries devastated, with a toll of many millions, not including the miserable victims of the enormous chemical warfare assault, including newborn infants today.[36]

There were a few at the margins who objected – 'wild men in the wings', as they were termed by Kennedy-Johnson National Security Adviser McGeorge Bundy, former Harvard Dean.[37] And by the time that the very survival of South Vietnam was in doubt, popular protest became quite strong. At the war's end in 1975, about seventy per cent of the population regarded the war as 'fundamentally wrong and immoral', not 'a mistake', figures that were sustained as long as the question was asked in polls.[38] In revealing contrast, at the dissident extreme of mainstream commentary the war was 'a mistake' because our noble objectives could not be achieved at a tolerable cost.

Another anniversary that should be in our minds today is of the massacre in the Santa Cruz graveyard in Dili just twenty years ago, the most publicised of a great many shocking atrocities during the Indonesian invasion and annexation of East Timor. Australia had joined the US in granting formal recognition to the Indonesian occupation, after its virtually genocidal invasion. The US State Department explained to Congress in 1982 that Washington recognised both the Indonesian occupation and the Khmer Rouge-based 'Democratic Kampuchea' regime. The justification offered was that 'unquestionably' Democratic Kampuchea was 'more representative of the Cambodian people than Fretilin was of the Timorese people' because

---

35 N. Chomsky, *Rethinking Camelot: JFK, the Vietnam War and US Political Culture*, Verso, London, 1993, pp. 49–56; Eric Bergerud, *The Dynamics of Defeat:* The Vietnam War In Hau Nghia Province, Westview, 1991; *The Pentagon Papers: The Defense Department History of United States Decisionmaking on Vietnam*, Senator Gravel Edition, Beacon Press, Boston, 1972, vol. II.
36 The first detailed study of the effects of Agent Orange on South Vietnamese, with effects on newborns right to the moment because of persisting genetic modifications, down to third or fourth generation, is Fred Wilcox, *Scorched Earth: Legacies of Chemical Warfare in Vietnam*, Seven Stories, 2011; See also the shattering photographic study by Philip Jones Griffiths, 'Agent Orange: "Collateral Damage"' in *Vietnam*, Trolley Ltd, 2003. J.B. Neilands, G. Orians, E. Pfeiffer, A. Vennema, and A. Westing, *Harvest of Death: Chemical Warfare In Vietnam and Cambodia*, Free Press, New York, 1972.
37 M. Bundy, 'The End of Either/Or', *Foreign Affairs*, vol. 45, no. 2, 1967, p.191.
38 John E. Rielly, ed., *American Public Opinion and U.S. Foreign Policy 1987*, Chicago Council on Foreign Relations, Chicago, 1987.

'there has been this continuity [in Cambodia] since the very beginning', in 1975, when the Khmer Rouge took over.[39]

The media and commentators have been polite enough to let all this languish in silence, not an inconsiderable feat.

A few months before the Santa Cruz massacre, Foreign Minister Gareth Evans made his famous statements dismissing concerns about the murderous invasion and annexation on the grounds that 'the world is a pretty unfair place ... littered ... with examples of acquisitions of force', so we can therefore look away as awesome crimes continue with strong support by the Western powers.[40] Not quite look away, because at the same time Evans was negotiating the robbery of East Timor's sole resource with his comrade Ali Alatas, foreign minister of Indonesia, producing what seems to be the only official Western document that recognises East Timor as an Indonesian province.

Years later, Evans declared that 'the notion that we had anything to answer for morally or otherwise over the way we handled the Indonesia-East Timor relationship, I absolutely reject'[41] – a stance that can be adopted, and even respected, by those who emerge victorious. In the US and Britain, the question is not even asked in polite society.

It is only fair to add that in sharp contrast, much of the Australian population, and media, were in the forefront of exposing and protesting the crimes, some of the worst of the past half-century. And in 1999, when the crimes were escalating once again, they had a significant role in convincing US president Clinton to inform the Indonesian generals in September that the game was over, at which point they immediately withdrew, allowing an Australian-led peacekeeping force to enter.[42]

There are lessons here too, for the public. Clinton's orders could have been delivered at any time in the preceding twenty-five years, terminating the crimes. Clinton himself could easily have delivered them four years earlier, in October 2005, when General Suharto was welcomed to Washington as 'our kind of guy'.[43] The same orders could have been given twenty years earlier,

---

39 J. Holdridge, Hearing before the Subcommittee on Asian and Pacific Affairs of the Committee on Foreign Affairs, House of Representatives, 97th Congress, Second Session, 14 September 1982, p. 71.
40 *Background Briefing*, 28, 29, 30 October 1990, ABC Radio National.
41 P. Daley, 'Man for a Crisis', *The Age*, 5 March 2001.
42 C. Fernandes, *The Independence of East Timor: Multidimensional Perspectives*, Sussex Academic Press, Eastbourne, 2011.
43 David Sanger, 'Real Politics: Why Suharto Is In and Castro Is Out', *New York Times*, 31 October 1995.

when Henry Kissinger gave the 'green light' to the Indonesian invasion, and US Ambassador to the UN, Daniel Patrick Moynihan, expressed his pride in having rendered the United Nations 'utterly ineffective' in any measures to deter the Indonesian invasion – later to be revered for his courageous defense of international law.[44]

There could hardly be a more painful illustration of the consequences of the failure to attend to Muste's lesson. It should be added that in a shameful display of subordination to power, some respected Western intellectuals have actually sunk to describing this disgraceful record as a stellar illustration of the humanitarian norm of the 'responsibility to protect'.

Consistent with Muste's 'revolutionary pacifism', the Sydney Peace Foundation has always emphasised peace *with justice*. The demands of justice can remain unfulfilled long after peace has been declared. The Santa Cruz massacre twenty years ago can serve as an illustration. One year after the massacre the United Nations adopted The Declaration on the Protection of All Persons from Enforced Disappearance, which states that 'Acts constituting enforced disappearance shall be considered a continuing offence as long as the perpetrators continue to conceal the fate and the whereabouts of persons who have disappeared and these facts remain unclarified.'[45] The massacre is therefore a continuing offence: the fate of the disappeared is unknown, and the offenders have not been brought to justice, including those who continue to conceal the crimes of complicity and participation. Only one indication of how far we must go to rise to some respectable level of civilised behaviour.

---

44 D.P. Moynihan, *A Dangerous Place*, Berkley, New York, 1978, p. 279: 'The United States wished things to turn out as they did, and worked to bring this about. The Department of State desired that the United Nations prove utterly ineffective in whatever measures it undertook. This task was given to me, and I carried it forward with no inconsiderable success.'

45 After Santa Cruz, the UN's Special Rapporteur emphasised Article 17, Paragraph 1 of the Declaration on the Protection of All Persons from Enforced Disappearance: 'Acts constituting enforced disappearance shall be considered a continuing offence as long as the perpetrators continue to conceal the fate and the whereabouts of persons who have disappeared and these facts remain unclarified.' (UN, Report by the Special Rapporteur Bacre Waly Ndiaye, on his mission to Indonesia and East Timor from 3 to 13 July 1994', E/CN.4/1995/61/Add.1, 1 November 1994, Paragraph 69.)

Sydney Peace Prize acceptance speech

2011 City of Sydney Peace Gala Dinner

MacLaurin Hall, University of Sydney, 3 November 2011[1]

Thank you. Well, it's unnecessary to say much about how grateful I am for the honour and the wonderful atmosphere, and how gratifying it is to join a group of people I greatly admire and respect, some of whom, former recipients, are close personal friends, for many years.

On an occasion like this, there's this phrase that resonates in my mind – often does in fact. It's a declaration that was issued by Bertrand Russell and Albert Einstein in 1955.[2] It was a call to the people of the world, a plea actually, to face a question that's, as they put it, 'stark and dreadful and inescapable: Shall we put an end to the human race; or shall mankind renounce war?' They were thinking, of course, of nuclear war, primarily. And since that time, we have come very close to virtually terminal nuclear war a number of times. The danger continues, in fact right today it's very much alive.

The area of primary concern now is West and South Asia. If you happen to have been reading the papers carefully for the last few days, you'll notice that there have been exercises in the Eastern Mediterranean, either actually intended or psychological warfare, aimed at the bombing of Iran. There's been a rash of newspaper articles in newspaper reports in the Israeli press about an apparent decision of the government to proceed with bombing Iran's nuclear sites. Very strikingly, for some months now there's been a long series of statements by former high security officials in Israel. They're former heads of Mossad and so on – people who rarely say anything – speaking quite

---

1 Chomsky spoke extemporaneously here.
2 Russell-Einstein Manifesto, 9 July 1955. Bertrand Russell read it to the world's press in London, explaining that Einstein's last act before he died was to sign the appeal. The Manifesto concluded thus: 'There lies before us, if we choose, continual progress in happiness, knowledge, and wisdom. Shall we, instead, choose death, because we cannot forget our quarrels? We appeal as human beings to human beings: Remember your humanity, and forget the rest. If you can do so, the way lies open to a new Paradise; if you cannot, there lies before you the risk of universal death.'

strongly, denouncing the plan, saying there'll be disastrous, horrible effects.[3] They wouldn't be coming out publicly unless they had some information that these plans are actually in the works. It's worth remembering that Israel did strike a nuclear reactor once before – the Osirak reactor in Iraq. Although it's not too well-known, there was credible information right away, and it has since been confirmed even by US intelligence, that the bombing attack actually initiated Saddam Hussein's nuclear weapons program.[4]

The reactor, it appears, was only capable of producing low-grade uranium for energy purposes. But after the attack, a secret nuclear weapons program was initiated and we know where that led to. And it's conceivable that that could happen again, along with other very threatening and dangerous consequences that could follow from an attack of that sort. We'll know very soon whether it's happened, but it's too close for comfort. There are things that can be done about these problems: I should say that for several years now, US analysts have been arguing that the most dangerous problem in the world – security problem – is Iran's possible development of nuclear weapons, and it's interesting to see why they think it's such a danger. The question's rarely asked, but there is an authoritative answer to it. The authoritative answer comes from the highest sources, namely the Pentagon and US intelligence.[5] They give annual reports to Congress on the global security situation; they do agree that the Iranian potential for nuclear weapons is an extreme danger, and the reason they say is that it's going to be part of Iran's deterrent strategy. They have a detailed analysis of the Iranian military: they argue that it's very small, its expenses are very low, even by the standards of the region.[6] And it's aimed specifically for defence. Its goal is to deter an invasion long enough for diplomacy to set in.[7]

---

3   Isabel Kershner, 'Israeli strike on Iran would be "stupid," ex-spy chief says', *New York Times*, 8 May 2011.
4   Richard Wilson, 'A Visit to the Bombed Nuclear Reactor at Tuwaitha, Iraq', *Nature*, vol. 302, no. 5907 (31 March–6 April 1983): pp. 373–76. Wayne White, *Middle East Policy*, Fall 2008. Michael Jansen, *Middle East International* 691 (10 January 2003). Imad Khadduri, *Uncritical Mass*, memoirs (manuscript), 2003. Scott D. Sagan and Kenneth N. Waltz, *The Spread of Nuclear Weapons: A Debate*, W. W. Norton, New York, 1995, pp. 18–19.
5   Lieutenant General Ronald L. Burgess, Director, Defense Intelligence Agency, Statement before the Committee on Armed Services, US Senate, 14 April 2010: 'The strategic objectives of Iran's leadership are first and foremost, regime survival ... Iran's military strategy is designed to defend against external threats, particularly from the United States and Israel. Its principles of military strategy include deterrence, asymmetrical retaliation, and attrition warfare ...'
6   Burgess, ibid.: 'Iran's defense spending as a share of GDP is relatively low compared to the rest of the region.'
7   Burgess, ibid.: 'This reflects its defensive military doctrine, which is designed to slow an invasion and force a diplomatic solution to hostilities. Iranian military training and public statements echo this defensive doctrine.'

And they add that if Iran is developing nuclear weapons, that would be part of the deterrence strategy.[8] So why is a deterrence strategy such a threat? Well, very simple, a deterrence strategy can deter; it can prevent the United States and its allies from free unconstrained military action in the region because there'll be a deterrent. And that's a threat, if you intend to carry out military attacks at will. That's the threat. We should recognise that our own countries interpret the possibility of a deterrent as a very serious threat. That tells us a lot about ourselves, and about the potential for very dangerous consequences, some of which are in process right now. Is there a way to deal with these problems? Well, there's a kind of narrow way, which has enormous international support, and that is to move towards developing a nuclear weapons free zone in the Middle East. Now there are several such initiatives around the world; Africa, Pacific Islands, other places. They have not really been implemented, and it's important to know why.

Take the African nuclear weapons free zone. There's one impediment to its being implemented: Britain and the United States insist that an African island, Diego Garcia, which was a former British dependency, be available for nuclear weapon storage, nuclear submarines, and so on.[9] They use it as one of the main bases for the bombing in Central Asia. Obama has recently built it up and extended it so it has facilities for nuclear submarines – that means submarines with nuclear tipped missiles. Well, as long as that is going on, the African nuclear free zone can't really be implemented. And the same is true in the Pacific area. The Pacific nuclear free zone was held up at first by France, which wanted to use its Pacific dependencies for nuclear weapons testing. They finally finished their tests, but now it's being held up by the United States and its British ally – and maybe Australia's involved – which want to use, and in effect are using the Pacific dependencies for the transit of nuclear-armed naval vessels. In fact, they're sustaining nuclear weapons bases there.

Well, what about the Middle East, the most dangerous one? There's an impediment there too. Support for a Middle East nuclear free zone is so broad that the United States has been compelled to formally agree to it at the Non-Proliferation Treaty Review Meeting that takes place every five years. The last one was in New York in 2010, and there was overwhelming support for

---

8   'Iran's nuclear program and its willingness to keep open the possibility of developing nuclear weapons is a central part of its deterrent strategy.' Unclassified Report on Military Power of Iran, April 2010; John J. Kruzel, American Forces Press Service, 'Report to Congress Outlines Iranian Threats', April 2010, http://www.defense.gov/news/newsarticle.aspx?id=58833.
9   Peter Sand, African Nuclear-Weapon-Free Zone in Force: What Next for Diego Garcia?, *American Society of International Law, Insight*, vol. 13, no. 12, 28 August 2009.

moving in this direction. The Obama administration agreed it was a very good idea, but with several qualifications: it's a good idea, but not right now, and furthermore there's a condition, any nuclear weapons free zone will have to exclude Israel, and in fact exclude any requirement that other states provide information about anything they're doing to support Israeli nuclear weapons.[10] Well, okay that kills that idea. So yes, now we have this tremendous danger – a danger of a deterrent to our actions. It may move on to a devastating war with all kinds of horrible consequences. Well, there are other ways, more far-reaching ways to deal with the problem, generally. A friend of mine – I've actually forgotten who – an Australian friend, who may be here, a while back sent me a book. It was a collection of Australian writings; short essays about nuclear weapons.[11] They were written in 1986, the International Year of Peace. An Aboriginal poet had a comment which is so eloquent that I don't want to paraphrase it, so if I can find it I'll actually read it.

The comment was this:

> There will come a time when our mother, whom the invader so ruthlessly raped by cutting down her trees, by slaughtering her creatures and mining her minerals, will retaliate. Are we so impudent as to expect that we can survive her backlash? The dangers of which I speak were long before the white man came to this land. In the Northern Territory, there's a green ant dreaming. It is a legend about what will happen if the yellow metal (uranium) is taken from the ground. A giant ant will grow, and will devour the living earth.

That was the point of the comment, and that in fact is what's happening. And one way to stop the proliferation of nuclear weapons is simply to prevent the materials from reaching the developers. The fact that it will devour the living earth is all too threatening; that's what Russell and Einstein were warning about.

Well these comments open up contemplation of a different threat, which actually wasn't evident at the time that Russell and Einstein were issuing their

---

10 General James L. Jones, *Statement by the National Security Advisor on the Non-Proliferation Treaty Review Conference*, May 28, 2010: 'The United States will not permit a conference or actions that could jeopardize Israel's national security. We will not accept any approach that singles out Israel or sets unrealistic expectations. The United States' long-standing position on Middle East peace and security remains unchanged, including its unshakeable commitment to Israel's security.'

11 Dorothy Green and David Headon, eds, *Imagining the real: Australian writing in the nuclear age*, ABC Enterprises for the Australian Broadcasting Corporation, Sydney, 1987.

warning, but it is very evident today. I learned about it myself, about forty years ago, when two personal friends, well-known scientists,[12] began to talk about the recent discoveries that were emerging about what we now know of as global warming. Those were the first indications that there was a serious problem coming. By now it's a very serious problem, and recognised as such.

A couple of months ago, the International Energy Agency issued a report that determined that greenhouse gas emissions had reached a record high, which is pretty striking, because it was a year of recession, and manufacturing had declined.[13] And they furthermore warned that the extent of global warming was coming very close to reaching what the main scientific consensus regards as a kind of a tipping point, a point beyond which it's irreversible. They said that two degrees centigrade warming was coming close, and if we reach that point – they don't put it this way – it'll devour the living earth. We can kiss each other goodbye; there won't be a possibility of a decent human existence. Well, there are things that can be done about that now, and there isn't a lot of time to waste. And things are being done; most countries are doing at least something, taking at least halting steps towards addressing the problem.

Unfortunately, that's not true of the countries where it matters most. A country where it matters most, is of course the United States, the richest, most powerful country in history, and not only is it not taking halting steps, it's taking steps backwards. The Republican congress now is dismantling programs instituted under Richard Nixon – that's an indication of what's happened in the past roughly forty years. They're now dismantling programs under Nixon, who was in fact the last liberal president, if you actually look at the programs.[14]

---

12   Raymond Siever (Earth Sciences, Harvard) and Jule Charney (Meteorology, MIT).
13   International Energy Agency, *Prospect of limiting the global increase in temperature to 2ºC is getting bleaker*, 30 May 2011: 'After a dip in 2009 caused by the global financial crisis, emissions are estimated to have climbed to a record 30.6 Gigatonnes (Gt), a 5% jump from the previous record year in 2008, when levels reached 29.3 Gt. In addition, the IEA has estimated that 80% of projected emissions from the power sector in 2020 are already locked in, as they will come from power plants that are currently in place or under construction today. "This significant increase in CO_2 emissions and the locking in of future emissions due to infrastructure investments represent a serious setback to our hopes of limiting the global rise in temperature to no more than 2ºC," said Dr Fatih Birol, Chief Economist at the IEA ... "Our latest estimates are another wake-up call. The world has edged incredibly close to the level of emissions that should not be reached until 2020 if the 2ºC target is to be attained."' http://www.iea.org/index_info.asp?id=1959 [accessed 13 February 2012].
14   Nixon signed the Endangered Species Act, the Environmental Policy Act, the Clean Air Act Amendments, the Population Research Act, the Marine Mammal Protection Act, the Coastal Zone Management Act, and other acts. He also extended the National Park System. See J. Brooks Flippen, *Nixon and the Environment*, University of New Mexico Press, 2000. See also Joan Smith, *Nixon Reconsidered*, Basic Books, New York, 1995.

And that's drawing backwards from the efforts to do something effective about global warming. There are much more positive directions; they are in fact mostly coming from the indigenous communities. In Ecuador, for example, where there is a substantial indigenous community, there are protests, serious protests; the government's kind of torn by them at the moment. The indigenous population is calling for an end to mining for oil, which is substantial. There's huge oil exploration with enormous environmental disaster associated with it, apparently much worse than the Gulf of Mexico disaster recently, actually in the Nigerian Delta there's no doubt that the pollution and destruction is far greater than the Gulf of Mexico. But these are poor people, people of colour, so it doesn't really matter what happens to them – no one pays attention, unlike the Gulf of Mexico. However, the native communities are demanding that all of this stop. They don't see any justification for destroying their lives, their culture, their societies so that people can sit in traffic jams in New York in their SUVs. They argue that's not a fair exchange. The most striking case, is actually Bolivia, where the indigenous population is a majority and have in the past ten years entered the political arena, successfully elected someone from their own ranks (as a poor peasant) as president, and have in fact taken the international lead now in taking steps towards doing something about global warming. That's the poorest country in South America, and it's kind of striking. That the poorest country in South America is taking the international lead on this program, and the richest country, not only in the western hemisphere, but anywhere in the world, and in fact in history, is not only not contributing, but is drawing back, eliminating efforts to deal with it.

One of the recent efforts in Bolivia was legislation granting rights to nature.[15] So in addition to human rights, there are now rights to nature. Nature has rights, and we have to observe them. Well, you know, sophisticated Westerners can mock this ridiculous idea, but the fact of the matter is that unless we are able to gain some of the sensibility of the indigenous populations, this is worldwide, the last laugh is almost certainly going to be on us.

Chomsky adds, '… when Richard Nixon – in many respects the last liberal president – declared a drug war in 1971, two-thirds of the funding went to treatment, which reached record numbers of addicts; there was a sharp drop in drug-related arrests and number of federal prison inmates, as well as crime rates.' The Columbia Plan, Z Magazine, June 2000.

15 *Ley de Derechos de la Madre Tierra,* December 2010. Borrowed from Orwell.

2011 Edward Said Memorial Lecture

Adelaide Town Hall, Saturday 5 November 2011

Thanks very much for the warm welcome.

This is actually the fourth time that I've had the privilege of giving a talk in memory of Edward Said, who was an old close friend for many years. The first time was in Beirut, then at Columbia University, where he taught and where we shared many platforms on these issues, and finally at Princeton. And it's of course always tinged with deep regret that he's no longer with us, enhanced by the recognition of how much we really need the incisive critical analysis that he provided and his simple integrity.

The topic I'd like to talk about is one that was of primary concern for Edward for most of his life. He was in fact one of the few who did not succumb to illusions or to powerful pressures, doctrinal and otherwise, and in his case, in fact quite serious threats to his life, taken very seriously by the police in fact. And he continued forthrightly to expose what was happening, in fact not sparing anyone his critical eye. Well a good place to start with this topic is to borrow a concept from a very fine young British diplomatic historian, Mark Curtis, author of quite important studies on Britain's post World War II imperial crimes. It's the concept 'unpeople', that is creatures who look human, but are not really human, they're not actually people.[1] And therefore they don't merit elementary human rights. That happens to be highly relevant to this topic.

That distinction is ever present. Take a couple of weeks ago for example, there was an assassination in Yemen of Anwar al-Awlaki. He's an American citizen – and a Muslim cleric – who was killed by a drone. The headline in the *New York Times* read, 'The West celebrates a cleric's death'.[2] 'Death' is not quite accurate. It was an assassination; an important escalation of President Obama's global assassination campaign. Not everyone celebrated; there were a few critics. Among them, almost all were critics because the person assassinated was an American citizen. That is, a person, unlike suspects who

---

1 Mark Curtis, *Unpeople: Britain's Secret Human Rights Abuses*, Vintage, 2004.
2 A. Shadid and D. Kirkpatrick, 'As the West Celebrates a Cleric's Death, the Mideast Shrugs', *New York Times*, 1 October 2011.

are intentionally murdered or victims of what's called 'collateral damage' – somebody who happens to be in the wrong place, or who isn't a citizen. There there's no problem because they are 'unpeople'. And therefore they can be freely murdered. I used the word 'suspect' because being old-fashioned I can recall that a long time ago there was a crucial conception in Anglo-American law called 'presumption of innocence'. That is, a person is innocent until proven guilty in proper proceedings in a court of law. That has so long been abandoned, and it's so deeply hidden that it sounds like you're talking about the Stone Age when you bring it up. It's never discussed.

Some of the critics brought up the Fifth Amendment to the US Constitution, which states unequivocally that no person shall be deprived of life, liberty or property without due process of law. Now, notice that that was not intended to be applied to 'unpeople', even those within US territory, actual territory or soon to be acquired territory. The native population were 'unpeople', so they could be deprived of life and property quite freely. Nor was it intended to apply to those who the Constitution determined to be only three-fifths human, that is the huge slave population.[3] In fact it barely applied to women, who had very restricted rights. The three-fifth humans advanced to full human with the Fourteenth Amendment a couple of years after the Civil War. At least, they did so in theory but not in fact. The war was followed by a decade of partial freedom for African Americans, but by 1877, with the end of Reconstruction, slavery was reconstituted in a new and even more sadistic form. Black life was effectively criminalised and sentencing was rendered permanent by various means. Brutal prison labor provided a large part of the basis not only for agricultural production, as under chattel slavery, but also for the American industrial revolution of the late nineteenth and early twentieth centuries.

The savagery of the practices lent some shameful support to the claims of slave owners that they were more humane than the northern capitalists who 'rented' labour, because those who owned people were concerned to sustain their capital investments. These horrifying practices continued until World War II, when free Black labour was needed, and in the post-war boom there was a window of opportunity for the Black population. The neoliberal turn in the past thirty years substantially closed the window. A new form of

---

3   US Constitution, Article I, Section 2: 'Representatives and direct Taxes shall be apportioned among the several States which may be included within this Union, according to their respective Numbers, which shall be determined by adding to the whole Number of free Persons, including those bound to Service for a Term of Years, and excluding Indians not taxed, three fifths of all other Persons.'

criminalisation was instituted, much of it in the context of the 'drug wars', leading to a huge increase in incarceration, mostly targeting minorities, reaching to levels vastly beyond comparable countries – in fact beyond any countries that have meaningful statistics. It's an extremely ugly story, not as well known as it should be. The past thirty years of very high criminalisation have had essentially the same effect, the same targets and the same period of severe social and moral regression, and not just in the United States.[4]

Well the Fourteenth Amendment was recognised right away to be problematic; the problem was that the concept 'person' was too narrow and too broad. And the courts went to work right away to remedy these flaws. They broadened the concept 'person' to include collectivist legal fictions, established and sustained by state power. They were called corporations.[5] And over the years, the courts and other agreements have given them rights that go far beyond persons of flesh and blood. That includes, in the last few years, the misnamed 'free trade agreements'. The concept was also narrowed to exclude undocumented aliens; they had to be 'unpeople', that is, not covered by the Constitution. And in fact both of these issues, the broadening of the concept, and the narrowing of it are very live issues in the courts and in public discussion right now. Of course, the concept excludes foreigners, particularly if they're suspected of terrorism. And now the notion of 'unpeople' has been extended to American citizens, which as I say aroused a little bit of discussion.

The concept of 'terrorists' also has taken on quite an interesting meaning in the past thirty years, in the context of the 'global war on terror', as it was called. That was actually initiated by Ronald Reagan in 1981 and re-declared by George W. Bush twenty years later.[6] There's a lot to say about this thirty year global war on terror, but I won't go into it, except to note how the term terrorist is now used, and indeed used without comment. That's a matter that bears quite directly on the obstacles to a just peace in the form of Palestine. Take, for example, Omar Khadr.[7] He's the first person to have

---

4   For a graphic and shocking account of post-Civil War slavery, see Douglas Blackmon, *Slavery by Another Name*, Anchor Books, New York, 2009. On the current scale and character, see Randall Shelden, *Our Punitive Society*, Waveland Press, Long Grove, 2010.
5   Morton Horwitz, *The Transformation of American Law*, Harvard University Press, 1992.
6   For general review of the first phase of the 'war on terror', see Chomsky's 'International Terrorism: Image and Reality' in Alexander George, ed., *Western State Terrorism*, Polity/Blackwell, 1991.
7   Andrea Prasow, *Khadr's Plea Agreement and Sentencing: Questions Never to be Answered*, JURIST – Forum, Nov. 5, 2010, http://jurist.org/forum/2010/11/khadrs-plea-agreement-and-sentencing-questions-never-to-be-answered.php; American Civil Liberties Union, Human Rights Watch and Juvenile Law Center, Letter to US Attorney General Holder

been brought before a military commission under President Obama. There had been some brought to military commissions under Bush, but those cases were all thrown out by the Supreme Court. It was a very right-wing Supreme Court, but those violations of due process were too much even for them. So Omar Khadr is the first one brought under Obama's very marginal revisions of the provisions thrown out by the court.

And Omar Khadr was accused of a very serious crime. He is a fifteen year-old boy. He was accused of having defended his village in Afghanistan when American soldiers attacked it. He was even accused of picking up a grenade and throwing it at the invading soldiers. Well, that's pretty serious. So, a fifteen year-old child was sent to the secret prison in Bagram, and after a year sent on to Guantanamo for another seven years, against quite explicit provisions of international law about the proper treatment of juveniles. Remember that he's a fifteen year-old boy, but those provisions are ignored by powerful states, so there's no comment about them.

The first few years he couldn't see a lawyer – you know what goes on in Guantanamo, so I won't discuss it – but after eight years of detention, he was brought to trial. And he pleaded guilty to avoid a very long prison sentence for this serious crime. We all know what it means to plead guilty under those conditions. He was therefore given only eight years additional sentencing. Now, he's a Canadian citizen, Canada can have him extradited, but courageously Canada's unwilling to offend the master. There may be some resonances of that decision here, and I leave that to you.

The crime of resisting aggression is a very interesting category of terrorism; it's not entirely new. Some of you may remember the slogan 'Terror against terror', used by the Gestapo.[8] None of this arouses any interest; none of it arouses any discussion. Omar Khadr belongs to the category of 'unpeople' so he's fair game. And pretty much the same is true in the Occupied Territories. There's a very fine Israeli human rights group, B'Tselem, which just came out a couple of weeks ago with a new report called *No Minor Matter*.[9] It's about

---

and Defense Secretary Gates Urging Repatriation of Omar Khadr, 12 March 2010. http://www.hrw.org/news/2010/03/12/letter-holder-and-gates-urging-repatriation-omar-khadr.

8   Magnus Linklater, Isabel Hilton and Neal Ascherson, *The Fourth Reich*, Hodder & Stoughton, London, 1984, p. 111. Incidentally, 'Terror Against Terror' (TNT – Terror Neged Terror) was the name adopted by Israeli terrorists in the West Bank.

9   B'Tselem – The Israeli Information Centre for Human Rights in the Occupied Territories, *No Minor Matter: Violation of the rights of Palestinian minors arrested by Israel on suspicion of stone-throwing*, July 2011. http://www.btselem.org/publications/summaries/2011-no-minor-matter.

the treatment of minors under the Occupation, and it's worth reading. It gives many ugly illustrations to support their conclusion. I'll just read it, 'the rights of Palestinian minors are flagrantly violated at every stage of the proceedings conducted against them, from the initial arrest and removal from their homes, through interrogation and trial, to serving the prison sentence', and follows with release. More generally, the concept of 'unpeople' is central to any consideration of tonight's topic, Israeli Jews are people, Palestinians are 'unpeople'. And almost everything that happens follows from that.

There are clear illustrations regularly in the press. In fact, in the Australian press this morning, the *Age* and the *Sydney Morning Herald*, there's a very graphic story of the treatment of 'unpeople'.[10] It's about a Palestinian woman who is also an Israeli citizen and a Bedouin, living in the South of Israel. Her name is Rifa al-Oqbi. The story describes what happened in her village recently. There's a picture of the young woman and her two little boys. The Israeli army showed up and ordered them to leave their home because it was going to be bulldozed. She asked for twenty-four hours to collect some furniture and possessions, but she wasn't allowed that. When she tried to reach for something, she was beaten and thrown to the ground. Somebody tried to help her; he was beaten up too. Then they destroyed the home. This is part of a broader program of getting rid of forty-five unregistered villages. They're villages into which Bedouins were driven when they were driven off their lands in 1948. I've visited some of them and heard plenty of complaints about what happens. They don't get services: they don't get running water, electricity, social services or schools. Remember that these are Israeli citizens; they serve in the army, they vote, they pay taxes, but they're 'unpeople'.

Prime Minister Netanyahu met with the mayors of these forty-five villages, and he explained to them that this is really a humanitarian endeavour. He gave two reasons: one is that Israel is replacing the 'unpeople' with people. That is, the Israeli cabinet gave the green light for work to begin on ten Jewish settlements in the area 'to attract a new population to the Negev'. And nobody could object to replacing 'unpeople' with people, obviously. The second reason it's a humanitarian gesture is that the plan would 'allow the Bedouin, for the first time, to realise their assets and turn them from dead capital into living capital to receive ownership of the land, which will allow for home construction, according to law, and for the development of enterprises and employment. This will jump the population forward and

---

10 Ruth Pollard, 'Bedouin battle to stay in their village ends in rubble', *Sydney Morning Herald*, 5 November 2011.

provide it with economic independence'. In short, they were living in villages but that's dead capital and was treated that way. But now, as a gesture of humanitarianism, ten of the villages will be registered, so therefore they can be treated like other villages. And that gives the people living capital. Well, this is in today's paper, but you can find it almost any day that you look.

As you know, there was a prisoner exchange a couple of weeks ago – the release of Corporal Gilad Shalit. And the coverage shows how Israeli Jews are people but Palestinians are 'unpeople' – the *New York Times* had a front-page story[11] about it, and right next to it, running right across the top of the front page, is a picture of four women agonised over the fate of Gilad Shalit. They had been sitting in, protesting the fact that the government had not arranged an exchange that would release him. That's understandable; I think he should have been released a long time ago. But there's something missing from this story. What about the Palestinians? There were no pictures of anybody agonised over their fate. I can't find their names. There was no comment on how they were treated, when they were released, or what condition they were in. There was one question raised about the Palestinians: *will they become terrorists again?* Among the questions not asked was what happened to the elected legislature in Palestine. Remember that there was a free election – a carefully monitored one – in January 2006. Not long after that the United States, the European Union and Israel dissolved the only freely elected legislature in the Arab world. Then members of the Palestinian Legislative Council were hauled off to prison. But they're 'unpeople' – so you don't have to worry about that.

Also unmentioned were the Muamar brothers. The day before Corporal Shalit was captured – and he was a soldier on the front lines of the Israeli army that was attacking Gaza – Israeli forces entered Gaza City and kidnapped two civilians. They were the Muamar brothers, a doctor and his brother. They were kidnapped and taken to Israel in violation of the Geneva Conventions. They disappeared into Israel's prison population, which includes almost one thousand held without charge, often for long periods. Whatever one thinks about the capture of a soldier of an attacking army, which was what Gilad Shalit was, the kidnapping of civilians is an incomparably worse crime. It only received a few lines of comment, but no noticeable criticism.[12] The difference in treatment again reflects the difference between people and 'unpeople'.

---

11 'Deal With Hamas Will Free Israeli Held Since 2006', *New York Times*, 12 October 2011.
12 For a review of the coverage, see Epilogue, note 29 of Gilbert Achcar, Noam Chomsky and Stephen Shalom, *Perilous Power*, Paradigm Publishers, Boulder, 2007.

Israel routinely kidnaps civilians. It's been doing that regularly for decades in Lebanon and on the high seas, often imprisoning them without charge in Israel.[13] The Al Mezan Centre for Human Rights, a reliable Gazan human rights organisation, reported that on 6 September 2009 the Israeli Defence Force carried out another regular infiltration into Gaza and 'kidnapped five Palestinian children who were on their way home after grazing sheep', ages fifteen to seventeen, taking them to Israel under cover of helicopter fire around the Bedouin village from which they were abducted. Their press release provided the names.[14] The crime – needless to say far more severe than the capture of Shalit – passed unnoticed.

There are plenty of others in prison – hundreds of them, in fact. We don't know how many there are. They're often held without charge, and there are plenty of others we don't know about because there are also secret prisons. This was revealed in Israel a couple of years ago and reported in Europe. It was not mentioned in the mainstream reporting in the United States. I don't know whether it was mentioned here. There was a long exposure by an Israeli reporter of one of these secret prison facilities, Facility 1391.[15] About what you'd expect at a secret prison, without Red Cross or any other access. But again, there was no particular interest since the prisoners are 'unpeople'. In fact, the racism is so profound that it's kind of like the air you breathe; it's just part of the atmosphere. You don't notice it.

Well, according to Western doctrine, negotiations have been proceeding under the supervision of the United States, which is an honest broker desperately trying to bring together these two irrational opponents who are recalcitrant. You can move from doctrine to the real world, and then you find a rather different picture: if there were real negotiations, they would be under the supervision of some neutral party, maybe a country that has a certain amount of respect in the world, maybe Brazil. On one side of the negotiations there would be the US and Israel, and on the other side there'd be the world. That's not an exaggeration, and in fact it's extremely clear from

---

13 D. Shipler, *New York Times*, 25 November 1983; also 26 January 1984. Human Rights Watch, *Israel: Without Status or Protection: Lebanese Detainees in Israel* 9, vol. no. 11 (October 1997).
14 Al Mezan press release, 'IOF kidnaps five Palestinian children in North Gaza', 7 September 2009. Reference 74/2009, http://www.mezan.org/en/details.php?id=9028&ddname=&id_dept=9.
15 Aviv Lavie, 'Inside Israel's secret prison', *Haaretz*, 22 August 2003; Jonathan Cook, 'Facility 1391: Israel's Guantanamo', *Le Monde Diplomatique*, November 2003; Chris McGreal, 'Facility 1391: Israel's secret prison', *Guardian (UK)*, 14 November 2003.

the diplomatic record. Let me just mention a few high points, or maybe low points, just going back through the last forty years very quickly.

In 1971, President Sadat of Egypt made a peace offer to Israel through UN mediator Gunnar Jarring. From Israel's perspective, it was a better offer than the one he would make in 1977, which led to the Camp David negotiations. Sadat's offer was for a full peace treaty in accordance with UN Security Council Resolution 242. Sadat offered peace in return for Israel's withdrawal from the Occupied Territories (but all he cared about was Sinai, not the West Bank). So, in effect the offer was to withdraw from the Sinai in exchange for a full peace treaty. Sadat's offer didn't contain anything for the Palestinians. There was mention of refugees, but there was nothing about Palestinian national rights. Jordan made a similar offer a year later. I don't think Israel even responded to the Jordanian offer but they did consider the Egyptian offer.

In his memoirs, Yitzhak Rabin, then ambassador to the US, referred to the 'famous' offer as a 'milestone' on the path to peace. He writes that 'the UN ambassador dropped his bombshell in the form of the famous "Jarring questionnaire" addressed to Israel and Egypt. It was one of those black-and-white, no-nonsense moves … Straightforward and simple; no ifs, ands, or buts. Jarring was impatient and demanded immediate, binding answers.'[16] So Israel had a fateful choice: it could accept peace and integration into the region or insist on confrontation, hence inevitable dependency on the US. It chose the latter course, not on grounds of security but because of a commitment to expansion. That is clear in Israeli sources. General Haim Bar-Lev, a cabinet member in the Meir and Rabin governments, wrote in a Labor Party journal, 'I think that we could obtain a peace settlement on the basis of the earlier [pre-June 1967] borders. If I were persuaded that this is the maximum that we might obtain, I would say: agreed. But I think that it is not the maximum. I think that if we continue to hold out, we will obtain more.'[17]

The 'more' that was of primary interest at the time was northeastern Sinai. Israel was planning and beginning to implement massive programs of development there. The Israeli army moved in and kicked out thousands of Bedouin farmers. It drove them into the desert and destroyed towns and villages in order to make way for an all-Jewish city, Yamit. The choice was security versus expansion, and expansion won flat out. And that's been

---

16 Yitzhak Rabin, *The Rabin Memoirs*, University of California Press, Berkeley, 1996.
17 Labor Party journal *Ot*, 9 March 1972: cited in Chomsky, *Towards A New Cold War*, Pantheon, New York, 1982, p. 460.

policy ever since. Well, as always, the crucial question was how Washington would react. The offer was debated in the US government, there was a split: the State Department was in favour of accepting the proposal, which was pretty much in line with what was formal US policy. The National Security Adviser, Henry Kissinger, was strongly against it. He was in favour of what he calls 'stalemate', meaning no negotiations, just force. That's pretty typical of Kissinger's diplomacy; it's why he's called a famous realist. So he rejected it, and his view prevailed in the bureaucratic infighting that ensued. So the United States and Israel therefore rejected this offer.[18]

Well that was pretty significant, but nobody took the Egyptians seriously. It was a period of extreme racism in Israel. There's some pretty good literature about this. There's a book by Amnon Kapeliouk, in Hebrew, translated into French.[19] He was an outstanding Israeli journalist, and the book is the best account of Israeli government (Labor Party) policies from 1967–1973. I haven't been able to get anyone to translate it into English. But the general picture is that there was a conception in Israel that Arabs don't know which end of the gun to hold, so it doesn't matter what they say. We'll just do what we like.[20]

That was the US position as well.[21] When Sadat was placing pretty substantial armies on the Suez Canal, Israel of course knew about it but they didn't pay any attention. They left the other side of the canal virtually undefended. Well, then came the 1973 war, which was a very close thing for Israel, very close. It was a desperate situation; it actually almost led to a nuclear war – a major nuclear war.[22] It was not trivial. Well, Kissinger does understand force, and Israel understood that they better pay some attention to Egypt instead of just dismissing them. Then begins the famous shuttle diplomacy, finally leading to the Camp David peace treaty in 1979, which was very similar to the peace treaty that the United States and Israel rejected in 1971. Except from Israel's point of view Camp David was harsher because during the mid-seventies the question of Palestinian national rights had entered the international agenda. So in 1979, the US and Israel were

---

18 Henry Kissinger, *White House Years*, Little, Brown, Boston, 1979, p. 1279.
19 Amnon Kapeliouk, *Israel: la fin des mythes*, Albin Michel, Paris, 1975.
20 Norman Finkelstein, *Image And Reality Of The Israel-Palestine Conflict*, Verso, London, 1995, pp. 167–9.
21 Matti Golan, *The Secret Conversations of Henry Kissinger: Step-by-Step Diplomacy in the Middle East*, New York: Quadrangle/New York Times, 1976.
22 Douglas Little, 'The Cold War in the Middle East: Suez crisis to Camp David Accords', *The Cambridge History of the Cold War*, vol. II, Cambridge University Press, Cambridge, 2010, pp. 305–326.

compelled to make some gestures about Palestinian national rights, which of course they proceeded then to violate, but they accepted a harsher position in 1979 than the one that they'd rejected in 1971.

Well you look at the literature: the Camp David agreements are regarded as a great diplomatic triumph for Henry Kissinger and President Carter. The reality is they were a diplomatic catastrophe. The US and Israel's rejection of a peace offer in 1971 led to a major war, a very serious war not only for Israel, Egypt and Syria, but also globally. The US and Russia came close to a nuclear war. And then, finally, the US and Israel accepted a version of Sadat's 1971 offer which was harsher from their point of view than the one they'd rejected. In an honest history, that'd be called a diplomatic catastrophe, but take a look at the way it's treated in academic and general history and you learn something about ourselves.

Well, meanwhile other things have been happening. As I mentioned, the issue of Palestinian national rights entered the international agenda. In January 1976, the three major Arab states, Syria, Jordan and Egypt, brought a resolution that called for a two-state peace settlement to the UN Security Council. The Palestine Liberation Organisation supported the proposal, which was the first official proposal of the two-state settlement idea. There's an overwhelming international consensus in favour of it by now. And they included in the proposal the major wording of UN Resolution 242, which everybody on all sides regards as the kind of core diplomatic resolution. The 1976 resolution called for recognition of the rights of every state in the region, including Israel and the new Palestinian state – the right to live within secure and recognised borders. That's the basic wording of 242, and that was also in the January 1976 resolution. But it was vetoed by the United States.[23] Now, a US veto is a double veto: first of all the resolution is blocked, and it's also eliminated from history. Check and find out – look at the academic scholarly studies, the general reporting and so on, and you'd have to go pretty far to find even a recognition that any of this existed, but it existed, and you can easily discover it.[24]

In 1980 again there was a similar resolution, again vetoed by the United States, therefore out of history. Between 1973 and 1987, the United States

---

23 For the fullest discussion of this, see particularly note 25 of Noam Chomsky, 'Armageddon is well-located', in *Towards a New Cold War*, Pantheon, New York, 1982. Also, Kathleen Teltsch, 'US casts veto on Mideast Plan in UN's Council', *New York Times*, 27 January 1976; 'Palestine Guerrillas Seek to Close Ranks for War', *New York Times*, 1 March 1976.

24 Edward Said and Christopher Hitchens, eds, *Blaming the Victims: Spurious Scholarship and the Palestinian Question*, London: Verso, 1988.

vetoed nineteen Security Council resolutions concerning Israel and Middle East peace, voting alone.[25] After debate was blocked in the Security Council, it shifted over to the General Assembly. I won't run through the history, but year after year if you check you'll see that the General Assembly continued to advance peace proposals in its annual winter meetings. In 1989, the Assembly voted 151–3 (United States, Israel, Dominica) for a settlement incorporating the wording of UN 242, along with 'the right to self-determination' for the Palestinians. In December 1990, the resolution was voted 144–2 (United States and Israel) to call an international conference. The record is similar in earlier years and up to the present. That goes on year after year, but all of that's kind of out of history too.

In 1988 something important happened: the Palestinian National Council officially accepted the international consensus on a two state settlement, and of course Israel and the US responded. Israel's coalition government at the time – the Shamir-Peres government – issued a formal response. The response said that there can be no 'additional Palestinian state in the Gaza district and in the area between Israel and Jordan'. Notice the phrase 'additional Palestinian state'. They were declaring that Jordan is already a Palestinian state; of course, the Jordanians don't agree, and the Palestinians don't agree, but since they're 'unpeople' and their voices don't matter any more than those of their camels and donkeys, there can't be an additional Palestinian state, and everything will have to be settled in accordance with Israeli guidelines. The response also declared that 'There will be no change in the status of Judea, Samaria [the West Bank] and Gaza other than in accordance with the basic guidelines of the Government' of Israel, which reject Palestinian self-determination. Again, you're going to have to search pretty far to find a record of this, but it's there. Well the question is always, how's the US going to respond? That was during the first Bush administration; James Baker was Secretary of State, and a few months later Baker issued the Baker Plan, which simply reiterated the Israeli position. No additional Palestinian state, the fate of the territories will be settled in accordance with Israeli guidelines. I can give you sources if you like.[26]

Well, shortly after that there were negotiations beginning with the Madrid negotiations. Then came Oslo, which undercut the Palestinian negotiators, for interesting reasons, and that led to the famous event on the White House

---

25 Mark Curtis, 'Obstacles to Security in the Middle East', in Seizaburo Sato and Trevor Taylor, eds, *Prospects for Global Order*, vol. 2, Royal Institute of International Affairs and International Institute for Global Peace, London, 1993.
26 N. Chomsky, *World Orders, Old and New*, Pluto Press, London, 1996, p. 545 n. 69 and 70.

lawn – President Clinton standing over the two antagonists, Rabin and Arafat. Rabin reluctantly shook hands with Arafat. That was described in the US press as 'a day of awe', and that's the way it was treated in fact.[27] Not everyone was enthralled, although most people were. Edward Said in fact was one of the few who recognised at once what was happening.[28] I spoke and wrote about it too, along with a very tiny handful of others, but the most important reaction was by Haidar Abdel Shafi. He was probably the most respected person in the Occupied Territories – a dedicated, honest nationalist, and also the chief negotiator for the Palestinians in the Madrid accords. He was undercut. He refused even to attend the ceremony on the White House lawn, and strongly opposed the agreement because of its content.[29]

What was its content? Well, there was a Declaration of Principles in September 1993. If you bother reading it, you'll understand right away why it was just a total sell-out of the Palestinians. For almost two decades before these negotiations, there was general agreement (including by the PLO from the mid-1970s) that a settlement should be based on UN Security Council Resolution 242 (and on UNSCR 338, which endorses 242). There were two basic points of contention: 1) Do we interpret the withdrawal clause of 242 in accord with the international consensus (including the United States, pre-1971), or in accord with the position of Israel and US policy from 1971? 2) Is the settlement based *solely* on UN 242, which offers nothing to the Palestinians, or 242 *and other relevant UN resolutions*, as the PLO had long proposed in accord with the non-rejectionist international consensus? Thus, does the settlement incorporate the right of refugees to return and compensation, as the UN has insisted since 1948 (with US endorsement, long forgotten), and the Palestinian right to national self-determination

---

27 David Shribman, 'At White House, symbols of a Day of Awe', *Boston Globe*, 29 September 1995.
28 Edward W. Said, 'Arafat's Deal', *Nation*, 20 September 1993.
29 N. Chomsky, *World Orders, Old and New*, Pluto Press, London, 1996, p. 551 n. 138: 'In a talk in Bethlehem on 22 July 1993, just as Arafat was secretly moving to take matters into his own hands, undercutting local Palestinians, Haidar Abdel Shafi held out little hope for the "peace process," which excludes entirely the possibility "that Palestinians must be the main authority in the interim period for the people and for the land," leading to true national self-determination. He stressed, however, that "the negotiations are not worth fighting about. The critical issue is transforming our society. All else is inconsequential … We must decide amongst ourselves to use all our strength and resources to develop our collective leadership and the democratic institutions which will achieve our goals and guide us in the future … The important thing is for us to take care of our internal situation and to organize our society and correct those negative aspects from which it has been suffering for generations and which is the main reason for our losses against our foes."'

repeatedly endorsed by the UN (though blocked by Washington)? These are the crucial issues that have stood in the way of a political settlement.

On both major issues under dispute, (1) and (2), the agreement explicitly and without equivocation adopted the US-Israeli stand. Article I, outlining the 'Aim of the Negotiations', specifies that 'the negotiations on the permanent status will lead to the implementation of Security Council Resolutions 242 and 338'; nothing further is mentioned. Note that this refers to the *permanent* status – the long-term end to be achieved. Furthermore, Israel's Deputy Foreign Minister Yossi Beilin, a close associate of Foreign Minister Shimon Peres, made explicit that the withdrawal clause of UN 242 is to be understood in the terms unilaterally imposed by the United States (from 1971), entailing only partial withdrawal, as Washington determines. In fact, the agreement does not even preclude further Israeli settlement in the large areas of the West Bank it has taken over, or even new land takeovers. On such central matters as control of water, it refers only to 'cooperation in the management of water resources in the West Bank and Gaza Strip' and 'equitable utilization of joint water resources' in a manner to be determined by 'experts from both sides', some of them already cited. The outcome of cooperation between an elephant and a fly is not hard to predict.

Remember that UN 242 crucially mentions nothing about Palestinian rights. Palestinians are mentioned as refugees – maybe we should be nice to the refugees – but nothing about Palestinian national rights. Now there are further UN resolutions in all those years, of course, which did refer to Palestinian national rights, including the vetoed Security Council resolutions, but they were ignored. Well that's the final outcome, which of course undermines any possibility of any kind of diplomatic settlement, and Haidar Abdel Shafi for that reason just refused to attend. Then through the nineties, settlement expansion continued, almost linearly. So if you take a look at the record, it just keeps going straight up. The peak year of settlements was actually the year 2000, about forty per cent higher than the last year.[30]

Another policy that the US and Israel were following was to separate Gaza from the West Bank. Now the Oslo agreements declared that they are a territorial unity, but the US and Israel never intended to accept that, and they began to move right away in the early 1990s to break them apart. Now that's pretty crucial because it means that if ever there is some kind of limited Palestinian self-determination in the West Bank, it'll be encircled and

---

30 The most informative continuing analysis is in Geoffrey Aronson's *Report on Israeli Settlements in the Occupied Territories*, http://www.fmep.org.

imprisoned; the only outlet to the rest of the world would be Gaza. But that's going to be separated. In this manner, the famous Oslo process continues right to the present. It should be recognised – in fact, remembered, because it is recognised – that all the settlements are illegal; not just settlement *expansion* but the very existence of every single settlement is itself illegal. That's not really in doubt; that's been determined by every relevant significant legal authority.

Israel itself understood at once that its settlement projects in the Occupied Territories, and anything related to them, are illegal. When the settlement project was beginning, Israel's top legal authority on international law was Theodore Meron, a distinguished international lawyer and a leading figure in international tribunals. He informed the Israel government in September 1967 'that civilian settlement in the administered [occupied] territories contravenes the explicit provisions of the Fourth Geneva Conventions', the core of international humanitarian law. Justice Minister Ya'akov Shimshon Shapira had already informed the Israeli cabinet about this. A few weeks later Defence Minister Moshe Dayan, who was in charge of the Occupied Territories, informed his fellow ministers that 'we must consolidate our hold so that over time we will succeed in "digesting" Judea and Samaria [the West Bank] and merging them with "little" Israel', meanwhile 'dismember[ing] the territorial contiguity' of the West Bank. This would have to be done by expropriating land from Arab owners under the pretence 'that the step is necessary for military purposes', a subterfuge that had also worked quite well to deprive Israeli Arabs of the rights accorded to Jewish citizens.

Dayan had no illusions about the criminality of the enterprise he was recommending. 'Settling Israelis in occupied territory contravenes, as is known, international conventions', he observed, 'but there is nothing essentially new in that'. This criminality was underscored by UN Security Council resolutions and by the International Court of Justice, with the basic agreement of US Justice Buergenthal in a separate declaration.[31] Dayan was kind of at the dovish end of the Israeli spectrum; he actually had some sympathy for Palestinians. Israel, he informed his colleagues, should tell the

---

31 G. Gorenberg, *The Accidental Empire*, Times Books, New York, 2006. On the carefully planned and systematic execution of the project, and the leading role of Peres and others honoured in the West as 'moderates' and 'peacemakers', see Idith Zertal and Akiva Eldar, *Lords of the Land*, Nation Books, New York, 2007, also on the shameful behaviour of the courts, along with the most prominent legal commentator in the Israeli media, Moshe Negbi, *Kisdom Hayinu*, Keter Publishing House, Jerusalem, 2004 (Hebrew). For quotes from his harrowing account of what passes for law in Israel, and from other leading Israeli analysts who bring forth similar material, see N. Chomsky, *Failed States: The Abuse of Power and the Assault on Democracy*, Metropolitan Books, New York, 2006. *Ibid.* on the ICJ and Buergenthal.

Palestinian refugees in the Occupied Territories that 'we have no solution, you shall continue to live like dogs, and whoever wishes may leave, and we will see where this process leads'. He then produced an interesting image. He said to a Palestinian poet that 'the situation today resembles the complex relationship between a Bedouin man and the girl he kidnaps against her will ... You Palestinians, as a nation, don't want us today, but we'll change your attitude by forcing our presence on you'. Not an original thought. When reports arrived of the massacres of Mexican civilians and rapes of local women by US soldiers during what Mexican historians call 'the American invasion' of 1846–48, the *New York Herald* thoughtfully observed that 'like the Sabine virgins, she will soon learn to love her ravisher'.[32]

Of course, in what's called Jerusalem – a vastly expanded area, which Israel has annexed in violation of Security Council orders – settlements are doubly illegal; firstly because all settlements are illegal, and secondly because Jerusalem is the subject of explicit Security Council resolutions going back to 1968, ordering that any modification of the status of Jerusalem be stopped. At that point the US went along with the resolution – the US was still part of the world back then. But, you know, what does it matter really? The creatures who are being harmed are 'unpeople', so that isn't very interesting, except maybe to animal rights activists, and in fact there's no comment about it.

There was one interesting break in this series of events, and that was in the last month of President Clinton's term in office, January 2001. Some very instructive events took place.[33] There had been negotiations at Camp David in the year 2000; they broke down. The official story is, you know, the Palestinians are responsible. Clinton knew better. After they broke down he recognised openly that no Palestinians could possibly accept the terms that Israel and the United States had proposed at Camp David, and he presented what he called his 'parameters' – this is December 2000, a couple of months after Camp David. The parameters are kind of vague, but they were more forthcoming. Then a couple of days later Clinton made a speech in which he said that both sides have accepted his parameters, although both sides had reservations.

---

32 Yossi Beilin, *Mehiro shel Ihud,* Revivim, Tel Aviv, 1985, pp. 42, 147 (the primary source for Israeli cabinet records under the Labor coalition, 1967–77). Dayan's analogy in Gershom Gorenberg, *The Accidental Empire*, Times Books, New York, 2006, pp. 81–2. *Herald* cited by James Bradley, *The Imperial Cruise*, Little, Brown & Co., New York, 2009, p. 63. See also pp. 181–4 of Noam Chomsky, *Failed States: The abuse of power and the assault on democracy*, Allen & Unwin, Crows Nest, 2006.
33 Jeremy Pressman, *Visions in Collision: What happened at Camp David and Taba?* International Security, vol. 28, no. 2, Fall 2003, pp. 5–43.

From 21–27 January 2001, Israeli and Palestinian negotiators met in Taba, Egypt, to iron out the differences, and made considerable progress. In their final joint press conference, they announced that a full resolution could have been reached in a few more days. But Israeli Prime Minister Barak called off the negotiations prematurely, and they have not been formally resumed. We have pretty extensive record of those negotiations, most of it is unfortunately in Hebrew; a very extensive Hebrew record. But a lot of it is in English, and there was also an international observer from the European Union, Miguel Moratinos, who gave his interpretation. You can find it also in the Israeli press.[34] They all agreed on what happened – in fact the final press conference of the two sides stated that they were coming pretty close to a settlement.[35] The settlement was along the lines of the international consensus that everybody knows: a two state settlement along the international border and various modalities for the other problems that arise.[36] They said if they had a little more time they might iron out everything – which would have resolved it. Well, Israel called off the negotiations prematurely, and that ended formal negotiations between the two sides. But that sort of tells us something. It tells us that the term 'international consensus' is correct – it includes every relevant party: the Arab League, the Organisation of Islamic Cooperation, which includes Iran, Hamas, just about everyone – at least on paper. Except the US and Israel.

It came very close. The formal negotiations ended but international diplomacy continued. The next step a couple of years later was the formation of what's called the 'Quartet' – the US, the European Union, Russia and the United Nations. The Quartet issued what they called their 'Roadmap to peace', which was a series of steps to be taken to lead to a settlement. Hamas is constantly denounced for failing to agree to the Roadmap; you have to look harder to find the fact that Israel instantly rejected the Roadmap. They did it in the usual way that states behave: they said, fine, we accept it, but we add reservations. And they added fourteen reservations. If you bother to read the reservations, you'll see that that's the end of the Roadmap. This had been kept rather quiet; activists know about it and people talk about it in meetings like this, but there was nothing mentioned publicly until President Carter's

---

34 For the Moratinos summary, see Akiva Eldar, *The Peace That Nearly Was at Taba*, Ha'aretz, 14 February 2002, pp. 4, 9.
35 'The sides declare that they have never been closer to reaching an agreement and it is thus our shared belief that the remaining gaps could be bridged with the resumption of negotiations following the Israeli elections.' Israeli-Palestinian Joint Statement at Taba, 27 January 2001, http://mondediplo.com/ focus/mideast/a3275.
36 Hussein Agha and Robert Malley, 'The Last Negotiation: How to End the Middle East Peace Process', *Foreign Affairs*, vol. 81, no. 3 (May–June 2002): p. 10ff.

book appeared. That was the great merit of Jimmy Carter's *Palestine: Peace Not Apartheid*: it brought these facts to public attention for the first time. It caused a huge furore; it was bitterly denounced, and major efforts were made to try to undermine it.[37] But one thing was not mentioned: the fact that it contained the first exposition in the mainstream of Israel's fourteen reservations, which undercut the Roadmap. Try to find a reference to it; it's unmentionable, it's another one of those things you can't say. But it's there.

Well, then came the January 2006 elections in Palestine that I mentioned. They were carefully monitored elections, recognised to be free and fair. Actually, they were the only free and fair ones in the Arab world. But there was a problem with them: the wrong side won. Our conception of democracy in the West is that it's not democracy unless the guys we like win. This is not the only case, incidentally. It's worth keeping in mind, when you hear the rhetoric about our yearning for democracy and so on, that this happens to be a striking example, but it's very far from the only one. Within days the United States and Israel announced that they were going to punish the Palestinians severely for the crime of voting the wrong way in a free election. It was a perfectly public announcement, incidentally, and the European Union went along too. So that's when the sanctions began. You can't do things like voting the wrong way in a free election, and expect to get away with it. The US immediately initiated the standard operating procedure when elections come out the wrong way – organise a military coup. It happens over and over, dozens of times, in various places since the Second World War.

So the US and Israel began planning a military coup – together with the Palestinian Authority, incidentally, because they didn't like the outcome either. Although it's commonly described as a Hamas military coup, the reality is quite different. The US and Israel incited a civil war in a crude attempt to overturn the elections that brought Hamas to power. That has been public knowledge since at least April 2008, when David Rose published a detailed and documented account of how Bush, Condoleezza Rice and Deputy National Security Adviser Elliott Abrams 'backed an armed force under Fatah strongman Muhammad Dahlan, touching off a bloody civil war in Gaza and leaving Hamas stronger than ever'.[38] The account was corroborated by Norman Olsen, who served for twenty-six years in the

---

37 There were great efforts to find trivial errors, but the one serious error was also ignored: Carter's repetition of the conventional myth that Israel's 1982 invasion of Lebanon was in defence against PLO rockets. For more, see Chapter Five of N. Chomsky, *Fateful Triangle*, Pluto Press, London, 1999.
38 David Rose, 'The Gaza Bombshell', *Vanity Fair*, April 2008.

Foreign Service, including four years working in the Gaza Strip and four years at the US Embassy in Tel Aviv, and then moved on to become associate coordinator for counterterrorism at the Department of State. Olson and his son detail the State Department shenanigans intended to ensure that their candidate, Abbas, would win in the January 2006 elections – in which case it would have been hailed as a triumph of democracy, warming the hearts of loyalists. After the election-fixing failed, the US and Israel turned to the punishment of Palestinians for voting the wrong way, and began arming a militia run by Dahlan. But 'Dahlan's thugs moved too soon', the Olsens write, and a Hamas preemptive strike undermined the coup attempt.[39]

So the elected government won, but they were soon in jail. The siege became much harsher in June 2007 after the military coup failed to overthrow the elected government. An important event took place in July 2008: a truce was signed between Israel and the Hamas government. Israel never lived up to its side of the truce. It was supposed to end the siege, those were the terms of the truce, but it refused to do so because of Gilad Shalit; it said that as long as he's in captivity we can't live up to the terms of the truce that we just signed.

So Israel maintained its siege, which we may recall is an act of war. In fact, Israel has always insisted on an even stronger principle: hampering access to the outside world, even well short of a siege, is an act of war, justifying massive violence in response. Interference with Israel's passage through the Straits of Tiran was a large part of the justification offered for Israel's invasion of Egypt (with France and England) in 1956, and for its launching of the June 1967 war. The siege of Gaza is total, not partial, apart from occasional willingness of the occupiers to relax it slightly to allow bare survival. And it is vastly more harmful to Gazans than closing the Straits of Tiran was to Israel.

However, Hamas did live up to the terms of the truce. You look at the Israeli official records, they recognised that there were no Hamas rockets. None of the famous rockets was shot – zero. There were some rockets, but not from Hamas. The spokesperson for the prime minister, Mark Regev, acknowledged that there was not a single Hamas rocket among the few that were launched from the onset of the June 2008 cease-fire until 4 November, when Israel violated the cease-fire even more egregiously with a raid into Gaza, killing six Hamas activists and eliciting a retaliatory barrage of rockets (with no injuries). The Israeli government acknowledged the same on its official website.[40]

---

39 Norman Olsen and Matthew Olsen, op-ed, *Christian Science Monitor*, 12 January 2009.
40 Mark Regev interviewed by David Fuller, Channel 4, UK, http://www.youtube.com/watch?v=N6e-elrgYL0. Editorial, *The Other Israel*, Holon Israel, December-January 2008–9.

The 4 November raid was on the evening of the US presidential elections, when the world's attention wasn't on Israel and Palestine. The pretext for the raid was that Israel had detected a tunnel in Gaza that *might* have been intended for use to capture another Israeli soldier; a 'ticking tunnel', in official communiqués. The pretext was transparently absurd, as a number of Israeli commentators noted. If such a tunnel existed, and reached the border, Israel could easily have barred it right there. But as usual, the ludicrous Israeli pretext was deemed credible, and the timing was overlooked. It went on for a couple of weeks. In late December, Hamas offered to renew the truce. The Israeli cabinet considered it and rejected it. It chose instead to bomb Gaza. That's the Cast Lead invasion and bombing. In the West, including the major reports on this, like the Goldstone Report, they all take for granted that Israel had a right to attack. The argument is that any state has a right of self-defence, which is true. But no state or no person for that matter has a right of self-defence unless you have exhausted peaceful means. Not only had they not exhausted peaceful means, they'd refused to try them, presumably because they knew they were going to work. If the truce had been renewed, it would have again stopped the rocket firing.

Well there were shocking war crimes during Cast Lead. If you read nothing more about it I'd recommend a book by two extremely courageous Norwegian doctors, Mads Gilbert and Erik Fosse, who were working in the main hospital in Gaza, right through this period.[41] It's a graphic, shattering, day-to-day account of the horrendous events that were taking place. You know, it doesn't have all the detail of the major reports, but you get a sense that it goes beyond the reporting. They describe the attack as 'infanticide' because of the hundreds of infants who were slaughtered during this attack that came into the hospital.

The US blocked a ceasefire attempt. Obama had been elected President but he hadn't been inaugurated. He refused to say anything about it; his line was there's only one President, and I'm not the President yet so I can't say anything. He was saying things about every other topic, but not that one. In fact his campaign did issue a statement. They repeated a comment he'd made when he visited the Israeli town of Sderot in July 2008: 'If missiles were falling where my two daughters sleep, I would do everything in order to stop that.' (As it happened, no Hamas missiles were falling, because Hamas was strictly observing the cease-fire, as I said, even though Israel had not relieved

---

41   M. Gilbert and E. Fosse, *Eyes in Gaza*, Quartet Books, London, 2010. See also M. Gilbert and E. Fosse, 'Inside Gaza's Al-Shifa hospital', *The Lancet*, vol. 373, no. 9659, pp. 200–202, 17 January 2009.

the punishing siege, an act of war.) But Obama did nothing, not even make a statement, when US jets and helicopters with Israeli pilots were causing incomparably worse suffering to Palestinian children. In fact, the Pentagon hired a German merchant ship to transport 3000 tons of unidentified ammunition from Greece to Israel during the assault on Gaza.[42] Greece to its credit wouldn't allow the ships to go; the Greek government barred the use of any port in Greece for the supplying of the Israeli army.

The attack was very carefully timed to end just before Obama was inaugurated. So it ended, making sure that he didn't have to say anything, and then as President he was able to say something. He said what he says about Bush's war crimes and everything else: it's better to look forward than to look backward, so let's forget about it and look forward. That's the usual, familiar rhetoric about how we must move on and put the past behind us – when it's our crimes, that is; the crimes of others can never be forgotten or forgiven. So then we get to the Obama period, which is in fact the worst period yet. It began right away. I can go through the details if you like but it's the worst record of any American President with regard to this issue. One striking example was last February, when Obama vetoed a Security Council Resolution, which called for implementation of official US policy.[43] That was extreme enough so it actually got some mention; this was a resolution calling for an end to expansion of settlements. Remember the settlements themselves are the problem, not just expansion. The US vetoed it, and that incidentally ended the discussion of settlement expansion. And since then it goes on without discussion. And it goes on right now. So when the Palestinian Authority went to the United Nations a couple of weeks ago, Israel responded at once, very brazenly, by announcing a new settlement called Givat HaMatos. It's right between Bethlehem and Jerusalem; it breaks the very limited connection between the two towns, which are in eyesight.[44]

It was done explicitly in order to respond to the Palestinian approach to the United Nations. Well that just happened again a couple of days ago

---

42 Stefano Ambrogi, 'US seeks ship to move arms to Israel', *Reuters*, 9 January 2009.
43 Brad Knickerbocker, 'If Obama opposes Israeli settlement activity, why did US veto UN vote?' *Christian Science Monitor*, 18 February 2011: '… the vote Friday is in line with stated US policy. That is, it favors direct talks between the parties without a role for the UN in establishing a lasting peace between Israel and its neighbors – especially with Palestinians. Friday's veto was the 10th time in the past 11 years that the US has voted against a UN measure considered critical of Israel. Over a longer period, there have been dozens of such votes on behalf of Israel.'
44 Chris McGreal, 'Israel plans new settlement of 2,600 that will isolate Arab East Jerusalem', *Guardian*, 16 October 2011.

when the Palestinians were accepted by UNESCO. The Israeli government responded by announcing new settlements both in Jerusalem and the West Bank – with kind of an interesting comment, namely that it really didn't matter because Israel is going to annex these areas anyway. And in fact they understand that they can do whatever they like because Obama is just going to genuflect – in ways which are kind of embarrassing actually, but it happens every step of the way. That's a change: earlier American presidents kind of went along, but not in this humiliating fashion. So George Bush I, for example, he and his Secretary of State James Baker were kind of offended by the insulting, brazen way in which Israel was expanding settlements right under their nose. Like, they announced a new settlement when Baker went to Jerusalem. The US was pretty irritated about this. It instituted real but very limited sanctions; they were essentially withdrawn under Clinton.[45]

Bush II went beyond that; the US several times under George W. Bush ordered Israel to stop carrying out actions that the US didn't like. Israel has a high-tech militarised economy. They need a market; the big market is China, so they wanted to upgrade Chinese Harpy Killer drone aircraft. The United States told them, you're not going to do it. They said they were going to do it anyway. The US then proceeded to humiliate them; not just to stop them but to humiliate them.[46] They refused to allow the Defense Secretary Shaoul Mofaz to visit Washington, Pentagon officials broke off their contacts with Israeli connections and they began to threaten sanctions. They insisted that Israel pass legislation to bar these sales and furthermore they were to write a letter of apology to the United States for planning to do it. Well of course they had to do it all. But Obama just goes along. Well, meanwhile Israel and the United States are perfectly happy to let the negotiations go on indefinitely. Then they can continue carrying out the programs in the West Bank and Gaza.

That means the takeover of the West Bank can continue, and Gaza can be crushed. And it's getting pretty serious: the United Nations Relief and Works Agency for Palestine Refugees (UNRWA) just announced that they're running out of money.[47] UNRWA is the UN organisation that just

---

45 Amir Oren, *Ha'aretz*, 29 November 2002; Ze'ev Schiff, *Ha'aretz*, 27 and 29 July 2005. Cited and discussed in Noam Chomsky, *Failed States*, Allen & Unwin, p. 190 and *passim*. See also 'Excerpts from President Bush's news session on Israel loan guarantees', *New York Times*, 13 September 1991; Andrew Rosenthal, 'Bush and Israel', *New York Times*, 14 September 1991.
46 Jeremy M. Sharp, *US Foreign Aid to Israel*, Congressional Research Service, 4 December 2009.
47 UNRWA, Statement on Payments, 4 November 2011. http://www.unrwa.org/etemplate.php?id=1138.

keeps the refugees alive; schoolchildren get maybe their only meal of the day in school from UNRWA. They're running out of money, partly because of the US withdrawal of funds after the UNESCO bid. Canada, incidentally, went along with that. I don't know about Australia. And they say that by January they won't be able to feed schoolchildren anymore. And that's not only Gaza; that's also Lebanese refugee camps. This is pretty serious. It's not a lot of money: it's only $100,000, something like that, just to keep going for a while – not huge amounts of money. And in general the process goes on. Well, the US and Israel do want the negotiations to proceed, but they have to meet several preconditions. Now the standard line is that the Palestinians are demanding preconditions and Israel says, No, let's just negotiate. The truth of the matter is exactly the opposite: the US and Israel have three crucial preconditions. The first precondition is the negotiations must be under the aegis of the United States, which is a joke: you can't have negotiations with one of the partners running them. That's part of Washington's long-term commitment – it goes back to the Second World War – to make sure it controls that important region. So the US must run the negotiations. The second precondition is that settlement expansion must continue unhindered; that's a very crucial precondition. And the third precondition is in fact what I already mentioned, and Netanyahu openly stated it: certain areas are going to be annexed. Period. Okay, that's a major precondition.

If there were time I could go through the details, but I'm sure you know how it works. They're essentially implementing what was called the 'Sharon Plan' at one time. If you want I can go through it later. In disgust over the pointlessness of these negotiations the Palestinian authority did turn to the United Nations. Israel was deeply concerned. An illustration of that was quite an important meeting – it was intended to be secret, but it leaked. It was published in the Hebrew press. It was a meeting of the oligarchs, the few dozen people that basically own the country. They had a meeting in which they warned that if the Palestinians are accepted as a state in the United Nations, Israel is going to face a situation of what they called 'South Africanisation':

> the morning after the expected recognition of a Palestinian state, a dramatic and painful process of South Africanisation of the state of Israel will commence. The economic quiet existing today in Israel is illusionary, and is very likely to explode immediately following the declaration. I continue even today to receive messages from senior Palestinian officials that the Palestinian side prefers a peace agreement

over a unilateral move. Therefore, the (Israeli) prime minister must initiate a real political process which will allow this, and prevent a catastrophe from an Israeli perspective.[48]

That's not a small point, and they therefore actually urged Netanyahu to enter into serious agreement – to accept something like two state settlement. They had a specific proposal, not unlike what was discussed in Taba. Well, they didn't do it.

The crucial question, and it's alive right now, is how Europe is going to react. We know how most of the world feels: there's overwhelming support for a Palestinian state. We know what the US position is: the US is going to veto anything at the Security Council, and is working overtime to reduce support at the General Assembly. But how will Europe react? Europe's an independent force in the world, or could be if it wanted to. Well, they capitulated, as usual. Europe capitulated to the master, and to make it very clear they sent a message delivered by the utterly pathetic Tony Blair telling the Palestinians to forget it, and to go back to the negotiations run by the US with these preconditions. The Palestinian authority had the dignity to announce publicly that they were never going to have any further discussions with Blair. Now the stand of Australia is important. Australia is of course not a major player in world affairs, but it's important nevertheless. And in the international arena it's been unusually strong in support for US policy, and support for Israel. I think a pretty good account of the reasons was given by the President of Bar-Ilan University, when he granted an honorary degree to John Howard a couple of years ago. He said that the ties between Israel and Australia are 'culturally deep, and spiritually intimate', and I think that's more than the usual rhetorical vacuity.[49] That contributes to US/Israeli rejectionism, which is the major obstacle to peace.

Now in the contemporary discussion of this issue, it's very widely assumed, sort of across the spectrum that there are two options. One option is the international consensus on a two state settlement. The other option is Israel takes over the whole region, and there can be a civil rights struggle, something like the anti-Apartheid movement. And a lot of the international solidarity activists are actually proposing the second as a preferable alternative. It's proposed also by some of the Palestinians. But it's a total illusion. Those two options are not

---

48 Calcalist, quoting Dani Gillerman, former Israeli ambassador to the United Nations: http://www.calcalist.co.il/local/articles/0,7340,L-3517511,00.html.
49 Tom Hyland, 'The ties that bind', *The Age*, 11 January 2009.

the only options – there's a third option namely that Israel and the US will continue doing exactly what they're doing. There's no reason whatsoever why anyone should expect them to agree to take over the territory. They don't want the 'unpeople' – they can kind of rot in isolated cantons. Meanwhile, Israel will take over exactly like they're systematically doing with US support: annex everything inside the so-called 'separation wall'; vastly expand Jerusalem; take over the Jordan Valley, which is important Arab land with a lot of water and so on. They're driving out Palestinians, sinking wells, and have a couple of salients cutting through the West Bank, breaking it up into cantons. I mean the plans are very clear and obvious; they're right in front of your eyes. And they're implementing them – big infrastructure projects, so Israelis can go wherever they feel like while Palestinians will be up in the hills somewhere. We'll give them Ramallah; they can have elegant restaurants and nice theatres, like any colonial society where there's something offered to the elite, who often live very well. That's what's developing, and there isn't the slightest reason why the US and Israel will accept the so-called second option, taking over the population. In fact there won't be any so-called 'demographic problem' – the problem of too many Arabs in a Jewish state – because they're bringing none in.

They'll be picturesque figures in hills; tourists will see them leading their donkeys and so on. But that's the other option, it's either going to be a two state settlement or it's going to be this. There's no other option on the table. You can talk about it in philosophical, academic seminars, if you like but it's not there in the real world. Well, of all the problems in the world, this is actually one of the easiest to solve. There are plenty of problems where it's really hard to think of a feasible solution, like Kashmir, let's say, or Eastern Congo. They're really hard problems. This one's quite straight-forward. We all know the outline of a short-term settlement: it's the international consensus, and it enjoys overwhelming agreement. There are some problems, but they're kind of side problems: the main structure of an agreement is very clear. What's required is an end to US rejectionism. Well, is that possible? For one thing, international pressure can make a difference. Here's where Australia can have a role.

There are also internal developments in the United States that may be significant. Public opposition to Israeli policy is growing quite rapidly. That's been particularly true after the Gaza atrocities; they struck home in many ways. That's true within the Jewish community, incidentally, particularly among the younger Jews. Support is just falling away; they don't want a part of this. You can see it very clearly on college campuses, where the atmosphere has just changed enormously. I mean a couple of years ago if say Ed Said or I were giving talks on a college campus you needed police protection, literally. Meetings were physically broken up, even in my own university. It was much more serious then. Police would insist on, say, walking me back to the car because they had had threats that were taken seriously. That's completely gone. By now there are enormous audiences, kind of like this: a huge number of invitations, and you can barely get a hostile question. Today it's one of the major issues on campus. That's a big change.

Furthermore the major institutions have taken a pretty strong stand. It doesn't get reported much but it is important. Amnesty International a couple of years ago called for an arms embargo.[50] They pointed out that arms shipments are illegal under international law, which they are. And you can add that the arms are illegal under US law too; that can be a campaign that can be pushed. Perhaps more interesting is Human Rights Watch, which has been pretty quiet on this issue for the most part. But they've come out with some pretty strong positions: just recently, about a year ago Human Rights Watch issued a call to the United States government to withhold any aid to Israel that has anything to do with the Occupied Territories, or with discrimination within Israel.[51] Like the report this morning in the *Age* – withhold all aid – that's pretty far-reaching. They also called on the US government to investigate the tax free status of groups that are carrying out funding, either in Israel or anywhere in the Occupied Territories, and are involved in illegal acts, like support for settlements, or discrimination within Israel. That's far-reaching. If that were implemented it would have a huge effect, and Human Rights Watch is not a particularly radical organisation.

There's another dimension which is significant as well. You may recall that General Petraeus, the head of Central Command, a while back made some statements warning the government that Israeli intransigence was harming US forces in the field, all over the Middle East.[52] He was told to shut up, and he stopped talking about it, but others in the military, and pretty high up in the intelligence system, are continuing to say this. It's also coming out in the right wing think tanks. One of the major military think tanks – Middle East oriented, quite conservative – is the Centre for Strategic and International

---

50 Amnesty International, *Full arms embargo vital as US munitions reported on way to Israel*, Press Release, 14 January 2009.
51 Human Rights Watch, *Separate and Unequal: Israel's discriminatory treatment of Palestinians in the Occupied Palestinians Territories*, December 2010.
52 David Petraeus, Statement – Senate Armed Services Committee, 16 March 2010. http://armed-services.senate.gov/statemnt/2010/03%20March/Petraeus%2003-16-10.pdf Petraeus spoke a week after Israel announced its plans to build 1600 housing units in East Jerusalem publicly while US Vice President Joe Biden was visiting the country.

Studies. It's Anthony Cordesman, for those of you who follow this. They came out with a study recently that the US should rethink its relations with Israel because they may be harming US interests.[53] There was a pretty surprising article in the *Washington Post* a couple of weeks ago by one of their lead correspondents, Walter Pincus, urging that the United States rethink whether it should be giving any aid to Israel.[54] That would have been unthinkable a year or two ago. There's quite a lot going on like that.[55] Well, suppose the United States shifted policy to adopting, say, the position of Human Rights Watch, Amnesty International. Suppose it were to cut support for the occupation and take the position that the IDF – the Israeli military – must withdraw from the Occupied Territories. Well, what happens to the settlers?

There's a myth that it's going to be a big problem because the settlers would have to be forcibly removed. In fact that's not true; they don't have to touch the settlers. All that's necessary is to send lorries to the West Bank and give them assistance in moving from their highly subsidised homes in the West Bank to highly subsidised homes within Israel, and they'll probably practically all go. Maybe a couple of people want to stay and hang onto every rock – somebody from Brooklyn or whatever. Okay, they can stay, you don't have to remove them. You don't have to remove anybody, just give them the opportunity and assistance to do what they want. Every analyst thinks almost all of them will go. If some of them want to stay, who cares? They can stay. But there's no issue of forcible removal. Actually the same was true in Gaza in 2005. There was a kind of staged trauma, mostly for the goyim – as the Israelis put it – for the Gentiles. We've got to stage a trauma when we decide to withdraw a couple of thousand settlers from Gaza. You have photographs, pictures in the newspapers of little children pleading with soldiers not to destroy their homes and so on. It was all staged, totally staged.

All they had to do is announce that the IDF is going to withdraw from Gaza on 1 August. The settlers will all climb into the lorries and go to their subsidised homes in Israel. But then you don't get the propaganda version of it. What made this particularly ludicrous was that it was almost an exact replay of something they did in 1981, after the Camp David accords when they had to withdraw from the Sinai, meaning withdraw from Yamit and so

---

53 Anthony Cordesman, *Israel as a Strategic Liability?* Center for Strategic and International Studies, 2 June 2010.
54 Walter Pincus, 'United States needs to reevaluate its assistance to Israel', *Washington Post*, 18 October 2011.
55 Helene Cooper, 'Washington Asks: What to do about Israel?' *New York Times*, 5 June 2010.

on. And the same thing was done: instead of just withdrawing, they staged a big trauma. In fact I remember a headline in a leading Israeli journal that said 'National Trauma '82', ridiculing the whole show.[56]

Amnon Kapeliouk described the Yamit evacuation as 'one of the largest brain-washing operations conducted by the government in order to convince the Israeli people that they have suffered a national trauma the effect of which will be felt for generations' and which will create 'a national consensus opposed to similar withdrawals in the remaining Occupied Territories'. He quoted General Chaim Erez, commander of the Yamit evacuation, who said that 'Everything was planned and agreed from the beginning' with the settlers who were to offer a show of resistance. Thus, Kapeliouk writes, 'While the hospitals of the West Bank were full of scores of Palestinian victims of 'trigger happy' Israeli soldiers, a miracle occurred in Yamit: no demonstrators required even first-aid attention'.[57] All this was redone in Gaza for propaganda reasons, but you could redo it if you want for the West Bank. It's totally unnecessary; this is just not an issue.

There are precedents for this; it wouldn't be something unheard of. The most interesting precedent actually is South Africa. There are a lot of analogies drawn constantly between Israel and South Africa – most of them pretty dubious – but there's one that's quite real, and it's worth thinking about. Go back more than fifty years ago: the white nationalist government recognised that they were becoming a pariah state. We have the records. In 1958, the South African foreign minister informed the American ambassador that strong UN resolutions against South Africa passed by the majority of countries do not matter: 'What matters more than … all other votes put together is [the position] of [the] US in view of its predominant position of leadership in [the] Western world.'[58] In brief, there is really only one vote at the UN.

And that's pretty much what happened. If you look at what happened in the following years, you'll see that by the 1970s there was a UN arms embargo. Decades of protest against apartheid had expanded to initiatives of boycott, divestment, and sanctions (BDS). Corporations were beginning to abide by the 1977 Sullivan principles of pulling out, and Congress was soon to pass sanctions over Reagan's veto. But it had no effect. The South African minister's insight into world affairs retained its force. Through the 1980s, US trade with South Africa increased despite the 1985 congressional

---

56 *Ha'aretz*, 27 April 1982.
57 Amnon Kapeliouk, 'Conjuring up a trauma', *New Statesman*, 7 May 1982.
58 Ryan Irwin, 'A Wind of Change?' *Diplomatic History*, November 2009.

sanctions, which Reagan evaded. Reagan continued to back South African depredations in neighbouring countries that led to an estimated 1.5 million deaths. As late as 1988 the US condemned Nelson Mandela's African National Congress as one of the world's 'more notorious terrorist groups'.[59] The Apartheid regime remained strong, some thought invulnerable. But by 1990 policy changed. Mandela was let out of Robben Island, and within a few years apartheid was gone.

It's not the only case; the case of Indonesia and East Timor is kind of similar. The Indonesian generals' atrocities mounted right through to 1999. They were saying they're never going to pull out of East Timor, that it was a province of Indonesia – as Australia also insisted. In September 1999, under a lot of pressure, Clinton decided to shift course. He quietly informed the Indonesian generals that the game was over. They immediately pulled out – within days – allowing an Australian-led peacekeeping force to enter.[60] Well, things like that can happen. If it doesn't happen, and soon, the prospects for Palestinians and I think Israelis and others look rather grim.

Question and Answer

The BDS campaign: Last year you were prevented from entering the occupied West Bank area in Palestine to deliver a lecture at Birzeit University – a sort of boycott imposed on Birzeit by the Israelis; you are reported as saying that the episode makes Israel look like 1960s-era apartheid South Africa which realised it was an international outcast but hoped good PR would resolve its problems. If Israel is behaving like apartheid South Africa and is boycotting Palestinian universities, do you have a clear position on the nonviolent boycott, sanctions and divestment campaign against Israel?

I kind of remember what I said, it wasn't exactly this, I don't know where the quote comes from. What I said was pretty much what I just repeated here – about South Africa and the course of what happened in South Africa. At the time I was very much in favour of sanctions, boycotts and so on in the case of South Africa. And it makes perfect sense in the case of Palestine. Incidentally, I was involved in BDS programs long before the

---

59 Joseba Zulaika and William A Douglass, *Terror and Taboo*, Routledge, New York, 1996.
60 Clinton Fernandes, *The Independence of East Timor: Multidimensional Perspectives*, Sussex Academic Press, Eastbourne, 2011.

formal organisation of the group, so sure I think it's fine. In fact I think the BDS programs don't go far enough. They ought to go at least as far as Human Rights Watch and Amnesty International. I mean, that's not asking a lot; these are pretty conservative, mainstream organisations with a lot of public support. I told you their positions; I think those are good positions. And they're actually beyond what the BDS groups have called for.

However, before you carry out any tactic at all – whether it's civil disobedience, demonstrations, petitions, whatever it may be – if you care about the people you're trying to help you're going to ask whether that tactic is well-fashioned for the existing circumstances. You ask, for example, what the reaction's going to be in the audience you're trying to reach. This is kind of second nature to activists, except in the BDS movement. A lot of them haven't thought about this. The view that they're taking is that you've got to act on principle. But that doesn't make any sense, not if you care about the people who are the victims. You have to ask what the effects are going to be. That's true for everything. I mean this came up all the time during the Vietnam War, for example. There were groups at the most extreme end, like the Weathermen. I knew a lot of them. But they were so angry about what was happening, they said, we're just going to go out and smash up bank windows and so on. The Vietnamese were very strongly opposed to that. They wanted to survive. They didn't want American protesters to feel good – they didn't care about that. So they recommended things that from the point of view of the anti-war movement were considered outlandishly mild.

I remember discussions with Vietnamese when they were urging tactics like, say, women standing quietly around the graves of American soldiers. They much preferred that to the Weathermen tactics because they wanted to survive. They were concerned with the consequences of the tactics. Now, you just have to take that into account. Anybody who is an activist has to make a distinction between what you might call 'feel-good tactics', (it makes me feel good to do this), and 'do good tactics', (it's going to have a good effect). And that requires careful thought. You can't avoid the issue if you're serious about results. So I think the BDS organisations are on the right track, but they should really think these things through more carefully.

The Arab Spring: *In recent months the Egyptian government has seemingly adopted a more pro-Palestinian foreign policy, relaxing restrictions at the Rafah border crossing with Gaza and brokering Hamas-Fatah unity and the Israel-Hamas prisoner exchange deals respectively. Considering that the majority of the Egyptian regime has remained in power since Mubarak's* *removal and still receives millions of dollars in military aid from the United States, do these gestures really indicate a new Egyptian foreign policy direction towards the Israel-Palestine conflict?*

Egypt and Tunisia are the two countries where the Arab Spring has really had an effect. And not coincidentally, these are the two countries that have a militant labour movement that's been carrying out important actions for years. They've usually been crushed by the dictatorship, though they've won some victories. Actually, the Egyptian movement, the Tahrir Square Movement, is called the April 6 Movement. And there's a reason for the name: the young, tech-savvy people with the social media were kind of in the forefront, but they remember that on 6 April 2008 there were major industrial actions at the biggest plants in Egypt, calling for decent wages, the right to form independent unions, and overcoming the disastrous effects of the neoliberal policies. They were mostly crushed by the dictatorship then, but they were recalled, and that's the April 6 Movement today. They've had some significant victories: the press is a lot freer, labour organising is proceeding, and there are other victories. It has also affected policy. On the other hand, the regime's power doesn't go away easily. The military is still in control; they run a lot of the economy, and the US and the West are backing them, naturally. So the conflict is continuing; it's an ongoing conflict. How it turns out will relate to this question.

Even the small steps towardss democratisation – democratisation, remember, means having public opinion influence policy – to the extent that that happens you can say that there's a functioning democracy. (The West doesn't look so good by that criterion, I should say. You just saw it in Greece. What happened in Greece is very revealing. It's almost like the 2006 election in Palestine. The Greek government proposed having the Greek people express an opinion on what's happening to them and the roof fell in. Totally. The US and Europe reacted with utter denunciation. I mean, how could you dare allow the people to have a voice when we already made a decision about what should be done? The hatred of democracy is so profound. It shows up over and over.)

So the struggle is continuing. To the extent that the Egyptian population has been able to influence policy – a limited extent – it's been significant. A couple of important things have happened. For one thing, for the first time in thirty years, Egypt permitted Iranian ships, including military vessels, to transit the Suez Canal. That's serious. The Mediterranean is supposed to be an American lake: nobody else is allowed in there. Maybe Britain, but Britain does what it's told. Certainly not Iran. But now they've been permitted. Egypt is also moving towards establishing formal relations with Iran. In the case of Israel-Palestine, they sort of pushed through the tentative Hamas-Fatah agreement, which is significant if it's implemented, if it's really developed. Since 1991, the US and Israel have been trying to separate Gaza from the West Bank. If this unification move works, it would undermine their attempts. It would also lay the basis for redoing something like the 2006 elections that were such a shock to the West. That's important.

In the background is something very important: the 1979 peace treaty. The Egyptians have not indicated that they want to abrogate the treaty – they don't want to go back to war – but there's an important question about how the treaty is interpreted. The US and Israel instantly and quite publicly interpreted the 1979 treaty as giving Israel a license to do whatever it wanted. Once the Egyptian deterrent went, Israel was free to withdraw forces from the south, attack Lebanon – as it did almost immediately – and expand its operations in the Occupied Territories. Well, the Egyptian people never liked that interpretation.[61] The Mubarak dictatorship went along with it but that interpretation could be threatened now. And it's taken very seriously in the West. You look at Western commentary, they're worried about that. Israel and the United States themselves are worried because it could reduce their flexibility to carry out operations freely. They're very worried about deterrence.

Take a look today: a high US military official today reiterated that the greatest threat to US interests in the world is Iran.[62] Incidentally, on the same day, a poll of European public opinion was reported; it said the greatest threat to peace is Israel. That's their opinion. But for the US government and for Israel the greatest threat is Iran. And you've heard that a thousand times: we're keeping all options open, threatening them with war and so on. What exactly is the threat? Take a look and see if you find a discussion of what the Iranian threat is. Well, actually, there is an authoritative answer on that; I don't know if it's been published here, but it's very explicit. It's given by the Pentagon and US intelligence. They give presentations to Congress every year on the global security situation. Of course, they have a long discussion on Iran, and they make it very clear what the threat is. The threat is that Iran

---

61 e.g. Pew Research Centre, *Egyptians Embrace Revolt Leaders, Religious Parties and Military, As Well*, 25 April 2011. http://pewglobal.org/files/2011/04/Pew-Global-Attitudes-Egypt-Report-FINAL-April-25-2011.pdf
62 'Iran now top threat to US, says military official', *Reuters*, 4 November 2011.

may develop a deterrent to US-Israeli freedom of action.[63] That's the threat. Nobody in their right mind thinks that Iran is ever going to use a nuclear weapon even if it had one – the country would be vaporised in five seconds. So that's not expected. Instead, what they're worried about is that if Iran develops nuclear weapons, it could limit the freedom of the United States and Israel to carry out aggression and violence freely. And of course that's intolerable; if you own the world you don't want to be deterred.

The same is true of the Israel-Egyptian treaty: if it's not interpreted as a license to invade, occupy and so on, then it's a problem. And that's a developing situation. How it will develop depends on the conflict that's going on inside the Arab world. The traditional ruling groups are of course hanging on to power as assiduously as they can, and the West of course supports them. The West is terrified at the idea that there might be authentic democracy in the Arab world. You look at public opinion and you can understand exactly why: there are good studies of Arab public opinion, done by the most prestigious US polling agencies. They're not reported widely in the press, but planners certainly know them.[64] So take a look at say Egypt, the most important country. About ninety per cent of Egyptians regard the US and Israel as the main threat that's facing them. They kind of agree with Europe. About ten per cent regard Iran as a threat; they don't like Iran, for all kinds of reasons, many of them good reasons, but they don't regard them as a threat. In fact, opposition to US policy is so strong that about eighty per cent of Egyptians think the region would be better off if Iran had nuclear weapons.

They don't want Iran to have nuclear weapons – separate polls say No, we don't want them to have nuclear weapons. In fact what they want is a nuclear weapons free zone in the region, including Iran, Israel and US

---

63 Lieutenant General Ronald L. Burgess, Director, Defense Intelligence Agency, Statement before the Committee on Armed Services, US Senate, 14 April 2010: 'The strategic objectives of Iran's leadership are first and foremost, regime survival... Iran's military strategy is designed to defend against external threats, particularly from the United States and Israel. Its principles of military strategy include deterrence, asymmetrical retaliation, and attrition warfare ...' Also, http://www.huffingtonpost.com/john-zogby/polls-egypt-obama_b_818192.html reports a Zogby poll, which gives the figures mentioned on Egypt.

64 e.g. The Brookings Institution, *2010 Arab Public Opinion Poll: Results of Arab Opinion Survey Conducted June 29 – July 20, 2010.* 'On Iran's potential nuclear weapons status, results show another dramatic shift in public opinion. While the results vary from country to country, the weighted average across the six countries is telling: in 2009, only 29% of those polled said that Iran's acquisition of nuclear weapons would be "positive" for the Middle East; in 2010, 57% of those polled indicate that such an outcome would be "positive" for the Middle East.' http://www.brookings.edu/topics/polling-and-public-opinion.aspx.

forces. There's overwhelming international support for that but the US is blocking it. The last thing that the US and Europe want is for opinions like that to influence policy. So of course they're going to try to block democracy. They'll say democracy is wonderful, and we love it, and so on but they're going to try to block it. Actually, polls by World Public Opinion found that Americans and Iranians agree on basic issues. A large majority of Iranians support Iran's participation in the Nuclear Nonproliferation Treaty, and a Middle East nuclear free zone, and the ultimate elimination of all nuclear weapons. Americans agree with Iranians in their support for the NPT regime including the elimination of all nuclear weapons.[65] And it's an ongoing conflict. In the countries that really matter to the West – the oil dictatorships – they've held on very tightly. In Saudi Arabia, the most extreme radical Islamist country in the world, long the major ally for the United States and Britain, there was an attempt to have a demonstration. But the security presence was so extreme that people were afraid to get out into the streets, and there was no protest in the West. The same thing happened in Bahrain. I'm sure you've read about it; it's been crushed by force. So they're hanging on; they're maintaining control. What will happen in countries like Egypt and Tunisia? Well, you know it's an ongoing struggle. It's not easy; they're facing very harsh conditions. It's not like the Melbourne Police – who weren't very nice, but it's much worse there.

---

65 'Public Opinion in Iran and America on Key International Issues', Poll, World Public Opinion.org, 24 January 2007. http://www.worldpublicopinion.org/pipa/pdf/jan07/Iran_Jan07_rpt.pdf.

Changing contours of global order

Deakin University lecture

The Plenary, Melbourne Convention and Exhibition Centre, 4 November 2011

There are quite definitely changes in world order that are undoubtedly of considerable significance. I think there are some questions about how they are interpreted. One prominent concern these days is what is called 'American Decline'. In the leading political science journal in the United States, you can read that it is a 'common theme' that the United States, which 'only a few years ago was hailed to stride the world as a colossus with unparalleled power and unmatched appeal – is in decline, ominously facing its prospects of its final decay'.[1]

There's a common corollary to that, which holds that there has been a long-term shift of power: first to northwest Europe, then across the Atlantic to the United States, and now moving across the Pacific to the rising powers, China and India. If that were true it would mean we were going back to something like the eighteenth century when they were in fact the commercial and industrial centres of the world, before the imperial period. Well, American decline is very real; the corollary, however, I think is quite dubious.

There certainly has been impressive economic growth in China and India, but they remain very poor countries, with severe internal problems that are not faced in the rich countries.[2] China, for all of its enormous growth, still remains largely an assembly plant for parts and components. High technology is provided by the peripheral industrial powers: Japan, South Korea and Taiwan, and also by the West. It presumably will ultimately move up the technology ladder, but that's a long hard path and the internal problems are enormous; even more so in India. American decline is entirely real, but in the foreseeable future I don't see any indication that there's any competitor

---

1   Giacomo Chiozza, 'Review, America's Global Advantage: US Hegemony and International Cooperation by Carla Norrlof', *Political Science Quarterly*, Summer 2011, p. 336.
2   Xizhe Peng, 'China's Demographic History and Future Challenges', Science vol. 333 no. 6042 pp. 581–7, 29 July 2011.

for hegemonic global power. The world is getting a lot more diverse, but that's a different matter.

There are further qualifications in order. One is that American decline is not new, contrary to the common theme; in fact it's been going on since the end of the Second World War. 1945 was the peak of American power. At that point, American global power was just colossal; the United States literally had fifty per cent of the world's wealth. Other industrial powers had been severely damaged or destroyed during the Second World War, which was economically of enormous benefit to the United States. It ended the Depression; US industrial production almost quadrupled during the Second World War, while its competitors were severely harmed. Long before the war, the US had already been far and away the richest country in the world. Also, the United States had enormous unparalleled security: it controlled the entire western hemisphere, both oceans, and the opposite sides of both oceans. There had never been a system of power even closely approaching that in world history. However, the decline began right away. In 1949, there was a very serious blow to US global power. It has a name – it's called the 'loss of China'. China became independent.

That phrase, 'loss of China', is an interesting one. It's also interesting that it's never questioned but if you think about it, there's something very instructive about it. I can't 'lose' *your* computer, I can only lose something *I* possess, and the phrase 'loss of China' presupposes that we possessed China. That's supposed to be taken for granted, and is taken for granted. It's a reflection of the deeply rooted imperial conception that the rich Western powers, with the United States in the lead, own the world. And therefore if anything moves on an independent path, they've 'lost' it, and the events that the 'loss of China' describes have been a major issue in world affairs ever since. Well, the so-called 'loss of China' was a very serious blow to plans that were laid during the Second World War. President Roosevelt's planners were well aware during the war that the United States was going to emerge as a power of overwhelming dominance. They laid careful, sophisticated plans for how the postwar world should be organised.

In the early stages of the war, they assumed that Germany would emerge from the war as a major force in Eurasia, so there would essentially be two global systems – a German-run world in Europe and parts of Asia, and an American-run world. The American-run world was called 'the Grand Area', and its contours were sketched closely. The Grand Area was to include the entire western hemisphere, the entire far east – that's why the 'loss of China' was so serious – and the former British Empire, including the Middle East, with its enormous energy resources. That's the Grand Area at a minimum. As the Russian armies began to grind the Germans down after Stalingrad it was recognised that Germany would not survive the war. The contours of the Grand Area were expanded to include the commercial and industrial centres of western Europe; southern Europe, which was of great significance because of the sea lanes for energy transit from the Middle East; and as much of Eurasia as possible. So, that's the Grand Area. Britain, meanwhile would become 'our lieutenant (the fashionable word is partner)', as a senior Kennedy adviser put it.[3] Before the war, Britain of course had been the dominant global power.

The energy resources of the Middle East, West Asia, were in fact recognised already to be staggering. The State Department in 1945 described them as a 'stupendous source of strategic power, one of the greatest material prizes in world history'. Shortly after, President Eisenhower described the region as 'the strategically most important part of the world'. One of Roosevelt's leading advisers, an important statesman, A.A. Berle, observed that whoever controls the Middle East can gain 'substantial control of the world'.[4] Well, the United States did not intend to give that up then, and it doesn't intend to give it up now. That's highly relevant to current affairs: today's headlines and tomorrow's events. Summarising the very distinguished British diplomatic historian Geoffrey Warner, one of the leading specialists on this topic, the documentary record shows clearly that President Roosevelt was aiming at US hegemony in the postwar world. That's quite correct, and it was a very plausible assumption, given the objective circumstances. Well, within these vast domains, the Grand Area, there were specific plans that were carefully implemented. The plans implemented in the early postwar years follow very closely the planning documents of the 'War and Peace Studies Project' – high officials in the State Department and extra-governmental specialists from the Council on Foreign Relations during the 1939–1945 period. Incidentally, this documentary material is open; in fact right away it was never classified. It's kind of strange that it hasn't been used much by diplomatic historians.[5] It's very revealing about Second World War plans and the way they were later implemented.

---

3   For sources, see Chapter Two of N. Chomsky, *Year 501: The Conquest Continues*, South End Press, Boston, 1993.
4   Joyce Kolko and Gabriel Kolko, *The Limits of Power*, Harper & Row, New York, 1972. Berle Papers, 11 May 1951, cited by Lloyd Gardner, *Three Kings*, New Press, New York, 2009.
5   The only careful study is Larry Shoup and William Minter, *Imperial Brain Trust*, Monthly Review Press, New York, 1977.

Planners and analysts concluded that in the postwar world the US would seek 'to hold unquestioned power', acting to ensure the 'limitation of any exercise of sovereignty' by states that might interfere with its global designs. They recognised further that 'the foremost requirement' to secure these ends was 'the rapid fulfilment of a program of complete rearmament' – then, as now, a central component of 'an integrated policy to achieve military and economic supremacy for the United States'.[6] That's quite an expansive vision, and the doctrines still prevail. But the power to implement them has significantly declined, and so that's what's regarded as American decline. The planning, as I said, was sophisticated, and it continued to be as it began to be implemented in the early postwar years. One of the major figures was George Kennan, head of the State Department planning staff. Kennan, incidentally, was more or less on the dovish end of the spectrum. In fact, he was soon kicked out; he was considered not to be tough enough for this harsh world. Kennan and his staff assigned every section of the world what they called its 'function' within the overall Grand Area.

So, for example Southeast Asia had the function of providing resources and raw materials to the former colonial masters, crucially Britain but also Japan, which was to be granted 'some sort of empire toward the south'.[7] This was in order that they might reconstruct and be in a position to purchase the manufacturing surplus of the United States. The US had a huge manufacturing system but few markets; the only plausible market was Europe, and Southeast Asia had the function of helping them reconstruct. And so it went, throughout the world. There was one part of the world that the US had no particular interest in at the time: Africa. Kennan therefore proposed that Africa should be handed over to Europe to 'exploit' – that's his word – for its reconstruction.[8] Looking at the historical relations between Europe and Africa you can imagine a different conception for the postwar world, an obvious one, but that of course was never considered. Incidentally, that conception has changed in more recent years – the United States is now

---

6   Memorandum of the War and Peace Studies Project of the Council on Foreign Relations, with State Department participation, 19 October 1940; Laurence H. Shoup and William Minter, ibid., p. 130ff.
7   Michael Schaller, 'Securing the Great Crescent: Occupied Japan and the Origins of Containment in Southeast Asia', *Journal of American History*, September 1982; Melvyn Leffler, *A Preponderance of Power: National Security, the Truman Administration, and the Cold War*, Stanford University Press, Stanford, 1992, p. 339.
8   '... a union of Western European nations would undertake jointly the economic development and exploitation of the colonial and dependent areas of the African Continent ... it would lend to the idea of Western European union that tangible objective for which everyone has been rather unsuccessfully groping in recent months.' *Op. cit.*

unwilling to give up Africa to exploit; it wants to take part in it itself, and is working hard to set up military and diplomatic structures to gain substantial control over Africa. That's part of the important changing contours of the world.

By 1949, the grand vision was beginning to crumble. First came the loss of China, which was quite serious. Shortly after came the threat of loss of Southeast Asia. If Indochina became independent from French domination, the function of Southeast Asia in the Grand Area would be undermined. Actually, Indochina didn't matter that much in itself, but it was significant because of its relation to a much greater threat – the loss of Indonesia. You'll pardon me continuing to use the conventional phrase 'loss of' one or another region; it's an obnoxious phrase in my opinion for the reasons I mentioned, but it's standard usage so I'll keep to it. Indonesia has extremely rich resources, so its loss was considered to be quite serious, if it happened. In 1948 George Kennan said that he took 'the problem of Indonesia' to be the 'most crucial' issue of international affairs in 1948. 'Indonesia is the anchor in that chain of islands stretching from Hokkaido to Sumatra which we should develop as a politico-economic counter-force to communism', he continued, and a 'base area' for possible military action beyond. A Communist Indonesia would be an 'infection' that 'would sweep westward' through all of South Asia, even threatening US dominance in the Middle East.[9] The crucial issue was the prospect of independent economic nationalism. That's 1948. All of that enters into planning for the Vietnam War in ways that are worth understanding. The Vietnam War, the Indochina wars in general, are maybe the most important, certainly one of the most important events of the last half of the twentieth century. They went on of course until 1975, with residues that continue.

It's commonly said that the US suffered a defeat in Indochina, and that's not entirely false, but it's not entirely accurate either. It would be more accurate to say that the United States had a partial victory. It achieved its major war aims, but not its maximal war aims; and if you have a really expansive conception of the need for dominance, then failure to achieve your maximal aims is considered a kind of horrendous failure. The reasoning behind the concern over Indochina, and the long destructive war, was pretty straightforward. It's analysed clearly in the internal documents, and furthermore it's a theme that you find throughout modern history, a very important theme. Indochina was – to use Henry Kissinger's later term –

---

9   Melvyn P. Leffler, *A Preponderance of Power*, p. 260.

a virus that might spread contagion elsewhere. The virus was independent nationalism. If it was successful, others might be inspired to try to pursue the same course. So, the concern was that the contagion might reach Indonesia, which is significant, and then on to what Asia historian John Dower called the 'super-domino': Japan.[10] If Southeast Asia were infected by the virus, and the contagion spread, Japan might accommodate itself to an independent East Asia, becoming its technological and industrial centre and using the surrounding region as a market and resource space. In effect, that would be providing Japan with what it sought to obtain by military conquest during the Second World War.

Look back at the Pacific phase of the Second World War. Japan was trying to construct what it called a New Order in Asia,[11] which would have exactly that character, and the United States was not prepared to lose the Pacific phase of World War Two in the immediate postwar years. By this reasoning, the loss of Indochina (i.e. its move towards independent development) would be quite serious. Well, how do you deal with a virus that's going to spread contagion? What you do is try to destroy the virus, and try to protect the potential targets of the infection from the contagion. And that's exactly what was done, in that region and elsewhere too, commonly. Again, this is a major theme of postwar history. So the virus was destroyed; Vietnam was devastated, as was all of Indochina. It would never be a model of independent development that others would follow. And the region was inoculated by installing murderous and brutal dictators who could be counted on to block any move towards independence. That happened in country after country throughout the region, either instigated or supported by the United States and Britain, and sometimes France, when it could.

The most important case, again, was Indonesia. In 1965, there was a military coup in Indonesia – General Suharto's coup. It was openly supported by the United States, perhaps instigated by it, and it was very successful. It ended the threat that Indonesia might catch the virus – that it might move towards successful independent development. The coup killed hundreds of thousands of people, mostly landless peasants. It destroyed the major mass-based political party and ended the threat of democracy in Indonesia. This is a party that Australian specialist on Indonesia, Harold Crouch, calls a

---

10 John Dower, 'The Superdomino in Postwar Asia: Japan In and Out of the Pentagon Papers', in Noam Chomsky and Howard Zinn, eds, *The Pentagon Papers: The Senator Gravel Edition*, vol. 5, Beacon, 1972, 101–142.
11 William C. Johnstone, *The United States and Japan's New Order*, Oxford University Press, New York, 1941.

party that 'had won widespread support not as a revolutionary party but as an organisation defending the interests of the poor within the existing system'.[12] It was devastated along with its mass base, and the coup opened up Indonesia to the exploitation of its enormous resources by the West. It was extremely successful and it elicited unconstrained euphoria in the United States, in Australia, Britain, and the West generally.[13] And the descriptions were pretty accurate; the *New York Times*' leading liberal commentator, James Reston, for example, described what was happening as 'a gleam of light in Asia'.[14] *U.S. News & World Report* had a story called, 'Hope Where There Once Was None'.[15] *Time Magazine* claimed that the Indonesian army was 'scrupulously constitutional … based on law not on mere power', with a 'quietly determined' General Suharto and his 'almost innocent face'.[16]

The euphoria was understandable in the context of the unquestioned acceptance of a conception of global order of the kind that I outlined. You'll find that conception in the internal records. One of the more interesting commentaries on this was by McGeorge Bundy. He was the National Security Advisor for Presidents Kennedy and Johnson, and one of the main architects of the Vietnam War in those years. In later years, he said that the US should have terminated its war in Vietnam after the Indonesian massacres, because it was no longer necessary. The anti-Communist purges in Indonesia had already achieved the broader objective of preventing independent economic nationalism in the region.[17] Vietnam by that time was already virtually destroyed, and Indonesia was protected from contagion by the highly successful Suharto coup. So going on beyond that was kind of pointless.

Well similar things were happening in Latin America. It had been taken for granted in Grand Area planning that Latin America would simply be in the pocket of the United States. 'I think that it's not asking too much to have our little region over here which never has bothered anybody', as Secretary

---

12 H. Crouch, *The Army and Politics in Indonesia*, Cornell University Press, Ithaca, 1978, p. 351.
13 Scott Burchill, 'Absolving the Dictator', *AQ: Journal of Contemporary Analysis*, vol. 73, no. 3, May–June 2001.
14 James Reston, 'Washington: A Gleam of Light in Asia', *New York Times*, 19 June 1966.
15 Robert P. Martin, 'Indonesia: Hope … Where Once There Was None', *U.S. News & World Report*, 6 June 1966, p. 70.
16 'Indonesia: Vengeance with a Smile', *Time*, 15 July 1966.
17 D. Fromkin and J. Chace, What are the lessons of Vietnam?, *Foreign Affairs*, vol. 63, no. 4, 1985, pp. 722–746; H. Salisbury, ed., *Vietnam Reconsidered: Lessons from a War*, Harper and Row, New York, 1984, p. 52.

of War Stimson put it.[18] But that wasn't so simple; there was a problem very soon in Guatemala. Guatemala overthrew a dictatorship and instituted steps towards democratisation, land reform and so on. That was considered quite threatening. The Eisenhower government carried out a military coup, overthrowing the democratic system and installing a murderous and violent terror state, which to this day is carrying out horrifying atrocities. It's not so bad as before – the peak was actually in the Reagan years in the 1980s. In fact, a lot of the immigrants desperately seeking to enter the United States even today are Mayan refugees from the highlands in Guatemala where virtual genocide was carried out in the 1980s. Well, the concern about Guatemala was the same as Indochina – the concern was it might be a virus that might infect others. That virus was quickly stamped out.

And it continues that way pretty much throughout Latin America. There was one clear exception, and that was Cuba. In 1959, Cuba liberated itself for the first time. The United States reacted very harshly to the Castro victory; quite quickly, within a few months it began bombing Cuba from Florida bases. It took a formal decision in March 1960 to overthrow the government.[19] When John F Kennedy took office in 1961 he escalated the attacks on Cuba. The internal records are quite revealing. Kennedy had a special interest in Latin America, and he established a Latin American Mission to analyse how the United States should deal with Latin America. It was headed by Arthur Schlesinger, the famous liberal historian and Kennedy advisor. He was one of Kennedy's major advisors on Latin America in particular. This is before Kennedy came into office. It's a report intended for the incoming President.[20] Schlesinger pointed out to President Kennedy that the problem in Cuba is 'the spread of the Castro idea of taking matters into one's own hand'. It's an idea that might influence others in the region, who face similar problems and might try to do the same thing. So it's a virus that might spread contagion. And the usual cure was tried – first try to kill the virus. I'll come back in a moment to how that was done, although you know the basic story. Kill the virus and inoculate the region.

Right away the US began to support military coups throughout the region. The first and most important was in Brazil, the most important country in the region. There was a military coup planned under the Kennedy

---

18 Gabriel Kolko, *The Politics of War: The World and United States Foreign Policy, 1943–1945*, Pantheon, New York, 1968 p. 471.
19 *SHAFR Newsletter*, vol. 33, no. 3, September 2002, ibid.
20 'Report To The President On Latin American Mission', *Foreign Relations of the United States, 1961–1963*, vol. XII, US Government Printing Office, 1996.

administration, and carried out a few weeks after Kennedy's assassination.[21] It installed the first of a series of what were called 'national security states' – basically neo-Nazi terror and torture states which were very brutal and violent. They then spread throughout the region.[22] One of them was what in Latin America is called 'the First 9/11'. 9/11/1973. That's the overthrow of the Parliamentary Government of Chile on September 11, 1973. Actually, if you think about it, the first 9/11 was incomparably worse than the second 9/11 – the one *we* call 9/11. Just do a thought experiment: consider what we call 9/11, which was a horrific atrocity. Suppose for example the plane that was downed in Pennsylvania by the passengers had gone on and hit its target, which was probably the White House. Suppose it had hit the White House, killed the President – he didn't happen to be there, but suppose he was – established a military dictatorship in the United States, which immediately killed thousands of people, tortured tens of thousands, established a major terror centre in the United States which initiated and supported comparable military coups elsewhere in the hemisphere and beyond, carried out assassinations far and wide, brought in a group of economists who quickly drove the United States into the worst depression in its history. Suppose all of that had happened, well that would have been a lot worse than 9/11, but since we did it to them, it's out of history and nobody talks about the first 9/11 except in Latin America.

But, if you think it through I think you'll see that this kind of comparison is quite apt. Henry Kissinger, who was one of the architects of the coup, assured President Nixon, his boss, that what happened was 'nothing of very great consequence'.[23] In contrast, the second 9/11 is commonly claimed to have changed the world. Well, that's the difference between us and them, the rich and the powerful versus the weak and the victims. But it's worth thinking about. Well, this plague of repression that spread through Latin America included Brazil, Chile, Uruguay. The worst of the criminal states that was installed was Argentina – that was Ronald Reagan's darling. He loved Argentina, and supported the dictatorship, which was the most brutal

---

21 Peter Kornbluh, *Brazil marks 40th anniversary of military coup: Declassified documents shed light on US role*, National Security Archive, http://www.gwu.edu/~nsarchiv/NSAEBB/NSAEBB118/index.htm.
22 Jan Knippers Black, *United States Penetration of Brazil*, University of Pennsylvania Press, Philadelphia, 1977.
23 T. Blanton and W. Burr, eds, *The Kissinger Telcons*, National Security Archive Electronic Briefing Book No. 123, 26 May 2004: http://www.gwu.edu/~nsarchiv/NSAEBB/NSAEBB123/.

and vicious of all of them.[24] Then the plague spread to Central America in the 1980s with hundreds of thousands of people killed, and any threat of independent development crushed. So the region was inoculated, but the US couldn't quite exterminate the virus, though it was contained.

After the Bay of Pigs invasion was beaten back, Kennedy instituted Operation Mongoose – a major war of terror against Cuba beginning on 30 November 1961.[25] Arthur Schlesinger, who as I said was a liberal historian, described the policy as one of 'bringing the terrors of the Earth to Cuba'. That's Schlesinger's description in his biography of Robert Kennedy, the President's brother.[26] He points out that Robert Kennedy was given responsibility for bringing the terrors of the Earth to Cuba – that was his prime responsibility and he was dedicated to it. And the war was a very serious one.[27] We have plenty of documents from it. Thousands of people were killed, whether it was sabotage, destruction, sinking of ships, shelling of industrial installations, probably biological warfare, it was no joke. And it continued for a long time. Also, the United States instituted an embargo to try to strangle the country, and that still continues. The CIA explained what the problem was: it said the problem in Cuba is Cuba's successful defiance of US policies going back to the Monroe doctrine.

In 1823 the Monroe Doctrine proclaimed the US's right to essentially dominate the hemisphere. It couldn't do it at that time; it wasn't strong enough. There was a deterrent: Britain, which was much stronger. And the British were a deterrent, but the US planners as far back as the 1820s recognised that 'there are laws of political as well as of physical gravitation; and if an apple severed by the tempest from its native tree cannot choose

---

24 N. Chomsky, *Turning the Tide*, South End Press, Boston, 1985, p. 57: 'Reagan's devotion to human rights was clear before his accession to the Presidency, which permitted him to put it into practice. In 1978, when the mass murders of the Argentine generals had become an international scandal, he condemned the Carter Administration for raising a fuss about such trivialities: "In the process of rounding up hundreds of suspected terrorists, the Argentine authorities have no doubt locked up a few innocent people," he wrote: "This problem they should correct without delay. The incarceration of a few innocents, however, is no reason they should open the jails and let the terrorists run free." True to his commitments, he and Jeane Kirkpatrick [US Ambassador to the UN] quickly let the murderers know that such concerns were a thing of the past, after the 1980 elections.'
25 Raymond L. Garthoff, *Reflections on the Cuban Missile Crisis*, Brookings, Washington, 1989.
26 A. Schlesinger, Jr., *Robert Kennedy and His Times*, Houghton Mifflin, Boston, 1978, pp. 477–80.
27 Taylor Branch and George Crile III, 'The Kennedy Vendetta: How the C.I.A. waged a silent war against Cuba', *Harper's*, August 1975.

but fall to the ground, Cuba, forcibly disjoined from its own unnatural connection with Spain, and incapable of self-support, can gravitate only towards the North American Union, which by the same law of nature cannot cast her off from its bosom'.[28] I'm quoting John Quincy Adams, the intellectual author of the Monroe Doctrine and Manifest Destiny. And that indeed happened: through the nineteenth century the US became more powerful, British power declined, and in 1898, the US essentially invaded Cuba. It's called the Liberation of Cuba but in fact it was the prevention of Cuba's liberation from Spain. Cuba had pretty much liberated itself from Spain; the US invasion put an end to that and turned Cuba into a virtual colony, as it remained until 1959. And then came this danger – what the CIA called the 'successful defiance' of policies going back 150 years.[29] It had nothing to do with the Russians, of course, though they were always the pretext in those years. Schlesinger's analysis that it was a virus that would spread contagion was the typical one, the same one that's used in Indochina and many other places.

If you want to understand the history of this period, you have to recognise that these quite rational themes occur over and over. Sometimes they're called the 'domino theory', but that doesn't capture the significance and the meaning of what in fact happened over and over. Well, the case of Cuba gives a considerable insight into how policy is formed. It's worth studying for that reason, too. For about forty years, public opinion in the United States has been strongly opposed to the policies against Cuba. The large majority of the public wants to normalise relations with Cuba. Well, it's normal for public opinion to be dismissed in what we call 'democracies', but what's more interesting in this case, is that major sectors of American business have also been in favour of normalisation. Now quite typically they're the sectors that determine policy, but in this case they've been overruled. Which is why it's interesting. And these are not small parts of the American corporate sector; they're central parts: major business interests such as agribusiness,

---

28 Robert F. Smith, *What Happened in Cuba? A Documentary History*, Twayne, New York, 1963.
29 Central Intelligence Agency: 'Cuba will, of course, never present a direct military threat to the United States and it is unlikely that Cuba would attempt open invasion of any other Latin American country since the US could and almost certainly would enter the conflict on the side of the invaded country ... More importantly, the advent of Castro has provided the Communists with a friendly base for propaganda and agitation throughout the rest of Latin America and with a highly exploitable example of revolutionary achievement and successful defiance of the United States.' *Foreign Relations of the United States*, 1961–1963, vol. X.

pharmaceuticals and energy corporations – but they are dismissed. There's a state dedication to punishing successful defiance, and it overwhelms the usual modalities of policy formation, which are usually pretty much in the hands of private capital. That's not the only such case. There are other such cases, and they're worth looking at closely if you want to understand policy formation. Actually, Iran is another case like that.

Well, going back to postwar planning, the main concern of course was Europe. Europe had to be reconstructed, but there was a preliminary condition. First, it was necessary to destroy the anti-fascist resistance, which was basically kind of radical democratic, called 'the Left'. That was the first target of US and British forces as they landed on the continent. Greece and Italy in particular had extremely powerful resistance movements. The French resistance is better known, but it was a very small sector of the society.[30] In Italy, a worker- and peasant-based movement, led by the Communist party, had held down six German divisions during the war. Most of Italy had been liberated by the resistance before the British and the Americans got there. The society that the resistance developed had to be thrown out; the US and Britain destroyed it, bringing back the fascist collaborators and essentially reconstructing the old order.[31]

In Greece it was very bloody; there was a civil war in which maybe 150,000 people or so were killed.[32] It went on for years, and restored the pre-war quasi-fascist government. There was an actual fascist coup later that the US supported. Greece and Italy were of particular significance as I mentioned before, because in global planning, they were protecting the sea lanes along which energy was provided from the huge material prize in the Middle East. In fact, Greece was actually in the Near East section of the State Department until 1974, the overthrow of the dictatorship. It was considered part of the Middle East, not part of Europe. It's worth thinking about today when you notice what's going on.

Germany was of course particularly important; it was necessary in Germany to dismantle union constitutions, to terminate social experiments and in general 'to endeavour to rescue western zones of Germany by walling them off against eastern penetration and integrating them into the international

---

30 For a review of a good deal of scholarship on how the policies were carried out in Italy and the rest of western Europe, and also in Japan, see Chapter 11 of Noam Chomsky, *Deterring Democracy*, Hill & Wang, 1992.
31 B. Davidson, *Scenes From The Anti-Nazi War*, Monthly Review, New York, 1980.
32 Lawrence S. Wittner, *American Intervention in Greece, 1943–1949*, Columbia University Press, New York, 1982.

pattern of western Europe rather than into a unified Germany'. That phrase, incidentally, is George Kennan's again.[33] Well, it was always recognised that Europe might follow an independent path, perhaps something like de Gaulle's conception of Europe from the Atlantic to the Urals – an independent force in world affairs. That had to be stopped, and there were various measures taken to prevent it. One was NATO. Part of NATO's function was to ensure that Europe would not pull out of the Grand Area as an independent force. That remains a major issue.

Meanwhile, throughout this whole period, decolonisation was following its agonising course. And throughout this period, the decline continued. By 1970 the United States had about twenty-five per cent of global wealth. It still has approximately that, which is very substantial but it's not fifty per cent. So that's a sharp decline. The world by 1970 was becoming economically tripolar: a North American economic centre based in the United States, a comparable European economic centre, German based, and an East Asian centre, at that point Japan based, later Japan-China based, which is already the most dynamic economic area in the world. That's 1970. Twenty years later, in 1990, the Soviet Union collapsed. Those who are interested in the reality of the Cold War and what shapes foreign policy generally will find it highly instructive to look at how the United States reacted when the superpower enemy collapsed. It's kind of striking that scholarship pays almost no attention to that, but it's clearly of very great importance, and if you look closely, quite instructive.

And looking at them tells you quite a lot. One aspect was that they said it would be necessary to maintain a huge military system; not to protect the West from the Russians – they're not around any longer – but to protect the West from what was called 'the growing technical sophistication of Third World conflicts'. It said, 'In the 1980s, our military engagements – in Lebanon in 1983–84, Libya in 1986, and the Persian Gulf in 1987–88 – were in response to threats that could not be laid at the Kremlin's door. The necessity to defend our interests will continue.'[34] Now if you're a well-educated intellectual you don't laugh when you hear that; you take it seriously. We need a huge military system to protect ourselves from 'the growing technical sophistication of Third World conflicts'. That's a sign of a proper education: to take that seriously. You're not supposed to laugh. What it meant of course

---

33 *Foreign Relations of the United States 1946*, vol. V, 1969.
34 *National Security Strategy of the United States: 1990–1991*, The White House, March 1990.

was that the huge military system never was intended to defend the West from the Russian hordes, but rather to maintain Grand Area control and that was still necessary.

The second element of the new system was that it was necessary to protect what they called 'the defence industrial base'. What's the defence industrial base? That's a euphemism for the high-tech economy. Free markets are fine for the weak, but not for us – we the powerful need a powerful state that sustains the economy, saves the wealthy when they're in trouble and so on. The modern high-tech economy, very largely, derives from what's called the defence industrial base: research and development funded by the Pentagon. That includes computers, the internet, in fact virtually the entire information technology revolution, microelectronics, satellites, on and on. After about thirty years in the state sector largely, these were handed over to private power for profit. And this system had to be maintained – that's what it means to maintain the defence industrial base. Actually there's nothing really new about that. It goes back to the earliest days of modern industrialisation: Britain and the United States, other developing powers such as Japan and the East Asian tigers and so on. In fact, every developed society has had something of this character.[35]

The third element of the planning in the immediate period of the collapse of the Soviet Union had to do with military intervention. The new defence strategy and military budget insisted that military intervention forces aimed at the Middle East must be maintained: 'The Middle East is a vivid example, however, of a region in which, even as East-West tensions diminish, American strategic concerns remain'. And then came an interesting phrase – these intervention forces must be directed toward the Middle East, where the serious problems we faced were 'threats that could not be laid at the Kremlin's door'. Contrary to fifty years of deception. So, it wasn't because of the Russians, and the Russian threat, that we were directing military intervention forces towards the Middle East. Sorry folks, we've been lying to you for fifty years but now we have to tell you the truth: the Russians aren't there, we can't blame them, and the problem is indeed what it always was and is in other parts of the world too – what's called radical nationalism,

---

35 F. Clairmonte, *Economic Liberalism and Underdevelopment: Studies in the Disintegration of an Idea*, Asia Publishing House, New York, 1960; A. Gerschenkron, *Economic Backwardness in Historical Perspective*, Harvard University Press, Cambridge, 1962; W. Lazonick, *Business Organization and the Myth of the Market Economy*, Cambridge University Press, Cambridge, 1991; Ha-Joon Chang, *Kicking Away The Ladder, Development Strategy in Historical Perspective*, Anthem Press, London, 2005.

or independent nationalism which might tear apart the system of imperial control.

Well, that's quietly conceded at that point, but that didn't matter much because none of this is ever reported; in fact you can barely find it even in academic scholarship, but it's there, in very open and perfectly public documents. Well, in the Middle East, as elsewhere, there had been viruses which threatened contagion. They had to be dealt with in the usual way. One was in 1953 where Britain and the United States intervened in Iran to overthrow a parliamentary democracy and install the tyranny of the Shah. There was another military coup in Iraq in 1963, initiated by the CIA. The most important case was 1967: the Israeli destruction of Nasser. He was the leader of the virus of secular nationalism. The 1967 war is conventionally described, and not inaccurately, as a war between Israel and mainly Egypt, which is true. But there was another war going on, highly relevant, between Saudi Arabia and Egypt. They were at war in the mid-1960s, in a conflict between radical Islamic fundamentalism centred in Saudi Arabia, and secular nationalism centred in Nasser's Egypt. The United States and Britain have fairly consistently over the years supported radical Islamic fundamentalism as a barrier to the much greater danger of secular nationalism, and 1967 is an important case in point.

In 1967 Israel performed an enormous service to the United States and Saudi Arabia, its major ally in the region, because that's where most of the oil is. It destroyed the major threat to radical Islamism and the secular nationalist efforts that might, it was feared, have tried to convert the resources of the region to domestic needs. That's the danger, and the service that Israel performed established US-Israeli relations in their present, kind of unique form. Before that the relations were nothing special. Right after that came what's called the 'Nixon doctrine'. It presented the structure of control of the Middle East: primarily, support for radical fundamentalist Islamic dictatorships, like in Saudi Arabia. That's where the oil is, so they're our main allies; but they have to be protected, mainly from their own populations, by what Nixon's Defense Secretary, Melvin Laird, called the local 'cops on the beat in their own neighbourhoods': local gendarmes who would protect the ruling dictatorships from their populations.[36] The responsibility of the Middle East cops was outlined in 1973 by the Senate's leading expert on the topic, Henry Jackson: to 'inhibit and contain those

---

36 D. van Atta, *With Honor: Melvin Laird in War, Peace and Politics*, University of Wisconsin Press, Madison, 2008.

irresponsible and radical elements in certain Arab States ... who, were they free to do so, would pose a grave threat indeed to our principal sources of petroleum in the Persian Gulf'.[37]

And there's an array of these cops. Preferably non-Arab – they do a better job of killing Arabs. The Shah of Iran was one of the main ones; also Turkey, Pakistan (which provided a lot of the military force for the Saudi dictatorship) and Israel, which was added to the list. Those are the cops on the beat; police headquarters of course stays in Washington and there's a kind of branch office in London in case we need our junior partner to do something. Well that was the Nixon doctrine, and Israel had a fundamental role in that framework: when the Shah was overthrown in 1979, that role actually increased. And that framework still is the core of the US-Israeli relationship, despite many changes since.

Let's go back to the end of the Cold War in 1990. The fate of NATO is quite instructive. The Russian hordes were gone, so you no longer needed NATO to protect Europe from the Russian hordes. Well, if anyone had believed the propaganda of the preceding years they would have expected that NATO would dissolve – the reason for its existence was gone. That's not what happened; instead NATO expanded to the east, in violation of explicit pledges to Prime Minister Gorbachev, who was willing to permit German unification within a hostile military alliance, on condition that NATO would not expand 'one inch to the East' – that was the phrase that the Bush administration promised to Gorbachev. Actually, Gorbachev's concession was quite significant in the light of history; after all Germany alone had practically destroyed Russia in that century and now Gorbachev was willing to allow a unified, militarised Germany to be part of a hostile military alliance, in return for the concession that NATO would not expand one inch to the east. Well NATO immediately expanded to East Germany in violation of the promise, and then beyond.

Gorbachev was pretty annoyed, as you can imagine, but when he complained, Washington explained to him that if he was naïve enough to accept verbal promises from the United States, that was his problem.[38] And NATO now continues to expand. By now its official mission, apart from serving as a US-run global intervention force, is to protect what's called the infrastructure of the global energy system. That means the sea lanes and

---

37 Senate Committee on Energy and Natural Resources, *Access to Oil – the US' relationships with Saudi Arabia and Iran*, US Government Printing Office, Washington, 1977.
38 N. Chomsky, *Hopes and Prospects*, Hamish Hamilton, Camberwell, 2010, pp. 278–280.

pipelines in most of the world. Well, I mentioned before that there was great euphoria in the 1990s about our magnificence. In fact that's kind of a strange period of intellectual history – worth looking at closely. The rhetoric was pretty astonishing. I'm quoting now from liberal intellectuals, historians and so on. These intellectuals were awe-struck at the sight of the 'idealistic new world bent on ending inhumanity'. Clinton's foreign policy was praised as having entered a 'noble phase' in its foreign policy with a 'saintly glow' as for the first time in history a state is dedicated to 'principles and values', acting from 'altruism' and 'moral fervour' alone as the leader of the 'enlightened states', hence free to use force where its leaders 'believe it to be just'.[39] This went on and on through the 1990s; well of course not everybody was so enraptured, the global South, for example – the traditional victims. They saw it quite differently. They bitterly condemned the so-called right of humanitarian intervention, which they saw as just the old right of imperialist domination. That continues up until today.

After Bush Jnr. took over, the hostility to the United States in the global South, particularly the Middle East, grew enormously. Obama in fact has carried out a major feat: he's succeeded in lowering his popularity in the Arab world even below Bush. That's not a small achievement; Obama's approval in Egypt, the most important country, is about five per cent, meaning essentially nobody.[40] There are similar numbers elsewhere. Meanwhile, the decline continued. In the last decade – the first decade of this millennium – something extremely significant happened: South America was 'lost' (in the conventional sense of the term). The threat had been around for a long time. There were plenty of brutal interventions, but it finally happened. For the first time in half a millennium, the first time since the European explorers arrived, South America has begun to move towards integration, and towards independence. It's begun to face quite severe internal problems.

One sign of its independence is that US military bases have been entirely thrown out of South America; that's pretty significant. A new organisation is just forming – CELAC.[41] It includes all countries of the western hemisphere, except for the United States and Canada. If it actually functions it'll be quite significant – another great loss to Grand Area planning. And that's pretty

---

39 Michael Mandelbaum, *The Ideas That Conquered the World: Peace, Democracy, and Free Markets in the Twenty-First Century*, Public Affairs, New York, 2002. See also Chomsky's *New Military Humanism*, Common Courage, 1999.
40 Jason Ukman, Arab world's views of US, President Obama increasingly negative, new poll finds, *Washington Post*, 12 July 2011.
41 *Comunidad de Estados Latinoamericanos y Caribeños, or the Community of Latin American and Caribbean States.*

serious; when the Nixon administration was planning to destroy another virus, namely in Chile, the National Security Council advised that if the United States could not control Latin America, it could not expect to achieve a successful order elsewhere in the world. That is, it won't be able to run the rest of the world. Now control over Latin America has been substantially lost. Well, that's bad enough, but the Middle East is far more important and that's beginning to happen. I've already quoted government assessments of the significance of Middle East oil back in the 1940s; planners recognised that if we can control the Middle East we can control the world. And, as a corollary, if we lose control of the Middle East, control of the world declines. Well the policies remain pretty much the same.

Notice that it's not a matter of access; it's a matter of control. In fact during the period when the US was the major oil exporter, it wasn't taking a drop of oil from the Middle East but it maintained the same policies. There's a further danger to US hegemony: the possibility that what's called MENA (Middle East-North Africa) may move towards some form of democracy. That would be really frightening. There's lots of rhetoric about the yearning for democracy and so on, but there are very good reasons why the United States and its allies will do whatever they can to prevent functioning democracy, authentic democracy in the Middle East.

Just take a look at the polls. A lot is known about Arab public opinion; the Arab world is carefully polled by leading US polling agencies. Polls are released by prestigious institutions. It's easy to find them. They're not reported but planners certainly know about them. And what they say is very significant. So take say again Egypt, the most important country. About a year ago, right before the Arab Spring broke out, polls in Egypt showed that about ninety per cent of Egyptians regarded the US and Israel as the main threats to Egypt. About ten per cent think Iran is a threat. In fact opposition to US policy was so strong that about eighty per cent of Egyptians thought that the region would be more secure if Iran had nuclear weapons. On separate questions, they do not want Iran to have nuclear weapons, not surprisingly. But they think the region would be more secure if Iran had them to balance the real threat: the US and Israel. Figures throughout the region vary a little bit, but they're more or less similar. Well, you know the last thing that the three traditional imperial powers, the US and Britain and France, want is for public opinion to have an influence on policy. That's pretty obvious and that's what democracy means, so it follows they'll do whatever they can to stifle democracy.

Well, of course there have been some victories in Egypt – partial victories – but the traditional military regime is still intact and there's plenty of ongoing conflict about that. One shouldn't underestimate the victories, incidentally. The press in Egypt is quite free but it wasn't before. The labour movement, which has been at the core of the protest, is now much more free. That's significant, but the basic regime is still in place. And even with the partial democratisation, the partial move of the public towards some influence, Egypt has taken steps that are very threatening to the power of the US and Israel. For one thing Egypt for the first time in thirty years has permitted Iranian ships including military vessels to transit the Suez Canal into the Mediterranean, which is supposed to be an American lake. They're moving towards diplomatic relations with Iran. Egypt has led a unification effort to unify the two Palestinian factions: Hamas and Fatah. That's quite threatening to the US and Israel, and if you notice they reacted in a very hostile way. The reason is that for twenty years, since the early 1990s, US-Israeli policy has been devoted to separating Gaza from the West Bank. That happens to be an explicit violation of the Oslo accords, which describe the West Bank and Gaza as a territorial unity.

If this unification move works, it would undermine their attempts. It would also lay the basis for redoing something like the 2006 elections that were such a shock to the West. That's important. There's a more serious problem, still on the agenda and that's the 1979 Israel-Egypt peace treaty. Public opinion in Egypt doesn't want to get rid of the treaty – they don't want a war – but they don't like the way in which the dictatorship had interpreted the treaty. Right away, the 1979 treaty was interpreted by the Egyptian dictatorship and of course by the US and Israel as eliminating the Egyptian deterrent and therefore giving Israel a license to do anything it wanted: to attack its northern neighbour, Lebanon, as it did almost immediately; or to escalate its operations in the West Bank. Well the Egyptian public didn't like it and still doesn't.

If public opinion has any influence, that is if democracy actually progresses, then they might threaten that interpretation of the treaty. It's kind of interesting to see the way that's described in the West. It's described as the cornerstone of stability in the Middle East. 'Stability' here is used in its technical meaning: do what we say, that's stability. In the literal meaning, the treaty is the cornerstone of instability in the Middle East, like invading Lebanon and taking over the West Bank, but not from the Western point of view.

Well, there's a lot more to say about all of this but I want to make a final comment about another crucial fact: while American decline is quite real, and has been going on since 1945, it's important to understand that in large measure it's been self-inflicted. There was a major change in world order in the 1970s. Take the United States: throughout its history, with some ups and downs and not in very attractive ways, the United States had been a growing, advancing power. It started as an agricultural country. By the end of the nineteenth century it was already the richest country in the world. After the Second World War and in the several decades beyond, the fifties and sixties, it experienced a period of maximum growth. Throughout this entire period, the US was a growing, advancing industrial power and there was a psychological aspect to it; there was always, even in the darkest days, a sense of hopefulness. There was the feeing that we'll go on, our children will be better off than we will, and so on and so forth. Well that goes on until the 1970s, and at that point there was a turn. From then on the United States has been a de-industrialising power. And the sense of hopefulness has declined very severely.

Two major things happened in the 1970s in the United States – and in other industrial countries too, but let's talk about the US. One change was a shift of the economy from production of useful things to finance: games with money, speculation, manipulation, financial shenanigans and so on. That grew enormously since the 1970s. Production continued, but it was exported offshore. There's a kind of a common core to those two moves: they both had to do with the fact that the rate of profit in manufacturing was declining. So you could make more profit from financial shenanigans and offshore production. But it took place. The financial sector of the economy doesn't help the economy, it probably harms it; and it's become huge.[42] By 2007, right before the last crash it was about forty per cent of corporate profits – that's not small.

Well, these things have effects. One effect is high concentration of income, in the hands primarily of financial sectors. The top one-tenth of one per cent of the income spectrum, a sector so small that the census can't even pick it up, is the core reason for the tremendous inequality that's developed. And concentration of capital of course leads to concentration of political power, which in turn leads to legislation that increases the concentration of capital, and the vicious circle continues. Meanwhile, for the mass of the population – a large majority – wealth and income have pretty much stagnated, sometimes declined. Well, what the West has been doing is living out a kind of nightmare that was actually described by the classical economists, Adam Smith and David Ricardo, the founders of modern economics. Their concern

---

42 Robert M. Solow, 'The Bigger They Are ...' *Daedalus*, Fall 2010.

of course was England. The term 'invisible hand' appears only once in Adam Smith's classic *Wealth of Nations*. Smith warned that if English merchants and manufacturers were free to import, export, and invest abroad, they would profit while English society would be harmed. But that is unlikely to happen, he argued. The reason is that an English capitalist, 'preferring the support of domestic to that of foreign industry', would be 'in this, as in many other cases, led by an invisible hand to promote an end which was no part of his intention', and thus England would be spared the ravages of economic liberalism.

Now that's a pretty hard passage to miss. That's the one single use of the famous phrase 'invisible hand', in *Wealth of Nations*, in what amounts to a critique of neoliberal globalisation. The other great founder of classical economics, David Ricardo, said pretty much the same thing. Using his famous example of English textiles and Portuguese wines, he concluded that his theory of comparative advantage would collapse if it were advantageous to the capitalists of England to invest in Portugal for both manufacturing and agriculture. But, he argued, thanks to 'the natural disinclination which every man has to quit the country of his birth and connections', and 'fancied or real insecurity of capital' abroad, most men of property would 'be satisfied with the low rate of profits in their own country, rather than seek a more advantageous employment for their wealth in foreign nations', feelings that 'I should be sorry to see weakened', he added.[43]

The instincts of the classical economists were insightful. They knew what they were talking about. For a long time, what they described was more or less accurate. And we're now living in the middle of the nightmare that they predicted. The effect, as I said, is a very narrow concentration of wealth, increasing concentration of political power, further measures to concentrate wealth and power, fiscal measures, rules of corporate governance and deregulation. It's catastrophic for the economy, very harmful for most of the population and it's had a quite considerable effect on the nature of the society. It's enriching and empowering a tiny sector, but it's contributing to the decline of the United States as a functioning society. That's an important aspect of American Decline. It's also succeeding in shredding the remnants of political democracy, hence laying the basis for carrying the lethal process forward. And it will continue to do so as long as the victims are willing to suffer in silence.

---

43 Adam Smith, *Wealth of Nations*, bk. IV, chap. II; David Ricardo, *Principles of Political Economy and Taxation*, Dover, 2004, pp. 83–4.

Question and answer session with Dr Scott Burchill

Over the past decade, we have seen the assassination of Osama Bin Laden, the Guantanamo Bay detention of David Hicks and many individuals' rights significantly curtailed as a result of being labelled a "terrorist". Yet, many of these "terrorists" do not consider themselves terrorists. As the consequences for being labelled a terrorist continue to intensify, what, in your opinion, is the difference between a terrorist and a freedom fighter? Is it merely a difference in perspective?

That framework is commonly used to discuss the issue. A common phrase you've heard a thousand times is that 'one man's terrorist is another man's freedom fighter'. I think that's a pretty misleading way of describing the issue. If questions aren't formulated correctly, it often prevents you from getting to a reasonable answer. There's no dichotomy between freedom fighters and terrorists – freedom fighters are quite typically terrorists. Take, say, George Washington's army. They were, I suppose, freedom fighters – if anybody was. But they carried out brutal terrorist acts; that's why there was a huge flight of loyalists from the colonies after the rebels took over. They were fleeing in terror, you know, writing letters from Nova Scotia saying they're dying in the snow but they have to get away from these maniacs who won the war.

As British troops were withdrawn, more refugees fled, primarily to British American territories, including Nova Scotia. One of them described it as 'the most inhospitable clime that ever mortal set foot on'. There, 'women, delicately reared, cared for their infants beneath canvas tents, rendered habitable only by the banks of snow which lay six feet deep' while 'strong and proud men wept like children, and lay down in their snow-bound tents to die'.[44]

Remember that these loyalists were fleeing what was already the richest country in the world. And they weren't being drawn out; they were fleeing in terror. It was quite unlike Vietnam. We know that the percentage of people who fled in the American Revolution was about four per cent. You should compare that to the flight of refugees from Vietnam after 1975. Pretty typically, most wars of liberation are civil wars. That's pretty standard; the American Revolution for example was in fact a civil war. If you look at the

---

44 Sources cited in Noam Chomsky and Edward S. Herman, *After the Cataclysm: Postwar Indochina an the Reconstruction of Imperial Ideology*, South End Press, Boston, 1979, p. 45.

rough estimate, maybe a third of the population were with the rebels, a third were with the loyalists and a third wished they would all go away.[45] Carl van Doren summarised the exodus as follows:

> There are no accurate figures as to how many persons including women and children left the United States on account of loyalty to the British Empire, but it may have been as high as 100,000, of whom 35,000 may have gone from New York alone. About half the exiles settled in Canada, where they and their descendants were called United Empire Loyalists. The expulsion was so thorough that the next generation of Americans, with few former loyalists as reminders, almost forgot the civil aspects of the war and came to think of it as a war solely against England. The loyalists disappeared from American history, at least from ordinary knowledge of it.[46]

That's probably pretty normal. So, there's no dichotomy, and that's just one of innumerable examples.

Typically, wars of liberation do involve terror. I don't think they should; I'm not condoning it. I'm just describing a fact. So the real questions are: one, do we ever support terror? I don't think we should, no matter who is carrying it out. But the second question is: of the efforts at achieving some political goal, which ones do we approve of and which ones don't we approve of, and what are the reasons? Well, that puts things in a different framework. As far as the concept of terror is concerned, it's quite an interesting one. The concept gained prominence when the Reagan administration came into office in 1981. His administration declared that a prime focus of US policy would be what they called 'state-directed international terrorism'. Reagan described it as the 'evil scourge of terrorism', a plague spread by 'depraved opponents of civilization itself' in 'a return to barbarism in the modern age' (that was Secretary of State George Shultz, by the way). On and on it went, with similar rhetoric.

---

45 John Adams' estimate was that one third of the population supported the revolution, one third opposed it, and one third were neutral. John Shy, *A People Numerous and Armed*, Oxford, 1976, p. 166. Shy concludes that 'almost certainly a majority of the population, [the great middle group of Americans] were the people who were dubious, afraid, uncertain, indecisive' and unwilling to risk the hazards and suffering of revolutionary struggle; 'the prudent, politically apathetic majority of white American males was not eager to serve actively in the militia'. (pp. 215, 217).
46 Carl Van Doren, *Secret History of the American Revolution*, New York: Viking, 1941.

Debate and discussion about terrorism became a major topic in the media and everywhere else. Actually, I started writing about it too, along with some friends: Edward Herman and some others.[47] We began writing about terrorism, however the work we did on terrorism cannot be included in the canon. If you look back, you'll see it's been excluded, and there's a very simple reason. We defined 'terror' as it is defined officially in the US code and in British law, and in army manuals; and by now in the declarations of the Security Council and the General Assembly.[48] They all have definitions of terrorism, which in my mind are pretty good ones. And those are the definitions we kept to, but those definitions cannot be used for a very simple reason. If you use those definitions it follows almost immediately that the United States is the leading terrorist state, Britain is not lagging far behind, and France is right behind.

That's not terribly surprising – that's what imperial power is. Well, it's the wrong conclusion, and since it's the wrong conclusion, something must be wrong with the argument. And what's wrong with the argument? It's using the official definition of the word 'terror'. For this reason, weighty volumes have been written to try to define terror. It's a big topic in the academic profession and at international conferences. It's recognised by everyone that defining terror is a very difficult problem, and indeed it is. It's extremely difficult. Try to craft a definition which includes their terror against us, but not our much greater terror against them. That's hard, so therefore it's a difficult problem. But I think there's a simple solution: let's take the official definitions and just apply them honestly. If we don't like the conclusions, well it doesn't mean we're doing the wrong thing. It means we've got to rethink why we don't like the conclusions. As well as, of course, what policies do we not like.

So that's one question. The second question is which efforts do we approve of when it comes to using violence or the threat of violence to obtain political, ideological and other ends. Which ones do we disapprove of? I mentioned the American Revolution; I could have mentioned a ton of others. Take, say, the anti-apartheid struggle. By any measure I can think of, it was a liberation struggle. The African National Congress, which led it, was in the forefront of a major struggle for liberation. On the other hand, it was

---

47 N. Chomsky, *Culture of Terrorism*, South End, Boston, 1988; Edward Herman and Gerry O'Sullivan, *The 'terrorism' industry: The experts and institutions that shape our view of terror*, Pantheon, New York, 1989; Edward Herman, *The real terror network: Terrorism in fact and propaganda*, South End Press, Boston, 1982; N. Chomsky, *Pirates and emperors, old and new: International terrorism in the real world*, South End Press, Cambridge, 2002. Alexander George, ed., *Western state terrorism*, Polity Press, Cambridge, 1991.
48 Ben Saul, Definition of 'Terrorism' in he UN Security Council: 1985–2004, *Chinese Journal of International Law*, vol. 4. no.1.

a terrorist organisation. The Reagan administration was not lying when it declared that the African National Congress was a terrorist organisation. In fact, as they put it, it was one of the 'more notorious terrorist groups in the world' – that was in 1988, incidentally.[49]

In 1988, the Reagan administration denounced the ANC, Mandela's ANC, as one of the more notorious terrorist groups in the world. Well, that's a vast exaggeration; it didn't come close to the Reagan administration itself, for example. But nevertheless they did carry out terrorist acts, and on those grounds the United States under Reagan continued to support apartheid South Africa while it was carrying out crimes in neighbouring Angola and Mozambique. A UNICEF study estimated that South Africa's crimes caused the deaths of about 850,000 infants and young children in those two countries in 1988 alone, reversing the gains of the early post-independence years primarily through the weapon of mass terrorism.[50] That is putting aside South Africa's practices within its own borders. But the US had to support South Africa because the ANC was one of the 'more notorious terrorist groups in the world'. Actually, Nelson Mandela himself was just taken off the terrorist list two years ago. He can now come to the United States without special dispensation.

Well, this liberation struggle, which is a prime example of one, did use terror. We can say it shouldn't have done so – I don't think it should have – but it did, and it's just the wrong formulation. We should ask different questions. What is terror? Is there a reason why we don't use the official definitions? (Apart from the fact that they give conclusions which are considered unacceptable – not a good reason, of course.) And second, what kinds of violence or threat of violence do we condone, and which ones do we not. Those are hard questions, but important ones.

Alright, we're off to the Middle East now. The Australian government only a few days ago voted against Palestine's admission to UNESCO. There were 107 in favour, fourteen opposed and fifty-two abstentions. What does the two state solution really mean in 2011? It's still the official policy of the Australian government to support a two state solution. I think it's still the

---

49 Joseba Zulaika and William A Douglass, *Terror and Taboo*, Routledge, New York, 1996.
50 UN Inter-Agency Task Force, Africa Recovery Program/Economic Commission, *South African Destabilization: The Economic Cost of Frontline Resistance to Apartheid*, 1989, cited in Merle Bowen, 'Mozambique and the Politics of Economic Recovery', *Fletcher Forum of World Affairs*, vol. 15, no. 1, Winter 1991, pp. 45–55. Dereje Asrat et al, *Children on the Front Line*, UNICEF, New York and Geneva 1989.

Obama administration's official, stated position. But what does that really mean in 2011?

Well that's up to Australia to decide. Australia's not a major player in world affairs, but you know it has a role. Just like any one of us: we're not major players but we do have a role. I think the Israel-Palestine conflict at least in the short term has a very straightforward solution. It's one of the simplest problems to solve. When you think of Kashmir or Eastern Congo or something, it's extremely hard even to dream up what could be a satisfactory solution. In Israel-Palestine, there's a short term settlement, which is very straightforward, and is agreed by virtually the entire world. It's the official position you mentioned. It's been pretty well understood – a two state settlement on the internationally recognised border. That's the pre-June 1967 border, with 'minor and mutual modifications' – that phrase is from official US foreign policy in the early 1970s, when the US was still part of the world on this issue.

Then there are other questions about what to do about various other aspects. But the basic framework of a short-term settlement is quite clear. I don't think it's a great settlement, but it's at least a step towards maybe something better. And it could seriously cut down violence, destruction and threats, and make life better for everyone.

What's blocking it? For thirty-five years the United States has been blocking it, unilaterally. This proposal, pretty much along those lines, came to the Security Council in January 1976. It was advanced by the three major Arab states – Egypt, Syria and Jordan, the so-called 'confrontation states'. It was vetoed by the United States.[51] A similar proposal came up in 1980, and it was also vetoed by the United States. It shifted to the General Assembly, and practically every year there was a vote with more or less similar proposals. They varied in wording but the votes were like 151–3 (United States, Israel, Dominica in 1989), 144–2 (United States and Israel), something like that.

That pattern's been occurring year after year. Now the US and Israel have a definite position: they insist on negotiations with crucial preconditions. That's not the way it's often described. What's claimed is that the Palestinians insist on preconditions for negotiations, that Israel says let's have negotiations without preconditions, and that the United States is an honest broker throwing up its hands in despair at its inability to bring the two sides together. That's the official

---

51 Kathleen Teltsch, 'US casts veto on Mideast Plan in UN's Council', *New York Times*, 27 January 1976. See also 'Palestine Guerrillas Seek to Close Ranks for War', *New York Times*, 1 March 1976.

myth. The reality is that the US and Israel insist on crucial preconditions: one precondition is that the negotiations will be run by the United States. That essentially undermines any possibility of progress. If negotiations were meaningful, they would be run by some neutral party, with the US and Israel on one side, and the world on the other side. But the US insists on blocking a diplomatic settlement and controlling the negotiations. Well, that's consistent with what I was talking about all along. It's part of the system of making sure you control the Middle East and you don't permit others to interfere.

The second precondition is that Israel must be free to continue its settlements in the Occupied Territories. Those settlements are unequivocally criminal actions; not just the expansion of the settlements but the settlements themselves. The transfer of populations into Occupied Territories is a major crime; in fact, it's in violation of fundamental conventions of international law.[52] And that's been recognised by every relevant authority – the International Court of Justice, the Security Council, even Israel conceded it back in 1967.[53] But they said, we'll do it anyway, as long as the US backs us. So a second precondition is that they must continue to carry out these criminal acts, which are carefully designed to ensure that no viable Palestinian state can emerge. And, as I mentioned before, Gaza will be separated from the West Bank, and kept under a siege. That's the second precondition.

You can read the third precondition in the newspapers right in the last few days.[54] After Palestine asked for membership in UNESCO, Israel retaliated by immediately announcing new building programs in the West Bank and what they call Jerusalem – which is now a vastly expanded region that Israel has annexed. The settlement programs in Jerusalem, I should say, are doubly illegal. First, because all the settlements are illegal, and secondly because in Jerusalem they are in explicit violation of specific Security Council resolutions going back to 1968, demanding that the status of Jerusalem not be changed.[55] Now, if you look at Netanyahu's statements

---

52 Geneva Convention IV, Article 49, Para 6: 'The Occupying Power shall not deport or transfer parts of its own civilian population into the territory it occupies.' Additional Protocol I, Article 85(4)(a): 'the transfer by the Occupying Power of parts of its own civilian population into the territory it occupies' is a grave breach of the Protocol. Article 8(2)(b)(viii) of the ICC Statute: 'The transfer, directly or indirectly, by the Occupying Power of parts of its own civilian population into the territory it occupies' constitutes a war crime in international armed conflicts.
53 G. Gorenberg, *The Accidental Empire*, Times Books, New York, 2006.
54 Chris McGreal, 'Israel plans new settlement of 2,600 that will isolate Arab East Jerusalem', *Guardian*, 16 October 2011.
55 UNSCR 251 (2 May 1968); UNSCR 252 (21 May 1968); UNSCR 267 (3 July 1969); UNSCR 298 (25 September 1971); and others.

when he announced the current settlement programs in retaliation for the UN move, he said it doesn't really matter because these are in areas that will remain in Israel in any final settlement.

What does that mean? That means he's saying we've got a precondition for negotiations, namely that we will retain parts of the West Bank that we want to annex. Period. That's a precondition for negotiations. Well, you know with a framework like that, nothing is going to happen. This is of course a framework designed to allow meaningless negotiations that can go on forever, while Israel proceeds, with US backing, to take over what it wants in the Occupied Territories.

So what's the status of the two state settlement? Well, that depends on whether the world is willing to act. Most of the world, whatever it is, 140 countries, they already insist upon the international consensus, and have for decades. Australia has tended to go along with the United States, not completely, but tended to.

For example: On the Question of 'Permanent sovereignty of the Palestinian people in the Occupied Palestinian Territory, including Jerusalem, and of the Arab population in the occupied Syrian Golan over their natural resources', Australia's voting record for the past decade has been a Yes vote in 2000, 2001 and 2002, then it abstained in 2003 and 2004, and then voted No, along with Israel, the United States and a few countries (like the Marshall Islands, Micronesia) in 2005, 2006, 2007, 2008, 2009 and 2010.[56]

Okay, that's saying we don't want a settlement, we're willing to follow the master, we don't care what happens. Europe, with its typical courage, trails after the master. It's gone along with the United States on these issues. Europe is powerful enough to take an independent stand and follow an independent path. But that's a European decision. If Europe joins the United States, or it sort of backs away, Australia too, Canada too, then the United States and Israel will continue to block a settlement indefinitely. Until they get what they want. The Palestinians are lost.

So the status quo actually suits them?

It allows them to go further. The status quo is fine, as far as the US and Israel are concerned. Israel has quite definite plans; they're not a secret – they're approximately what was called the 'Sharon plan' at one time. It means that Israel takes over everything behind what they call the separation

---

56 Clinton Fernandes, 'Australia: General Assembly Voting on Palestine 2000–2010', MS, 2011.

wall – actually, it's an annexation wall. About eighty-five per cent of it cuts through the West Bank. It assigns to the Israeli side the arable land, some of the major water resources, the nice suburbs of Jerusalem and Tel Aviv, and so on. That is what Netanyahu says he's going to take over permanently. They're also settling the Jordan Valley. There's a recent study by B'Tselem, the Israeli human rights group, which gives some details of what Israel is doing in the Jordan Valley.[57] They're sinking hundreds of wells, establishing communities and barring Palestinians from vast areas. These are the traditional steps towards slowly taking over the region. So that means that what's left of Palestine would be trapped between Israel's Jordan Valley takeover and its takeover of the land behind the annexation wall. The vastly expanded Jerusalem is about five times its original size. That's been annexed illegally, and in addition to that there are salients cutting through; you can see it on the maps.[58]

East of Jerusalem, there's a salient that virtually bisects the West Bank, leading to the city of Ma'ale Adumim. It was begun in the 1970s, but it was built mostly under Clinton in the 1990s; it essentially bisects the West Bank. There's another one farther north, going through the town of Ariel. That bisects much of what's left, and there's another one even beyond to another town.[59] So, you've got these salients cutting through, leaving unviable cantons. They are huge infrastructure projects for Israelis only. As for the Palestinians, they can rot up in the hills. Israel has recognised recently that it makes sense to establish a traditional neo-colonial project: any imperial colony, or neo-colonial system has a sector of extreme wealth. You can go to the poorest country in sub-Saharan Africa, and there's a sector where people live in opulence way beyond what we can imagine. And Israel's doing the same thing. Not to that extent, but in Ramallah for example, you can live a kind of Western life: nice restaurants, theatres and so on. Meanwhile the rest of the country has become this kind of desperate world. Gaza of course is just a prison kept at the barest level of survival. Of course they don't want to have absolute genocide; there'd be too much reaction. Well, that's what's developing, and if Australia continues to vote with the US, they're helping it.

---

57 B'Tselem, Dispossession and Exploitation: Israel's Policy in the Jordan Valley and Northern Dead Sea, May 2011: http://www.btselem.org/publications/fulltext/dispossession_and_exploitation.
58 http://www.fmep.org/maps/.
59 Continuing analysis is at Geoffrey Aronson's *Report on Israeli Settlements in the Occupied Territories*, http://www.fmep.org.

I know you've been up since 6 am, and you must be tired. The Auslan simultaneous interpreters are doing a marvelous job. I won't keep you much longer. What on earth is going on with the Republican Party primaries? On this side of the Pacific we're not quite sure whether it's reality TV or whether they're preparing people to take over the country.

You're not the only one. I've been in Europe a couple of times recently, and people can't believe what's going on. In fact in the United States it's hard to believe. This is something that has no precedent as far as I know in the history of parliamentary democracy; it's kind of a freak show. It literally is. I don't know if you've been following it; it's kind of shocking. And it's a continuation of a process that's been going on thirty years. During this period I described – this kind of roughly neoliberal period – the Republican Party has increasingly ceased to become a traditional political party. You know, a party that participates in parliamentary interactions: maybe you like them, maybe you hate them but at least they're somehow functioning in a parliamentary framework. They've ceased that. Now, and for some years in fact the party has been so deep in the pockets of corporate America, and particularly the financial sector that you need a telescope to find them. Well, no political party can survive unless it has voters. And you're not going to get voters from one tenth of one per cent of the population.

So they've had to try to develop a different mass base – some mass base that will tolerate this. And what they've been compelled to do – since it's hard to think of an alternative – is to appeal to some of the elements of American society and culture that have always been there, but are not very attractive and have never been mobilised politically before. So, just to take one example, it's been known for decades, and there are plenty of studies, that if you do comparative studies of religious extremism, the United States is just off the spectrum. In the 1990s the US received a rating of sixty-seven on a study's 'Religion Index' whereas many European countries like the UK, Netherlands and France all scored in the thirties.[60] Literally, like about a third of the population believes in the literal truth of every word of the Bible. About half the population thinks the world was created a couple of thousand years ago with all the fossils and everything else. I think about eighty-five per cent believe in miracles. Roughly two-thirds expect the second coming, most of them within our lifetimes if we act properly. Whatever you think about these things, they're just off the international spectrum. Even in

---

60 G. Gallup, Jr. and J. Castelli, *The People's Religion*, Macmillan, New York, 1989.

extremist Islamic fundamentalist societies, you don't have comparable things. This goes way back to the colonists, who were pretty much religious fanatics. But, that's just a feature of American society, you know love it or hate it. And there are other things, like the fear; it's a very frightened society. It always has been, back to the earliest days. You see it in popular literature.[61] It's part of the gun culture. People have guns because they're afraid.

What are they afraid of? You know it's the most secure country in history, but they're terrified. There are people who are well-known scientists who are survivalists. Meaning they have a barn full of assault rifles or whatever you stick in those things. And they're going to defend themselves. Against whom? Well, look at the examples: it's frightening. The state of Indiana, a couple of years ago, had to tear down all of its highway signs. Why? (You know, the signs that say turn right at the next light or something.) Because the signs, it turns out, have a code on them, presumably for the people who clean the highways or something, and rumours started spreading that that code was for the United Nations, which is planning to commit genocide against the American people, and people see black helicopters coming, which are from the United Nations, and they're planning to descend on us and destroy us and those codes are for them. So people started tearing out the signs. And the state literally had to replace all the signs and take the codes off.[62] It's a very frightened society. You ask why people have guns? Well, one of the Republican congressmen, who's been in the lead of maintaining gun rights, told the *New York Times*, we have to have our guns, because when the federal government comes after us to take away our rights, we're going to defend ourselves.

You can't even call it paranoia, it's so far out. But it's a definite feeling, and there are a lot of things like this. And the Republicans, to the extent that they're a party, have mobilised them. That's their mass base. They can't have a mass base of people who support their policies, because nobody supports their policies. What you end up with is this show that you're seeing. I don't want to exaggerate – but I'm just about old enough so it has some resonances – it's a little bit like what happened in late Weimar Germany. There are plenty of differences, but enough similarities to be frightening; Germany, remember, in the 1920s was the absolute peak of Western civilisation in the sciences and in the arts. It was considered a model of democracy. It was

---

61 H. Bruce Franklin, *War Stars: the Superweapon and the American Imagination*, Oxford University Press, New York, 1988.
62 The Editors, 'The Evidence: Debunking FEMA Camp Myths', *Popular Mechanics*, 10 April 2009.

as advanced as Western civilisation could be. A couple of years later it was the absolute depths of history. Part of what happened is there was just a loss of respect for the central institutions of the society. People began to hate the political parties – they hated the wrangling in parliament, they wanted to get rid of everything, nothing was working, everyone was against them. The world was attacking them, they'd had an unfair Versailles settlement imposed on them, and a kind of a paranoia spread. Then a charismatic figure came along, and we know what happened next. It wasn't very nice. I don't think that's going to happen, but there are enough similarities for the current situation to be at least worrisome.

Interview with Phillip Adams

This interview with Phillip Adams was broadcast on ABC Radio National's *Late Night Live* program on 2 November 2011 and is reproduced here courtesy of the ABC.

Welcome beloved listeners, to our little wireless program. I've been trying to remember when the Sydney Peace Prize actually started. I think it was in 1998. And many of the winners passed almost without comment; they were so wonderfully respectable. Who could complain about Desmond Tutu or Sir William Deane or Mary Robinson? But once Hanan Ashrawi won in 2003, the critics of the prize started to get their knickers in a twist. There was much the same response to Arundhati Roy, to Hans Blix who got it in 2007, to John Pilger my old friend … Conniptions! Now it's gone to Noam Chomsky, and the right wing commentariat are enraged. I don't think that worries Noam Chomsky too much, does it Noam?

No, not particularly, unless there's something substantive – then I pay attention.

But it seems to me that you're almost as immune to accolades as you are to criticism; you seem to brush it all off. I mean, you're frequently described as the most important intellectual alive. You don't blush when that's said?

Well, when people quote that, they never quote the next sentence. It was in the *New York Times*. The next sentence was something like 'how can he write such terrible things about American foreign policy?' That somehow never gets quoted in print.[1]

---

1 Paul Robinson, 'The Chomsky Problem', *The New York Times Book Review*, 25 February 1979, BR1: 'Judged in terms of the power, range, novelty and influence of his thought, Noam Chomsky is arguably the most important intellectual alive today. He is also a disturbingly divided intellectual. On the one hand there is a large body of revolutionary and highly technical linguistic scholarship, much of it too difficult for anyone but the professional linguist or philosopher; on the other, an equally substantial body of political writings, accessible to any literate person but often maddeningly simple-minded. The "Chomsky problem" is to explain how these two fit together.'

Well, it's on the record now. And this is about our thirteenth or fourteenth chat. It's just wonderful to have you here. Let me add to this mountain of congratulations, on the one hand, as opposed to the attacks on the other. You must have a mantelpiece groaning with prizes?

There's a pile somewhere, not a mantelpiece.

Look, in all the times I've talked to you, I've never had a chance to ask you a little bit about your extraordinary youth. I'd like you to tell us a little bit about William and Elsie, your father and mother.

My parents were both first generation immigrants; my father came to the United States from the Ukraine in 1913, when he was about seventeen. He came essentially to escape the Tsar's draft, which was almost a death sentence for Jewish boys. He lived in a village that was later wiped out by the Nazis; there was nothing left. And when he came to the United States, he didn't know any English. He worked in a sweat shop in Baltimore and managed to learn the language. He got some education, finally went to John Hopkins, got a degree, and ended up a pretty important Hebrew scholar. He did a lot of work on medieval Hebrew grammar. In fact, when I was a child I was reading the draft of his dissertation on David Kimhi, a thirteenth century medieval grammarian.[2] He went on to be an educator – a kind of Deweyite educator – and taught in Hebrew college and in the graduate university of Jewish Studies in Philadelphia: Dropsie College. My mother was also an immigrant. She came to the United States when she was a baby – about a year old – from what's now Belarus. The family was in New York; both families are extreme, super orthodox. I remember my mother telling me that when she was with her friends in the streets of New York, as a young teenager, if she saw her father coming towards them, they would cross the street because she didn't want to be embarrassed in front of her friends by having her father pass by and act as if he didn't recognise her, a mere girl.

She was very smart and independent but she couldn't go to college; that was only for boys. So her younger brother was allowed to go to college, but she could only go to normal school. She became a teacher, an educator

---

2   William Chomsky, *David Kimhi's Hebrew Grammar: (Mikhlol) Systematically Presented and Critically Annotated*, Bloch, New York, 1952.

– also a Hebrew educator.[3] She wrote books – actually the two of us even wrote a play together once in Hebrew. But she became a pretty influential educator in the – Hebrew ghetto isn't exactly the right word, but where they lived in Philadelphia, where I grew up, there was a segment of the Jewish community, mostly first generation immigrants, who were deeply engaged in a revival of Hebrew and a modernisation of Jewish culture. They wanted to split from the diaspora tradition of Eastern Europe …

And split from Yiddish?

Yeah, both my parents' native language was Yiddish, but they wouldn't let us hear a word, so all I learned of Yiddish was what everybody learns from Woody Allen, or the secret language of your parents.

You drop the odd Yiddish word into your public performances though, don't you?

Occasionally.

So, who influenced you the most politically: mum or dad?

Politically, neither of them. This was the 1930s, so they were fairly conventional New Deal Democrats. I can remember listening to Roosevelt's fireside chats on I think Friday evenings; there was a mood of calm settling over the family, you know everything's going to be okay. But the influences on me politically, to the extent that they came from the family, came from a different part of the family. My mother's relatives were all in New York, which is a short train ride from Philadelphia. By the time I got old enough to travel by myself – about eleven or twelve– I'd take the train to New York all the time and stay with a couple of my relatives. They were working class mostly, most of them unemployed at the time, and there was a very lively working class culture in the 1930s. It's sort of forgotten now. One of my uncles, who was maybe the biggest influence on my life at that age, actually never went past fourth grade, and others had some education but not much.

Your uncle was a Trotskyite, wasn't he?

---

3 H. Feinberg, *Elsie Chomsky: A life in Jewish education*, Hadassah International Research Institute on Jewish Women, Waltham, 1999.

He had been through every sect that there was, and had rejected them all, so he was an ex-Trotskyite, but he was an ex- everything else as well.

You were never seduced by the Communist Party and the Soviet Union, were you?

By the time I was twelve years old, I was not only anti-Stalinist, but anti-Leninist – from the Left – and I was being led towards the anarchist movements and towards the Left Marxists. There was a major component of the Marx tradition which was very critical of Bolshevism from the Left – there was another from the Right, the Mensheviks – but there was an important one on the Left: people like Anton Pannekoek, who was one of the leading intellectuals of social democracy, but a left critic of Bolshevism, and others; those are the people I read. They were not too far from components of the anarchist movement; they were sort of close to the anarcho-syndicalists whom I was also interested in. I became very much interested in the Spanish revolution right around 1940, around that time.

Well, that was the impulse behind pretty much your first column or your first article – when you were ten?

I don't know if it was the first one, but it was an early one. I was the editor of the fourth grade newspaper – probably the only reader, except maybe for my mother, I don't know. But I did write an article which I half remember. It was right after the fall of Barcelona, so that would have been about February 1939. It wasn't specifically about the Spanish Civil War; it was about the spread of fascism in Europe, which as a child seemed very frightening and ominous. I mean, I listened to Hitler's speeches on the radio and I didn't understand anything, but you could pick up the mood and the threat, and knew some of the things that were happening. The article was about the fall of Austria, then Czechoslovakia, now Spain. It looked at the time as if fascism was unstoppable: it was going to spread over the world. That was frightening in itself, but it also tied in with personal experiences, which incidentally my parents never even knew about. Those days you didn't talk to your parents about personal things, at least boys didn't. It's not done. But we lived in a neighbourhood where we were the only Jewish family, and the neighbourhood was pretty pro-fascist.

Partly it was Irish Catholic – and they just hated the British – and partly it was German, and they were pro-Nazi. As a boy on the streets you get to run into these things. And I grew up with just a visceral fear of Catholics. I knew when the kids came out of the Catholic school down the street, they were going to be raving anti-Semites. And maybe later in the afternoon they'd calm down; we could play ball or something. But just part of experience was fear of violently anti-Semitic, mostly Catholic, kids coming from this Jesuit school.

Well with this momentum, with this background, why didn't you study politics when you went to university? Why did you suddenly opt for linguistics?

I didn't study politics because I really didn't believe in what was being taught. I thought I had better insight from other sources, and in retrospect I think that was probably a wise decision. Actually, I got into linguistics through political contacts. That's just a personal story, I don't know if it's of any general interest.

I'd love to hear it.

I went to a Deweyite experimental school.[4] As I said, my father was very much interested in Dewey's educational theories and practiced them. It was run by Temple University, which had a progressive education department. It was a terrific school. I was there from infancy – about eighteen months old, since my parents worked there – until high school: so until twelve. It was a very exciting experience. You weren't graded; there was no ranking. Actually I didn't know I was a good student until I got into high school. I mean I knew I had skipped a grade, but okay that just meant I was the smallest kid in the class; nobody paid any attention to it. And the teachers kind of inspired creative work, often cooperative; you worked with other people or you pursued your own interests. There was a curriculum, you followed it and then I got into high school. There was one academic high school in the city for boys and another for girls; my future wife went to the girl's one. And it was kind of like a black hole; I don't remember a thing. Everything was graded and you had to pass exams. It was extremely boring.

I was looking forward to going to college – a local college, of course, since there's no thought of going anywhere else. You live at home, you work, and you go to college. I was sixteen when I got into college. The catalogue looked very exciting. I was going to take courses in Greek, this, that and the other,

---

4 Oak Lane Country Day School.

all kinds of exciting stuff; when I started to take these courses I discovered it's high school. It was just boring, routine, and I was ready to drop out after about a year. I didn't see any point going on. And through political contacts – what now would be called anti-Zionist but then it was Zionist, left-Zionist, anti-state radical activism – I ran into a professor, Zellig Harris, who was very much involved in these things. In fact he was at the centre of many of these movements, and had a big influence on a lot of young Jewish intellectuals of the period. He didn't write much, and nobody knows about him, but he was very influential and kind of a charismatic person. I got to know him, and in retrospect I think he was trying to convince me to get back into college; he didn't say anything, but he just suggested that I start taking some of his graduate courses. So I took them, and—

Isn't life serendipitous, absolutely arbitrary in a way?

Extremely. The whole thing for me is totally … I don't even have professional qualifications, which is why I'm teaching at MIT – they didn't care. But I had no professional qualifications in any field. Through Harris' influence I started taking graduate courses. He directed me to faculty members at the university, who were pretty exciting people, but in different fields. One was in mathematics, another in philosophy, and I ended up with a strange hodge-podge of courses.

Well, you did pretty well because you finished up as Institute Professor, and Professor Emeritus of linguistics and philosophy at MIT, which isn't too bad for a sort of autodidact.

Well it was serendipitous, as you say; it was mostly accidental. I spent four years as a Junior Fellow at Harvard's Society of Fellows – a kind of graduate sub-institution of Harvard for select students – and that was very free also. It was kind of like elementary school again. But when I was finished with that I had no profession, and I had no particular job prospects. I had friends at MIT and they just suggested that I get a job in the electronics lab. I can't tell a radio from a tape recorder. To this day, if something goes wrong with my computer I have to check with my grandchildren. So I had an interview with the head of the Research Laboratory for Electronics. The person became pretty well known: Jerry Wiesner. He became Kennedy's science and technology adviser shortly after. We had an interview. He was interested in talking about what I was interested in. He thought it was interesting; he suggested that I work on a project that they had there on machine translation. And I told him I thought it was a silly project and wasn't going to work on it. The way to solve it was just brute force. There was nothing else you could do. Which turned out to be correct years later. But he thought that was a pretty good answer, so he said okay why don't you just work on what you're interested in. And it kind of went on from there. But it was luck, otherwise I would never have ended up in the academic world.

It's interesting that even if you had never made a public utterance on matters political, you were going to be a trailblazer. Because I vividly recall your great contribution, your great theoretical contribution to the notion of language: that it is innate and not learnt. And you argued, discovered the role of hormones in the emergence of human language in much the same way as hormones play such a part in the emergence of puberty.

Well, in a sense that's correct. There was a kind of general atmosphere in Cambridge, Massachusetts – it was all over the place but in Cambridge it was at the peak – in philosophy, social sciences, psychology, linguistics, practically all fields. It was called 'behavioural science'. That was an interesting period in American life altogether. It's worth remembering that before the Second World War, the United States was far and away the richest country in the world, but it wasn't a major player in world affairs. You know, Britain was the dominant power. And intellectually it was kind of a backwater. If you wanted to study physics or philosophy or math you went to Germany or England. If you wanted to be a writer you went to Paris. The United States was like central Iowa: you want to get out if you want to do anything. So much so that after the Second World War when I was teaching at MIT we were still teaching French and German to the graduate students because – as a holdover from the pre-war period – they had to know them because the work was in Europe.

The Second World War changed all that dramatically. Power shifted to the United States: it became the major technological centre, the major intellectual centre. A lot of European émigrés came. They fled fascism; Europe was devastated. So, there was a kind of Rome-Greece attitude towards Europe, you know: it's there and it's fading.

So your personal timing was perfect.

As luck had it, but it was more than that. I mean there was a sense in the United States in the 1950s – if you read the literature back then – that 'we can discard all of that old-fashioned stuff'. That was all old, European stuff. We're going to do it the right way; we're Americans and we'll do everything from scratch. And it had an objective basis: the United States at that time had literally half the world's wealth, incredible security and was in a position to dominate the world.[5] The planners knew it – there were careful plans laid for running the world – and in the intellectual spheres it was kind of at its peak in places like Cambridge: Harvard, MIT and so on. There was a sense that we could start everything all over. And there were a lot of new discoveries: in the 1930s it became possible to unify chemistry and physics with the new quantum theory, and that was a step forward. It included a major American scientist, Linus Pauling. Then during the war there was a lot of technological development. After the war, in the late 1940s, information theory looked like it could be a unifying concept for the human sciences. Then came radical behaviourism: Skinner's work in the late 1940s looked like the answer to human behaviour. A couple of years later, in the 1950s, came Crick and Watson's discovery of DNA. It looked as if somehow biology was going to be integrated into chemistry which already somehow had a link to physics. The concept of unified science – you know, 'we can unify all of science and march on', – was very dominant.

It's still just beyond our reach, isn't it.

There's a lot more modesty now, and rightly so. In the human sciences then, including in linguistics, there was a sense that everything was basically solved; we need to add a few touches here and there, but the basic ideas are understood. The most influential philosopher of the period was W.V. Quine at Harvard; a very influential philosopher. His view was, as he put it, language is essentially an arbitrary collection of 'conditioned responses' – learning a language is a matter of association of sentences to one another and to certain stimuli through conditioning.[6] And that was virtually dogma, that together with information theory: computers were just coming along, and it looked as if it would be possible to automate analytic techniques. That's where the machine translation interest came

---

5   Gabriel Kolko, *The Politics of War: The World and United States Foreign Policy, 1943–1945*, Pantheon, New York, 1968; Gabriel Kolko and Joyce Kolko, *The Limits of Power: The World and United States Foreign Policy, 1945–1954*, Harper & Row, New York, 1972.
6   W.V. Quine, *Word and Object*, MIT Press, Cambridge, 1960; Noam Chomsky, 'Quine's Empirical Assumptions', in D. Davidson and J. Hintikka, eds, *Words and Objections*, Reidel, Dordrecht, 1969.

from. There were three of us, graduate students, who didn't believe a word of it. We were at Harvard in the early 1950s and we tried to work out our own views. One of them died some years ago; he was the founder of modern biology of language.[7] Another is my office mate still, after sixty years at MIT; he's retired also.[8]

But we thought, first of all, with regard to language that the core problems were just being ignored, not even studied. I mean the core, the most elementary property of language when you think about it, and it was kind of understood in the seventeenth and eighteenth centuries, is a capacity which all humans share, and no other organism has: to act creatively with language; to produce an unbounded number of expressions which have a very specific meaning and very specific sound; not determined by stimuli either external or internal; appropriate to situations, not caused by them; intelligible to others, who recognise that they could have expressed the same thought the same way, if it ever occurred to them before. And it can go on without bounds, it's a kind of elementary aspect of human nature and a very distinctive one. If you go back to, say Descartes, that was kind of the core of Cartesian philosophy, and it spread and found its way into all sorts of directions, like classical liberalism, and much of Enlightenment thought. A lot of it's been forgotten since. It wasn't forgotten in the nineteenth century but in the twentieth century it turned into what I just described: behavioural science, analysis of data and so on. But it was missing all of these points.

And then the three of you come along, and?

Well, the three of us – there were a couple of other friends too, but it was mainly the three of us – thought first of all that this ought to be the core problem for the study of language. And the other thing we thought was that language should not be divorced from biology; that the capacity for language is a biological capacity, much like, say, the visual system or the immune system and so on. It is some sub-system of the cognitive faculties which can be studied on its own but also integrated with others. It later came to be called Biolinguistics. In pursuing those two directions, language and cognitive science sort of developed an interaction around

---

7   Eric Lenneberg, 'The Capacity of Language Acquisition' in Fodor and Katz, eds, *The Structure of Language, Englewood Cliff*, 1964.
8   Morris Halle.

the same time. It's still a very conflicted topic; it's not as though everyone accepts it, by any means.

I'm aware of that. You are under constant attack in that area of your life as you are politically.

It's a contested area, but I don't really think there should be much controversy about it. Then MIT just became the centre of it: we were all at MIT and one of us, Eric Lenneberg, went off to medical school and worked on biology of language. Morris Halle as I said is still my office mate, after all these years. We developed a department and students came and so on and so forth, and it spread all over the world.

And you were able to demonstrate quite convincingly that the capacity to learn language was at its greatest when the human being is pretty young?

It was kind of known intuitively, but as the topic became studied much more intensively, some of the best work has been done by a couple of scientists who are right here, now: Stephen Crain and Rosalind Thornton. By now there's intensive study of acquisition of language, and like other biological capacities, it appears to have what's called a 'critical period': it functions almost reflexively at a certain stage of life. In later stages, as it becomes harder, it has to be done differently. There are individual differences but that's generally true.

I asked you this years and years ago, but it's so long ago I can't quite remember the answer. There was a time when there was a cluster of languages that you were finding a bit recalcitrant, a bit hard to sort of fit in, and those were at least some of the Aboriginal languages in Australia.

Well, one of the early appointments in our departments, Kenneth Hale, became a very close friend. He died a couple of years ago. He was one of the founders of Australian linguistics. In fact, a lot of the people working here now are students of his, and so on. He did a lot of work with Aboriginal languages of Australia, with Native American languages, later others. Some of them seemed to have properties which looked quite different from familiar Western languages. Actually, I should say so did Japanese at the time: it looked quite different. One of the basic differences appeared to be – this was widely assumed right through the 1970s – that they had free word order, basically. Kind of like Latin, you know: you could put words in all sorts of orders. Whereas a language like English has got to be pretty rigid. So it was assumed that there's a property – it's called a parameter, technically – a distinction among languages as to whether they're word order free or have rigid word order.

Over the years there's been a lot of chipping away at that. First it was shown for Japanese and others that that just wasn't true. It now appears that they had basically the same structures: a few differences, but not these. Finally that came to be shown for every language that's known, including the ones that appeared to have extremely free word order. One of the main ones was Warlpiri, one of the languages that Ken studied. But more intensive study showed that if you looked more closely they had pretty much the same principles; there are differences, but small differences. In fact, it's kind of interesting that the same development has taken place within biology. So if you go back to the 1950s, in the study of language it was pretty widely assumed that languages can, I'm quoting, 'differ from each other without limit and in unpredictable ways' and therefore the study of each language must be approached 'without any preexistent scheme of what a language must be'.[9] It's sometimes called the Boasian tradition after the great anthropologist Frans Boas.

In biology, the same was assumed, it was assumed that organisms can vary from one another virtually without limit and they develop the way they do just by the accidents of natural selection over long periods. Both of these ideas are pretty much, well in biology it's gone, but by now it's so far gone that there are even proposals taken seriously, even if not totally accepted that there may be a universal genome that all complex, multicellular organisms develop – roughly half a billion years ago in the Cambrian Explosion and they're all fundamentally the same, from bacteria to humans. They have slight differences, what's been found as conservation of genetic mechanisms, which is extremely deep, and the way it was put back in the 1970s by one of the great figures who initiated this development, Francois Jacob, who was the great French biologist, Nobel laureate, that, as he put it, 'the difference between say an elephant and a fly is just slight differences in the arrangement of regulatory mechanisms'[10] And this went in parallel with

---

9   This was the formulation of the prominent theoretical linguist Martin Joos fifty years ago, summarising the reigning 'Boasian tradition', as he plausibly called it, tracing it to the work of one of the founders of modern anthropology and anthropological linguistics, Frans Boas.
10 Francois Jacob, *Le Jeu des Possibles: Essai sur la diversite du vivant*, Fayard, 1981.

similar developments in linguistics. Not unrelated, incidentally, we all knew each other, and there were influences.[11]

But what an exhilarating time it must have been for you!

It was quite exciting, yeah. By now what seemed very exotic in the early '50s for many, not for everyone by any means but for at least people in a pretty wide sector of study of mind seems kind of routine.

Are the studies in linguistics plateauing or are they accelerating? Is there still a hell of a lot more to know?

Well, it's like the other sciences, the more you learn the more you know that you don't understand anything. In fact it's very characteristic of the sciences; take a look at early modern science, which is instructive. So if you go back to say Galileo, there was a general assumption in the sciences that they sort of basically understood everything. So take something which we now know is complex, but was then considered very simple. Suppose I'm holding a cup with boiling water in it, and it's covered. If I take the cover off the cup, the steam rises. If I let go of the cup, the cup falls; so why does the cup fall but the steam rise? Well there was an answer that was accepted for several millennia; the answer was, they're going to their natural place, so that explains it. Game over. We understand everything. Galileo and others of the early seventeenth century were willing to be puzzled by it. The ability to be puzzled by simple things is quite a significant kind of intellectual achievement; and Galileo questioned – he's the famous one; there were among others too – why that happens. As soon as he began to question it, it turned out that not only that it's not trivial, but that one's intuitions about it are all wrong. So the intuition about it, is that if you have a heavy, a big ball and a small ball, the big one will drop faster. Turned out not to be true, they drop the same rate. It turned out that rate of fall didn't depend on mass, and so on and so forth.

Out of that puzzlement comes modern science and as you proceed in modern science, the more you learn the bigger the gaps are. It's kind of like mountain-climbing, you climb a hill, you think you've made the top, when you get there you see there's a bigger peak you didn't know about.

---

11 Noam Chomsky, *Rules and Representations*, Columbia University Press, 1980, p. 67.

You know over the years I've lost count of the scientists who have sat where you're sitting, and who have confidently told me that the theory of everything was just moments away. That the equation was going to go up on that blackboard at any minute.

Physics for example, has some slight problems; like finding ninety per cent of the universe. They haven't found it yet. It's what the CERN accelerator is for, trying to find some particle that's supposed to be there, but if it isn't there there's a big mystery about ninety of the mass energy in the universe.

I've had the pleasure of reading your speech for the Sydney Peace Prize, while under embargo. And needless to say, I thoroughly enjoyed it. And let me now do a segue into this whole issue of your political life. You make the point powerfully and endlessly that we voice great moral indignation about other people's atrocities but we are blind to our own.

That's pretty much a cultural universal, I think. When you look back over history, you find many examples of this, but very little willingness to sort of look into the mirror. Almost every culture I know of has a fringe of people who do it, and they're usually persecuted. So, one of them drank the hemlock in classical Greece; we go to the biblical prophets in the same period roughly. The prophets are what we would call dissident intellectuals, and they were very badly treated. One of them, a famous case – Elijah – was denounced by the evil king, the epitome of evil[12] in the bible, King Ahab, as a 'hater of Israel'. It's usually translated as 'troubler of Israel' but a proper translation should be 'hater of Israel'.[13] The reason is that he was criticising the evil king, so he must hate Israel. The evil king, like all totalitarians associated himself with the culture of the society, the people and so on.

And if you take a look at the biblical record, the people we honour, who were honoured centuries later as prophets, were treated extremely badly, after all one was crucified. That's again a historical pattern that replicates itself through the ages, so there's typically some fringe of critics who say 'look, we should look at ourselves', I mean you read the prophets; they were saying we should pay attention to *our* crimes. It was put in theological terms,

---

12 'Ahab son of Omri did evil in the sight of the LORD more than all who were before him'. 1 Kings 16:30.
13 1 Kings 18:17. See also A .J. Heschel, *The Prophets*, 2 vols, Harper & Row, New York, 1962.

you know 'God's going to punish us for violating his laws, but *we're* the ones who are sinning'.

But whenever you raise this issue, you are immediately categorised as anti-American. Mind you of course, that's the classic technique.

'Anti-American' is an interesting concept. Notice that it's used almost only for the United States. So if someone in Italy let's say, condemns Berlusconi, he's not called anti-Italian. The very concept is a totalitarian concept. It means that if you're criticising say state policies, you must be opposed to the society, the culture, the tradition and so on – which is a typical totalitarian concept. In the old Soviet Union for example, the dissidents were condemned as what was called anti-Soviet, in the Brazilian military dictatorship they were anti-Brazilian. It's kind of striking that I think the United States is about the only society where the term is used.

And primarily of course, used by the right.

I wouldn't call them totalitarian, but they're reflecting a totalitarian conception: that if you're a critic of the policies of the state you must hate the country.

But you're an even-handed critic of the United States, you've never been a great enthusiast for the rabid right of the Republican Party, but you're no great fan, for example of Obama's?

First of all I think the two parties barely differ. They're just, as the famous sociologist C. Wright Mills writes in the 1950s, two branches of the business party. So that's kind of interesting; I mean, there's a concept of objectivity. If you go to a journalism school in the United States you're taught a concept of objectivity. Objectivity means you tell the truth about debates going on within the Beltway: you know, in the Washington framework. If you object to that framework, you're subjective, biased, emotional, whatever it may be. That's – again, I don't want to exaggerate it, but – it has a totalitarian element to it.

Were you sympathetic to Ralph Nader's candidacies?

His campaigns? Well, I like Nader, I think he's done very interesting things but we had our personal, sharp disagreement about this. I don't think it makes a lot of sense for an individual to set himself up and say, I'm running for president. If he were running as part of an incipient political organisation which was trying to establish itself and become a voice in national affairs, say the Green Party, and he were picked as its candidate then I think you could give some justification for it. But when it's a personal campaign it doesn't make any sense. For one thing it's never going to get anywhere, but it's also the wrong idea. It's not individuals that change the world – popular movements can change the world. They may yield spokespersons who may be influential and significant, but they're not gods.

What do you make of the Occupy movement?

I think it's quite an exciting movement, in fact in many ways inspiring. There's a lot of pitfalls, a lot of problems, but it's the first organised, popular response to very significant changes that have taken place not only in the United States, but in other societies too. These changes have happened in roughly the last generation, the period of what sometimes is called neoliberal globalisation. That, I think, has been very destructive everywhere it's been applied. The concepts have been applied differently in different countries, but take in Egypt, where the policies were applied: they led to economic growth and also to a concentration of wealth that was very harmful to the general population. They resulted in a lot of resistance, a lot of militant labour action, which has finally crystallised itself in the Arab Spring. If you go to a rich society like the United States, the policies were not identical, but they were somewhat similar in character. Again, there's been economic growth, but it's gone into very few pockets and for the majority of the population it's been something like stagnation, even decline. That's a big shift in American history. Remember that since the early British colonists came, it was a developing society. It was industrialising, developing; it wasn't very pretty, I should say. It meant exterminating the indigenous population and slavery, and all sorts of horrible things like conquering half of Mexico. But the fact of the matter is that – whatever your judgment about the methods – it was a growing, developing society. I don't mean one hundred per cent of the time; there were setbacks. But it was also a hopeful society: you could expect that things were going to be better for your children. That went on until the 1970s, and at that point it reversed. It's quite a significant historical thing—

And it's not just the Occupy movement, it's also Tea Party in a strange way?

The Tea Party movement is expressing similar sentiments. It's based on similar resentments and anger, but it's a totally incoherent movement. For one thing, it's not a real popular movement; it's actually quite small. There are a lot of sympathisers: the people are angry about everything.[14] But their position is internally incoherent. In an interesting way, the United States is a very heavily polled society. We know a lot about people's opinions. When you look at a study of attitudes, which are carefully done, they're quite interesting. There are studies of people who we think of as Tea Party adherents: people who say, you know 'get the government off my back', that kind of thing, 'small government, let us alone, free markets'. Now if you look just at those people and their attitudes, it turns out they're social democrats.[15] Like, they think, Yeah, we want to get rid of the government, but what about spending on health? It should go up. Spending on education? It should go up. Spending on help for, say, poor women who have to take care of children? Yeah, it should go up. What about welfare? No, that should go down. That's because welfare's been demonised.

But even on things like foreign aid, you know, they have very standard attitudes. This has been the case for a long time in the United States: 'We give way too much away to the undeserving poor.' Then if you ask people what they estimate foreign aid is, they give an estimate that is way higher than it is. When you ask them what it ought to be, the answer is much higher than it actually is. In fact, across the board, what you have are these vague, unformulated but roughly social democratic attitudes connected with a doctrine that says get rid of the government, and hand it all over to corporations. And they hate the corporations.

As well as the orthodox polls, like Pew, there are the greasy poles which are run, you know, by the likes of Fox News. And looking at those, one is astonished from this side of the Pacific at the comings and goings in the Republican sort of rat race for the nomination. And I know a couple of days ago you were very concerned – or perhaps more amused – by the prospect of Texas governor Rick Perry getting the nomination. Now, I know he has fallen back, but isn't it funny that the Republican machine, or the organism, can produce someone as totally irrational as Perry.

---

14 Anthony DiMaggio, *The Rise of the Tea Party: Political Discontent and Corporate Media in the Age of Obama*, Monthly Review Press, New York, 2011.
15 Neil King, Jr and Scott Greenberg, 'Poll shows budget-buts dilemma', *Wall Street Journal*, 3 March 2011: 'Even tea party supporters, by a nearly 2-to-1 margin, declared significant cuts to Social Security "unacceptable."'

The Republican debates, I don't know if you followed them, but there's nothing in the history of parliamentary democracy that's anything like that, I think. They are totally irrational and very dangerous. There's a kind of catechism you have to sign on to if you want to be a part of that system, and some of it is not only irrational but extremely dangerous. For example, you have to be a global warming denier. Well, you know that spells doom for the species.

And you've also got to deny evolution.

You have to deny evolution, and there's a reason for that. For about the last thirty years, the Republicans have gradually ceased becoming a political party.

What are they, then?

What they are, at the core, is just an extreme faction of the very wealthy and tiny corporate elite. But the point is that they have to have a mass base. They can't participate in a political system if their policies are just 'enrich the super rich', and then 'empower the super powerful'. They can't go to the population that way, so they had to develop a mass base. How do they do it? They recognised around the early 1980s that there is a mass base. It is founded on precisely the kind of thing you're mentioning: a kind of religious extremism, irrationality, fear of foreigners, fear of everything. That base is quite large. So for example in the United States – I don't know what it's like here – but in the US, about a third of the population believes in the literal truth of every word in the Bible. That's why you get half the population thinking the world was created a couple of thousand years ago. About two-thirds of the population expects the second coming soon, and about a third expects it in their own lifetimes.

Right now you are in a much more agnostic country, you know: Australia. We don't have these sort of manias.

I don't think any other country has it. There's been a lot of comparative studies[16] of different …

---

16 W.D. Burnham, 'Social Stress and Political Response', in T. Ferguson and J. Rogers, eds, *The Hidden Election*, Pantheon, New York, 1981.

But why America?

This goes way back, whatever the reasons are, it goes back very far. The pilgrims, who were the first colonists, were religious fanatics. I mean, they were waving the Holy Book when they were destroying the Amalekites.[17] Then the Scotch Irish brought similar things. Anyway, whatever the reasons may be, it perpetuated. And Republican strategists recognised that you can appeal to that mass base and get enough votes to put into office the people that are going to cut taxes on the rich.

Noam, given that fear is rampant in the American political system, and given that we prefer not to be fearful, do you fear for the future of your country in the short term?

Well, if you fear for the future of the country, you're fearing for the future of the world. For example, take global warming again. That's not a joke. You look at the way it's presented: it's as if there are scientists that believe in global warming and skeptics who say that it isn't happening. But that picture is incorrect. There's another group that denies the scientific consensus: those are the scientists who say the consensus is much too moderate. They say that it's a lot worse than any of us thinks. So for example, just take MIT, where I am. There's a climate change group of very eminent scientists who are convinced that the truth is much worse. Actually, a big study just came out from University of California, which comes to the same conclusion. Even the International Energy Agency has recently warned we might be getting to a tipping point where there's not much that you can do.[18]

It may be too late already.

It may be, but whatever it is, it's very serious. Now, if you have a country, the most powerful and richest country in history, which says it's not happening, and furthermore that we're going to make it worse, the species is in trouble. Just about every country is taking some kind of maybe halting move to do something about it. But the United States has not only not taken action but is actually going backwards. Under the impact of this right-wing

---

17 The Bible, 1 Samuel 15.
18 International Energy Agency, *Prospect of limiting the global increase in temperature to 2°C is getting bleaker*, 30 May 2011.

Republicanism, they are now dismantling the efforts that were made by Richard Nixon; that's an indication of how the party's changed. When I say it's not a political party anymore, I mean it's developed a mass base based on fear, anger and irrationality. It also has policies which are totally destructive. And there are no longer any moderate republicans.

I want to ask you one final question, and then you can rest your poor voice. In the Sydney Peace Prize Lecture you ask the big, big question: Can we proceed to at least limit the scourge of war? Can we?

If you look at history, it's pretty hard to believe it. I mean, when you say we need to save 'succeeding generations from the scourge of war', you're quoting the founding document of the UN in 1945. And we certainly haven't limited the scourge of war. I mean, there has been one success – in fact, I mention it in the Lecture you just mentioned – and that's continental Europe. Europe for centuries had been the most savage, brutal place in the world. You go back to the seventeenth century: the thirty year war had killed maybe a third of the population of Germany. That's not small. And we already know about the twentieth century. But it stopped in 1945, and now European states don't go to war with one another anymore. There's a thesis about this in the political science literature, which I'm kind of skeptical about. It's called the 'thesis of the democratic peace' – democracies don't fight each other. However, there's another factor which you have to consider, and I suspect it's dominant: Europeans recognised after 1945 that if they play the traditional game of slaughtering each other, it's all going to be over. They had developed means of destruction so extraordinary that you just can't do it anymore. Powerful states can't go to war, so you attack the weak. And since 1945 there have been plenty of attacks on the weak and defenceless.

Problems of knowledge and freedom

In conversation with Mary Kostakidis

This public discussion hosted by Mary Kostakidis was conducted as part of the 'Ideas at the House' series presented by the Sydney Opera House and the Sydney Peace Foundation on 3 Nov 2011. Thank you to Mary Kostakidis for permission to reproduce her contribution to this discussion.

How can we reconcile what you're advocating [in your Sydney Peace Prize lecture last night] with the three most frequently used words to engender unquestionable public legitimacy: The National Interest. Indeed, given that so many of our problems are global, how are they to be tackled when we are each protecting our National Interests?

That's an interesting term: the national interest. Of course it's the core notion of academic international relations theory – so-called 'Realist' international relations theory, based on the concept that states pursue their national interests. It's always seemed to me that the concept is very far from realistic; in fact, there's a touch of mysticism about it. It assumes that there's a common national interest shared by everyone in the country. So the CEO of General Electric and the janitor who cleans the floor have the same interest. Well, actually, they have very different interests, often sharply conflicting interests. It turns out that the interest of the CEO is what ends up being the national interest, not the interest of the janitor.

So, it's a concept that relates to elite conceptions. There are some shared interests, of course, like not being destroyed by nuclear war or environmental destruction. Well, how do we protect ourselves from those things? Suppose for example the Australian national interest could be advanced by enslaving the population of sub-Saharan Africa and sending them to work under miserable conditions, in mines owned by Australian companies. And suppose that increased the wealth of Australia, and was hence the national interest. Should we therefore be in favour of it? Well I think if we took a vote among people, very few would be in favour of it. And I should say that this is not really a hypothetical example. After the Second World War, when the United States was in a position of just overwhelming power – I won't go into the details but there's nothing like it in history – the planners made detailed, sophisticated plans to organise the world so that it would serve what they took to be the American national interest.¹ They assigned every region of the world what they called its 'function'. The 'function' of Southeast Asia was to provide resources and raw materials. The United States was not particularly interested in Africa, but it was interested in the reconstruction of Europe. So it decided to hand over Africa to the Europeans to exploit, to help with their reconstruction. That was said to be in the American national interest because the former colonial powers would then be able to purchase US manufacturing exports.

Well, do we accept that? Thinking back, was it correct, would Americans even then have said that it's right to hand Africa over to Europe to exploit for its reconstruction? Not many would have accepted that, I hope, and certainly not now. And those are real issues. If it turns out to be in the so-called mostly mythical 'national interest' to exploit and harm and destroy others, is that a conflict? Are we in a conflict about whether to accept it or not? I don't think so.

The election of Obama engendered a lot of hope in the US and internationally. He was awarded the Nobel Peace Prize. The Rambo-style execution of Osama bin Laden under a Democratic president came as a disappointment and surprise, at least to some. Guantanamo Bay hasn't been shut down. Has the post-9/11 neo-conservative agenda been more successful, more entrenched and more pervasive than you anticipated?

I frankly did not share the hopefulness when Obama was elected. I thought it was mostly illusion; in fact I wrote about it even before the primaries, just basing myself on his record, his webpage and so on.² What I'm saying is not an afterthought. Nevertheless, it was worse than I expected. In many ways it's worse than Bush's programs, and that's been pointed out by conservative military analysts. Bush's way of dealing with suspects – now let me stress 'suspects', since there used to be a principle in Anglo-American legal tradition that people are innocent until proven guilty in a court of law – was to kidnap them and send them to Bagram or Guantanamo, and detain them without charge indefinitely. These are essentially torture chambers.

Why, incidentally, do they send them to Guantanamo rather than to, say, Kansas? It has nothing to do with security. That's ridiculous. It's because they

---

1   Gilbert Achcar, Noam Chomsky and Stephen Shalom, *Perilous Power*, Paradigm Publishers, Boulder, 2007.
2   See Chapter Nine of N. Chomsky, *Hopes and Prospects*, Hamish Hamilton, Camberwell, 2010.

anticipated that Guantanamo would be regarded by the courts as outside the applicability of American laws. The Supreme Court, even a conservative Supreme Court, disappointed them on that, and did rule that they have habeas corpus rights and so on – limited rights.³ Well, that was the Bush program: kidnap suspects, send them to the torture chambers, then maybe have military trials, which are no trials at all. Obama has expanded that. He does the same things, but the program has been expanded. Now the program is to assassinate suspects. So there are several places in the world, quite a few by now, in which people like us can be walking around the streets wondering whether a minute from now there's going to be a massive explosion directed by someone halfway across the world. That means a drone attack, which is aimed at killing a suspect and whoever else happens to be the so-called 'collateral damage'. That's the Obama global assassination program, and it continues to be extended bit by bit.⁴

For the first time it has been extended to the purposeful assassination of American citizens. There's been some criticism of this in the case of Anwar al-Awlaki and another American citizen who happened to be collateral damage.⁵ Well that's a little bit of an expansion; there's an elite assumption that American citizens are human beings and have certain rights. Others are what are sometimes called 'unpeople', a term used by the British diplomatic historian Mark Curtis in his discussions of crimes of the British Empire.⁶ There were people and 'unpeople', and the non-citizens were 'unpeople' – so it was okay to assassinate them. In many other ways – I won't get into the details here – Obama has stretched war and the violation of civil liberties beyond what I expected.

In Afghanistan, for example, the US and its allies, like Australia, now have forces well beyond the peak of Soviet forces during their occupation of Afghanistan. Last year was the most violent year in Afghanistan since 2001.⁷ It's not a pretty picture, and in many ways he's going beyond what I expected in pursuing pretty much the same agenda. It's not the whole story; I mean there have been a few steps I think that are positive and better than would have taken place under, say, a McCain administration. He appointed quite a

---

3   *Hamdan v Rumsfeld*, 548 U.S. 557 (2006); *Boumediene v Bush*, 553 U.S. 723 (2008).
4   Peter Bergen and Katherine Tiedemann, *The Year of the Drone: An Analysis of US drone strikes in Pakistan, 2004–2010*, New America Foundation, 24 February 2010.
5   A. Shadid and D. Kirkpatrick, 'As the West Celebrates a Cleric's Death, the Mideast Shrugs', *New York Times*, 1 October 2011.
6   Mark Curtis, *Unpeople: Britain's Secret Human Rights Abuses*, Vintage, 2004.
7   Afghanistan Annual Report 2011, *Protection of Civilians in Armed Conflict*, UN Assistance Mission in Afghanistan – UN Office, HCHR, Kabul, February 2012.

good Secretary of Labour, and some of the labour laws are beginning to be implemented, and there are a few other things. But in general the picture is not pretty and I think the strongest thing he has going for him, and what may in fact win the election, is just that the opposition is apparently off the planet. I don't know if you've been following this, but there's nothing like it in the history of parliamentary democracy that I can think of. Maybe for that reason he'll get re-elected, with maybe parts of his base voting for him. He's actually lost a large part of the base that enthusiastically worked for him – not just voted, but organised and so on – and are terribly disillusioned.

We turn to Israel and Palestine, and of course there are many issues we could take up but let's look at prospects. You said that under Obama the Palestinians will be offered fried chicken, nothing more. What do you mean by that?

That phrase, 'fried chicken' is actually not mine; it comes from the Netanyahu administration. In 1996, Shimon Peres was Prime Minister. He was then replaced by Binyamin Netanyahu in a vote in 1996. In Peres' last press conference, he was asked 'will there ever be a Palestinian state?' He said, 'there will never be a Palestinian state; we'll never permit it'.[8] That wasn't well-reported for an interesting reason; he was actually giving a press conference to a group of American correspondents – *Newsweek* and others, but there were some Israeli correspondents too. You can read about it in the Israeli press. The reason it wasn't in the American press was that in the middle of Peres' press conference, the news came through that a verdict was coming in the OJ Simpson trial. All the American reporters scampered out of the room to get the important news, and Peres could make these comments to a small number of Israeli reporters.

Well, that was the Peres administration. Then Netanyahu came along – this was his first term; he's now in his second term – and his Communications Director was asked whether there could be a Palestinian state. And he answered, Well, our plan is to leave a few fragments of the West Bank in Palestinian hands; we're not interested in them – we don't want to bother with the population – and if they want to call it a state we don't mind. Or they can call it fried chicken.[9] That's their conception of what a state would

---

8   Amnon Barzilai, Haaretz, 24 October 1995. For more detail, Epilogue of N. Chomsky, *World Orders, Old and New*, Pluto Press, London, 1997.
9   David Bar-Illan (Director of Communications and Policy Planning in the Office of the Prime Minister), 'Interview with Vidor Cygielman', *Palestine-Israel Journal* (Summer/Autumn 1996).

be. And that's essentially the conception that Obama has adopted. For thirty-five years the United States has almost unilaterally barred a diplomatic, negotiated settlement of the Israel-Palestine conflict. The settlement could be along lines that are well known, and in fact accepted by virtually the entire world. There's an overwhelming international consensus; the basic form of it is a two state settlement on the internationally recognised border, the pre-June 1967 border. And then there's a phrase from the formal US position in the early 1970s when the US was still part of the world on this: 'with minor and mutual modifications' (to straighten ceasefire lines, and so on).[10]

So that's the international consensus, and there are other provisions for other issues. The United States vetoed the resolution at the Security Council in 1976. I won't run through the record but it stays about the same.[11] Obama's pushed it even further. For example, his last veto, last February, did get some international attention because he was actually vetoing the Security Council resolution that called for the implementation of official US policy, namely barring settlement increases.[12] These are of course illegal, everyone agrees, even Israel.[13] It was pretty extreme so it got some notice. And in general, Obama has taken a position that is in many ways harsher and more extreme than previous American presidents, which is saying something. Now if you think about the current situation, and indeed the role of Australia, there's a standard conventional view: the United States has been a kind of honest broker, desperately trying to bring together two recalcitrant opponents, Israel and the Palestinians (the Palestinians being the guilty ones most of the time). And the conventional view is that the US has been trying to reach a settlement. But that's just totally untrue. If there were meaningful negotiations, they would be organised by some neutral party – pick it as you wish, maybe Brazil, a respected state that's fairly neutral. On one side would be the United States and Israel, and on the other side would be the rest of the world, almost without exception.

Well, the United States and its allies don't want honest negotiations. They want negotiations which meet a variety of crucial preconditions. Again, the conventional view is that the Palestinians are asking for preconditions, and

---

10 Donald Neff, 'The differing interpretations of Resolution 242', *Middle East International*, 13 September 1991.
11 Mark Curtis, 'Obstacles to Security in the Middle East', in Seizaburo Sato and Trevor Taylor, eds, *Prospects for Global Order*, vol. 2, Royal Institute of International Affairs and International Institute for Global Peace, London, 1993.
12 Brad Knickerbocker, 'If Obama opposes Israeli settlement activity, why did US veto UN vote?' *Christian Science Monitor*, 18 February 2011.
13 G. Gorenberg, *The Accidental Empire*, Times Books, New York, 2006.

Israel wants just negotiations, and of course the US is neutral. But if you look at it closely, it's the US and Israel who are imposing strict preconditions, and important ones. One is that it has to be run by the United States – an extremist rejectionist state which has been blocking a settlement for thirty-five years. So that's Precondition One.

The second precondition is that Israel must have the right to continue expanding settlements; that's a precondition. And again I stress that it's not in dispute that the settlements themselves are illegal, and certainly expansion of them is multiply so. Expansion in what's called Jerusalem – a vastly expanded region annexed by Israel – is doubly illegal. It's doubly illegal because it's also in violation of explicit Security Council demands that nothing be done to change the status of Jerusalem. That goes back to 1968. In fact the US, which at that time was part of the world, voted with everyone – it was a unanimous vote. So it's doubly illegal – but that's a precondition. Furthermore, Israel has made it clear, you can read it in today's paper, that the expansion is proceeding in regions which will be annexed to Israel – illegally, of course. That's a further precondition. They're already establishing the borders, officially, which they're going to illegally annex. That's another precondition. And under those preconditions, everyone who has a brain cell functioning can see that nothing will happen. Negotiations of this kind can go on indefinitely while Israel, with US diplomatic, military, economic support, simply takes over. They don't want parts of the West Bank; let the population sort of rot in these fragments. It'll be a kind of fried chicken – if you want to call it a state, okay.

Also, the US and Israel insist that the West Bank be separated from Gaza; that's been US and Israeli policy since the early 1990s, in explicit violation of the Oslo agreements, which insist that Gaza and the West Bank are a single territorial entity. But Israel and the United States have been trying hard to separate them since the early 1990s – an interesting story, we don't have time to go into it here, but you should know about it. The reasons are pretty obvious: if any fragments of Palestinians are left in the West Bank, they'll be completely imprisoned, with no access to the outside world. They'll be imprisoned between the regions annexed to Israel in the West Bank, Israel and the Jordanian dictatorship. Gaza would be the only access to the outside, so of course it has to be separated. Those are the preconditions. You can ask whether the Palestinian Authority made a wise or an unwise tactical move in trying to approach the United Nations to get around this, but it's perfectly understandable that they would seek some way to get around farcical negotiations of this kind, if there are obvious consequences.

You mentioned growth, and that's another term that has a terrific ring to it. I mean what could be bad about growth. We don't challenge the notion that growth is good. But are we breeding and consuming our way to extinction? And what's it going to take for us to recalibrate our expectations in a finite world?[14]

First of all, we should be careful to think about consumerism and the consumption culture. To a large extent, that's artificially created. And it's not my opinion: go back a century to the origins of the public relations industry, including the advertising industry. It's an interesting history. Back around a century ago, in the freest countries in the world, England and the United States, there was a recognition – a conscious, articulated recognition by elite sectors – that enough freedom has been won by popular struggles, and people can't be controlled by force anymore. So there have to be other ways to control them.[15] And one way is control of attitudes and opinions. That's when you get the call for the manufacture of consent on the part of progressive intellectuals.[16] We have to have manufacture of consent, but we also have to have creation of wants; people's 'lack of purpose in life' will have 'an effect on consumption similar to that of having a narrow life interest, that is, in concentrating human attention on the more superficial things that comprise much of *fashionable* consumption'.[17] We can control people if we can fabricate consumers with created wants. That was the term used by the great political economist Thorstein Veblen who understood this and wrote about it. If we can fabricate wants, create wants, we can trap people.[18] They can trap people into consumerism, debt and so on. And the way it was done was very interesting; if there was time I could go into it.

---

14 Kostakidis' preceding question about the Occupy movements has been excised and moved to a composite Q&A on pp. 146–152.
15 Alex Carey, *Taking the Risk Out of Democracy: Corporate Propaganda versus Freedom and Liberty*, University of Illinois Press, Urbana, 1997.
16 'The public must be put in its place, so that each of us may live free of the trampling and roar of a bewildered herd', Walter Lippmann, cited in C. Rossiter and J. Lare, eds, *The Essential Lippmann*, Random House, New York, 1963, pp. 91–2; 'That the manufacture of consent is capable of great refinements no one, I think, denies ... the opportunities for manipulation open to anyone who understands the process are plain enough. The creation of consent is not a new art. It is a very old one which was supposed to have died out with the appearance of democracy. But it has not died out. It has, in fact, improved enormously in technic, because it is now based on analysis rather than on rule of thumb.' W. Lippmann, *Public Opinion*, Macmillan, New York, 1922.
17 Paul Nystrom, *Economics of Fashion*, Ronald Press, New York, 1928. Emphasis in the original.
18 Thorstein Veblen, *The Theory of the Leisure Class: an economic study of institutions*, MacMillan, London, 1899.

To a large extent we live in a culture, a society, in which enormous resources are devoted to fabricating wants. I presume it's the same here as in the United States. Take a look at television directed to infants, two year olds: it's already trying to create a culture of demand for goods. In fact there's now an academic discipline, part of applied psychology, which is concerned with nagging – literally.[19] The reason is that the advertisers recognised a couple of decades ago that there's a big part of the population that doesn't have any money, so they can't buy; so we've got to do something to make them buy. And the way they can buy is by nagging their parents. So it's, say, 'I've got to have that video cam'. Advertising is aimed at children; it devises various types of nagging that could be used for different kinds of purchases. Well, the idea is to trap infants, children, into a culture of fabricated wants, so they can then be trapped into consumer culture, and then they can be effectively controlled, along with the manufacturing of opinions.

It's all very conscious. Incidentally, there are some quite good studies on this. If you're interested there's one very good book by a Canadian law professor, Joel Bakan. It's just come out. It's called *Childhood Under Siege*.[20] It's a very concerted effort. But quite apart from that, suppose we are to some extent trapped in it; how do we react to the fact that, as you say, it's a finite world with finite resources, and we're going to hit limits? Well, there are two ways: one is the way of the lemmings. We just march happily toward a cliff and when it turns out that there's a cliff, we go over it and we're finished – that's one way to react. That's what the business world is driving us to do, for the purposes of short term profit.

But they're going to fall off too

They'll fall off too, but you don't think about that, literally. So for example, in the United States, quite openly the Chamber of Commerce (the main business lobby), the American Petroleum Institute and others are very openly organising propaganda efforts to convince people that global warming is a liberal myth. And it's affected popular opinion; you can see the polls reacting as the campaign continues.[21] Now, the people who are

---

19 Holly K. M. Henry & Dina L. G. Borzekowski, 'The Nag Factor: A mixed-methodology study in the US of young children's requests for advertised products', *Journal of Children and Media*, vol. 5, no. 3, 2011, pp. 298–317.
20 Joel Bakan, *Childhood Under Siege: How Big Business Targets Children*, Penguin, 2011.
21 Sharon Beder, *Global Spin: The Corporate Assault On Environmentalism*, Chelsea Green, White River Junction, 1998.

running this campaign as individuals, probably share your attitudes. Maybe they're members of the Sierra Club and they contribute to environmental programs; but in the capacity of a CEO of a corporation, you have a duty that you must perform. If you don't perform it, you're out and someone else is in. This is an institutional property; much harder to deal with. The property is that you have to maximise short term profit and market share. In fact that's a legal requirement in Anglo-American law. If you don't do that, you're displaced and somebody else comes in. So there's an institutional imperative to destroy the planet, to march off the cliff. That's a serious problem. It traces back to well known inefficiencies of market systems which you probably learn about in your first economics class – they ignore externalities, technically. That's a built-in institutional property, and it does lead to the leaders of the lemmings knowing that they're going to fall off the cliff too. But we don't have to be lemmings; we can deal with these problems sensibly. Consuming more of the world's resources is the advertising industry's image of happiness but it doesn't have to be ours. And I think any sensible person knows that it isn't.

... all sensible people know anarchism is ridiculous and irresponsible. Common sense, right?

It depends what you mean by anarchism. If you mean by anarchism the media image, which goes back to the late nineteenth century, of people running wild, breaking windows and so on – okay, that conception of anarchism, I would agree with. But there is another conception, which is the actual conception, which is the core of traditional anarchist thought and activism. It goes back to the Enlightenment, in fact. It literally comes pretty much out of the origins of classical liberalism. One great anarchist and thinker, Rudolf Rocker, an anarcho-syndicalist, argued with some plausibility that, as he put it, 'Democracy with its motto of equality of all citizens before the law, and Liberalism with its right of man over his own person, both were wrecked on the realities of capitalist economy.'[22] Classical liberalism was blocked by capitalism; it couldn't survive capitalism. Rocker argues that this particular strain of anarchism – anarcho-syndicalism – was the natural outgrowth of classical liberalism in an age where you have to overcome the barriers introduced by the rise of capitalism, later corporate capitalism.

---

22 Rudolf Rocker, *Anarchism and Anarcho-syndicalism*, Pluto Press, London, 1989.

And I think there's some sense in that: that the core of the anarchist tradition, which again has Enlightenment roots, is to raise questions about authority, hierarchy and domination, and to point out that they are not self-justifying. Whatever structure they are. You know, master-slave, patriarchal husband-obedient wife, imperial power dominating the world, whatever the structure of authority is, it is not self-justifying and it should be challenged. And if it cannot justify itself, it should be dismantled. That's a core principle of anarchism. In that sense, I think everyone should be an anarchist. And if you look at the [interrupted by applause].

Notice, I say 'if it cannot be justified'. I think there are cases where justification can be given. So, just take a personal example: I once, only once, thankfully, slapped my little daughter on her hand. She didn't like it. You can ask her now what she thinks about it. She's grown up now – she slaps my hand. But the occasion was, when she was about two years old and we had an electric stove – as you know the grills or whatever they're called stay hot after they turn black – and she was reaching to put her hand on the stove. So I grabbed her hand, and slapped it – one and only time. I think you can give a justification for that, but it takes efforts to justify. It was an act of authority, of course; you have to work pretty hard to justify structures of authority and domination. Usually they're not self-justifying. As moral consciousness expands, which I think it does over time, there have been repeated challenges to these structures – in our own lifetimes, in fact. I think they are moves in the right direction, and that's the basic anarchist conception. It leads on to a conception of social order in which voluntary, free association, creative work under one's own control, and so on, assume major proportions and revise the nature of the society. Actually, these questions are coming up in the Occupy movements for long-range commitments, and I think that's good, that's the way social, moral evolution should go.

[Kostakidis asks a question about media regulation and balance.]

Money is of course doing the talking: that's inherent in what I was just talking about. For example, fabrication of the consumer culture. That's manufacturing consent, that's money talking. As for balance in public media – I can't comment on Australia, but I'll talk about the United States – there's a kind of balance in the public media. They're different than say Fox News. But the balance is a very specific kind which is actually taught in journalism schools. So if you go to one of the better journalism schools in the United States, you're taught the concept of objectivity. How can you be an objective reporter? You're an objective reporter and an honest reporter if you report accurately what's going on 'inside the beltway', meaning inside Washington circles. If you report that accurately – if you say the Democrats say this, the Republicans say that and so on – that's balance. But that balance excludes the opinions, often the overwhelming opinions, of a large majority of the public.

I gave an example, and it's not the only one by any means: the enormous gap between public opinion and public policy. The balance in the public media is to present the views of elite sectors accurately. You know, the Democrats say this and the Republicans say that. If you pointed out that a large majority of the population is against it all, that would be subjective bias. I think there are questions to raise about the notion of balance. But to return to your actual question, it's certainly true that money is going to talk. Personally I'd be against efforts to regulate that – because where would the regulation be coming from? It would be coming from state power. I think we should be very cautious about assigning the state the power to determine what's said and what isn't said. I think we have to go after the core problem, which is the fact that money is talking; the fact that there's such a disparity of wealth and power that a democratic system simply can't function properly. And that shows up at every point. For example the United States in the last thirty years has become rather extreme in this respect, but it's an extreme version of something that exists generally. So, for example, for the last thirty years in the United States, you know the Reagan-Thatcher neoliberal period, elections increasingly are simply bought. Literally. You can predict the outcome of an election quite well by just looking at the amount of campaign spending. And you can predict the policies that are pursued by asking about where that campaign spending comes from. So, it should surprise no one that Obama, despite his nice talk, is essentially pursuing the policies of a small financial elite. That's where his funding came from, and that's where it's going to come from in the next election.

Actually this goes back very far – there are good studies of it by fine political economists[23] – but it's been very sharply exaggerated by neoliberal structures, not just in the United States, but everywhere. And now it's reached a point where, even in Congress, the old traditions of parliamentary functioning have been pretty much dissolved. It used to be the case that someone in Congress would get a position of influence, say Chair of a Committee, on the basis of seniority and performance. Well, I have questions about that, but at least that was the idea. That's been pretty much thrown to the winds;

---

23 Thomas Ferguson, *Golden Rule: The Investment Theory of Party Competition and the Logic of Money-Driven Political Systems*, University of Chicago Press, Chicago, 1995.

if you want a committee chair at this point you have to buy it from the party. You have to put money in the party coffers, and maybe you'll get the chair. And that simply drives members of Congress into the pockets of the corporate sector, meaning mostly the financial sector. It further erodes democracy, and what you described in the media is part of that.[24]

I do write about the media, but personally I don't think it's very different from the general intellectual community. Take a look at the elite media, what's sometimes called the 'agenda setting media' – the ones that provide the framework that smaller newspapers adhere to – the *New York Times*, *CBS News* and so on. I don't think there's much difference between their conceptions and boundaries, and those you find in, say, the academic world. They share the same general intellectual culture. It's easier to study the media than to study scholarship – it's just easier to carry out careful analyses. I've written a lot about it, if you're interested, but I don't think it's very different. It all reflects to a substantial extent the actual distribution of power in society. That's an observation that's considered radical, but it's as old as Adam Smith.[25] Adam Smith was not the caricature that you read about in elementary school; he recognised that in the England of his day, people who basically owned the society (the 'merchants and manufacturers') are 'the principal architects' of government policy. They design policy so that their own interests are very well served, however grievous the impact on others, including the people of England. Well, *The Wealth of Nations* in 1776 is basically correct now – it's not merchants and manufacturers; instead it's multinational corporations, investment firms and so on. But the same principle holds, and it holds in an increasingly exaggerated form under the impact of neoliberal ideology – an almost grotesque form. Well, these are real problems, deep social problems, and I think we have to go after those rather than calling on state efforts to regulate speech and publication.

Why was the study of language important to you and what has it revealed about how the mind works?

Well, traditionally, the capacity for language has been understood to be almost a defining property of the human species. That's how it was regarded in Cartesian philosophy in the seventeenth century (the dominant philosophy

---

24 Thomas Ferguson, 'Best Buy targets are stopping a debt deal', *Financial Times*, 26 July 2011.
25 Patricia Werhane, *Adam Smith and His Legacy for Modern Capitalism*, Oxford University Press, Oxford, 1991.

out of which the Enlightenment grew).[26] For Descartes, it literally *was* the defining property. Remember for Descartes it was critical to distinguish creatures with souls or minds from those who didn't have them. The ones who didn't have souls and minds were machines – that mechanical philosophy was the basis for early modern science. They were machines. Those with souls and minds were human. Well, how would you determine whether some creature has a mind? The proposals that come from Descartes and his followers were: by testing their language abilities. You ask, do they have this fundamental and creative capacity that humans have, and that they exhibit in their normal use of language? What's the creative capacity? I think they captured the essence of it pretty accurately. It's the ability which all humans share, and according to them no animal or machine shares – to create and produce freely new expressions which are appropriate to situations, but not caused by situations. They're not the result of stimuli coming from the outside – or, for that matter, even internal stimuli. There's a big difference between being caused and being appropriate. A crucial difference. A hard one to capture but we recognise it.

So this innovative behaviour has no limits; it can go on indefinitely. In fact most linguistic performance is new sentences, maybe never produced in the history of the world, or your own experience at least. And they're also intelligible to others, who recognise that I could have expressed that thought in that way, if it had come to mind. Well, that creative aspect of language use was regarded, and I think plausibly, as a kind of core component of human cognition, human morality, moral judgment, and in fact human activity. This was connected, especially in the early days of classical liberalism – people like Smith and Humboldt and others – with the belief that humans basically have a fundamental need to carry out creative work under their own control. It was put very nicely by Wilhelm von Humboldt, the founder of the modern university system, also a great linguist, and one of the founders of classical liberalism. The way he put it is that if an artisan creates a beautiful piece of work on command, we may admire what he did but we despise what he is, namely a tool in the hands of others. On the other hand, if that artisan produces the same beautiful work under his own control and initiative, we admire not only the piece of work, but also the artisan himself.[27]

---

26 Noam Chomsky, *Cartesian Linguistics: A Chapter in the History of Rationalist Thought*, 3rd ed., Cambridge University Press, Cambridge, 2009.
27 If a man acts in a purely mechanical way, reacting to external demands or instruction rather than in ways determined by his own interests and energies and power, 'we may admire what he does, but we despise what he is'. Marianne Cowan, ed., *Humanist Without Portfolio: An Anthology*, Wayne State University Press, Detroit, 1963.

Actually, Adam Smith said the same thing. Everyone has read the first paragraph of *Wealth of Nations*, where he talks about 'the butcher does this and the baker does that, and everybody's happy'. That comes out in favour of the division of labour. Very few people have gone on a couple of hundred pages, into this rather dense book, when Smith returns to the notion of division of labour, and says that the division of labour cannot be tolerated because it will turn people into creatures as stupid and ignorant as a human being can possibly be.[28] They're just routinely, under command, performing the same actions over and over. He says that in any civilised society the government's going to have to step in to do something about it – education and other things. If you take a look at the scholarly edition of *Wealth of Nations*, the University of Chicago Bicentennial scholarly edition, take a look under the division of labour, and you'll notice this passage isn't even listed in the index: the most important passage about the division of labour. I'm sure it was not intended deceit; I think they just couldn't understand it. It's an unintelligible view in modern conceptions – they read the words but they don't get beyond the eyes. But that conception is really fundamental to classical liberalism. I think it's correct. They related it loosely to the creative aspect of language use. Well, we're very far from having answers to any of these questions, I should say. But there are steps towards it, and the major steps do happen to be in the study of language. There are thoughts about it elsewhere, but that's what the main work is.

Some surprising things have come out, I think. It's sort of useful to compare what's been done in the last roughly sixty years to the very early days of modern science. One of the great breakthroughs in modern science, say in the Galilean period, was to be willing to be puzzled about things that seemed obvious – that's a tremendous step forward. So, for example, for literally thousands of

---

28 Adam Smith, *The Wealth of Nations*, Chicago: University of Chicago Press, 1976 (original 1776): 'The man whose whole life is spent in performing a few simple operations, of which the effects too are, perhaps, always the same, or very nearly the same, has no occasion to exert his understanding, or to exercise his invention in finding out expedients for removing difficulties which never occur. He naturally loses, therefore, the habit of such exertion, and generally becomes as stupid and ignorant as it is possible for a human creature to become. The torpor of his mind renders him, not only incapable of relishing or bearing a part in any rational conversation, but of conceiving any generous, noble, or tender sentiment, and consequently of forming any just judgment concerning many even of the ordinary duties of private life ... His dexterity at his own particular trade seems, in this manner, to be acquired at the expense of his intellectual, social, and martial values. But in every improved and civilized society this is the state into which the labouring poor, that is, the great body of the people, must necessarily fall, unless government takes some pains to prevent it.' (Book V, ch. I).

years it had been accepted by important scientists that we have answers to some very simple questions; like, when I hold this thing up, if I let it go the cup's going to drop. If there happened to be boiling water inside, and I lift the lid, the steam will go up; so the cup drops and the steam rises. Well, Aristotle had an answer to why – they're seeking their natural place. And that was taken to be the appropriate answer for thousands of years. Then Galileo and others said, let's be puzzled about this. Let's just not take it for granted, because it comes from authority. And when you start being puzzled about it, modern science begins – you see you don't know the answers. When you try to find out the answers they break down; you see that all sorts of intuitions are just wildly off. And finally, out of this, comes modern science.

And I think that's what's been happening in the study of language, since roughly the early 1950s approximately. A lot of things that seemed completely obvious were looked at carefully, and they all turned out to be extremely puzzling. So, take a simple example, which kind of evolved in an industry of analysis. Take the sentence, 'can eagles that fly swim?' We all understand it. We know that the word 'can' is associated with 'swim', not 'fly'. We're asking if they can swim, not if they can fly. Similarly, you can say things, like 'are eagles that fly swimming?' but we can't say 'are eagles that flying swim'. Actually, if you think about it, that's a fine thought – it says, Are the eagles that are flying, swimming too. You just can't say it that way. That thought can't be expressed in that form. Well, if you think about it, it was taken for granted forever that that was just intuitively obvious. But if you think about it, it's not at all obvious.

Aristotle defined language as 'sound with meaning'. Well, the pursuit of this enquiry tends to show that that's not correct; that actually language is 'meaning with sound'. And it need not be sound; it can be sign or some other mode of externalisation. That's a big difference. It means that the core character of language is the set of principles that yield structured expressions and assign them a meaning. And that part of language is probably – you can't show it yet, but it looks like it's uniform among humans. It doesn't seem to vary, much; and if we knew enough, maybe doesn't vary at all. It's just a core property of humans – that we have this set of principles that yields an unbounded array of structured expressions that have a semantic interpretation – that means something – and when you look into it, it's pretty strange what it means.[29] And that just seems to be shared among humans

---

29 Noam Chomsky, 'Language and Nature', *Mind*, vol. 104, no. 413, January 1995, 1–61; Peter Ludlow, 'Referential Semantics for I-Languages?', and Noam Chomsky, 'Replies',

altogether. There's no known difference between remote tribes in Papua that haven't had other human contact for tens of thousands of years and children who grow up here. If you interchange them at infancy they'll grow into their own society without any problem.

So that seems to be a core property of human nature. The externalisation – the sound part – is marginal, and it also follows from that that communication is marginal. It's kind of a dogma among even scientists who write about these topics, that language is basically a means of communication, and evolved as a means of communication. You look at current publications on the evolution of language, that's just taken for granted. It apparently is all false. It turns out from a closer analysis of language that it's actually a tool for thought. It's a means of expressing thought – and on the side you can use it for communication, as you can use anything else for communication. Actually if we just introspect for a minute, that shouldn't be surprising. Just ask yourself, what is most of your own use of language? Well if you introspect it turns out that probably ninety-nine per cent of it is talking to yourself. Talking to yourself is not communicating. It takes a tremendous act of will not to talk to yourself – try it, it's very hard. You're walking down the street, you're talking to yourself in fragments of sentences. That goes on all night, unfortunately, and sometimes it's used for communication but even the external part is not much. Well, that's a radically different conception of fundamental human nature. And it does lead in other directions, like at least exploring these thoughts about creative work, about moral judgment and so on. I don't want to exaggerate, this is by no means universally accepted, even among scientists, but I think that's the direction in which we're moving. And I think it is a way of finding out basic things about what kind of creatures we are.

Can you comment briefly about the role of elite academic institutions. Can they contribute to social change or are they a barrier to change?

Well, my own institution is a good example. It is, I think it's fair to say, the greatest engineering, science-based university in the world, and it was in the 1950s when I got there. In the 1950s, first of all, it was almost entirely Pentagon-funded. But contrary to what a lot of people believe, that was the freest period; the Pentagon didn't care what you were doing. During the 1960s, the laboratory in which I worked, was 100 per cent funded by the

---

in *Chomsky and his Critics*, Louise M. Antony and Norbert Hornstein, eds, Wiley-Blackwell, 2003.

three armed services. It was also the centre of anti-war resistance, I don't mean protest, I mean resistance. That meant support for deserters, and tax resistance – technically criminal activities. I was coming up for a long jail sentence, other colleagues were involved in this too. It was the main academic centre in the country on this. And it was all coming out of the same laboratory that was 100 per cent funded by the three armed services. And that has to do with a fact about the advanced economies, which is pretty well understood by participants – you know, engineers – but it doesn't seem to be well understood by economists or the general public. And that is, that the modern economy depends very heavily on massive state intervention. If you use a computer or the internet, satellites, micro-electronics, the IT revolution and so on, you're feeding off of public funding and public initiative – and the Pentagon understood that.[30] It was the funnel for raiding the taxpayer under false pretences – you know, the Russians are coming – so it wasn't democratic at all.

But it was essentially telling the public, you pay us and we're going to create the technology of the future. They didn't say that, but that's what was happening. So they didn't really care what you were doing. You want to throw over the government, that's your business. Just do your work. But, although that was a fact, it was a very small part of the institute. Most of the institute was extremely conventional, and people did their work, they didn't ask questions. You just developed science and technology; there's that Tom Lehrer song about Wernher von Braun, which you might know: 'Once the rockets are up, who cares where they come down? That's not my department, says Wernher von Braun.' That was essentially the conception.

Well, there was a small group of students, a very small community, maybe a dozen or so in the 1960s, who began to be caught up in the general student activism of the 1960s, and worked quite hard to try to change the atmosphere. I won't go through the details, but they succeeded; succeeded to the point that by about the end of 1969, they'd gotten to the point where actually the administration called a day off, just to focus on seminars, discussions, talks and so on, about the uses of technology. Should we be concerned with how science and technology are used? And a lot of self-criticism came out of that.

---

30 Vernon Ruttan, *Is War Necessary for Economic Growth?* Oxford University Press, New York, 2006; David F. Noble, *Forces of Production: A Social History of Industrial Automation*, Knopf, New York, 1984; Kenneth Flamm, *Targeting the Computer: Government Support and International Competition*, Brookings Institution, Washington, 1987; Winfried Ruigrok and Rob van Tulder, *The Logic of International Restructuring*, Routledge, New York 1995.

Quite important groups formed – the Union of Concerned Scientists, and so on.[31] They just changed the atmosphere of the place. And by now those are common attitudes. What was once, You just do your work and shut up, has become, We have to think about what we're doing and why. And that extends into other forms of social activism too, in all sorts of ways. I mean one very dramatic change at MIT – you can just see it walking down the halls – when I got there in the 1950s, it was all white, male, well dressed conventional, do your work. You walk down the halls today, it's like universities elsewhere: half women, a third minorities, informal dress – which is not insignificant; that means informal relationships. And a lot of activism.

Those are quite big changes. They came about largely through the activism of a small group of students, a couple of faculty, but mostly students, who simply organised the place through their own activities. A lot of interesting actions took place, which changed things. So what is a university? It depends on the people in it. These are very free institutions. There are a lot of things wrong with them – I don't want to exaggerate – but among the institutions in a society, these are perhaps the most free. And that's particularly true in the sciences. In the sciences, you can't institute external controls and expect them to survive. You see that in the old Soviet Union: biology couldn't survive under external controls.[32] The sciences are basically anarchist in the sense that I was describing before. The students are expected in a good scientific university to not just repeat what they're told; they're expected to challenge it. In fact a lot of the new ideas and innovation comes from that, so students are expected to say, you know, I don't believe what you're saying, here's an argument to the contrary. That's good, that's what you try to encourage. And if you didn't try to encourage that, the sciences would die.

So there's a kind of built-in dynamic that kind of frees them up. It doesn't mean that they're going to go to the point of raising questions about the use of technology and science. They didn't, and in fact there are classic, crazed examples of this which people should think about.

So take say creating the atom bomb. There were two main institutions in the United States – Chicago and Los Alamos. In Chicago they were basically constructing the materials; in Los Alamos they were turning it into a weapon. Now you go to places like Chicago and Los Alamos, they had some of the most outstanding intellectuals in the world. These were,

---

31 Union of Concerned Scientists, *Founding Document: 1968 MIT Faculty Statement*. http://www.ucsusa.org/about/founding-document-1968.html.
32 Richard Levins and Richard Lewontin, *The Dialectical Biologist*, Harvard University Press, Cambridge, 1985.

many of them, European émigrés – Einstein types. Very impressive people – cultured, literate, many of them what we would call pretty radical, interested in music, the arts, thinking about things. They were working in closed environments in which about the only thing that they pursued was how to carry out huge, massive destruction in Japan – they were pretty sure they were never going to use it in Germany – which might end the human race. Because they weren't really sure. And it was a single-minded pursuit of that objective. Now if you look closely the first protests, questioning, came out of Chicago, not Los Alamos. And the reason was, that the Chicago phase of the operation was completed earlier. They were providing the materials, and of course that was prior to turning it into a weapon. And it wasn't until their phase of the scientific activities was over, that some of them began to raise questions about what in the heck are we doing.

There were things like the Pugwash Movement and so on that grew out of that. But in Los Alamos it didn't happen until after the bomb went off, literally. And when they began reflecting about it later, there was a lot of justified self-criticism. I mean, here you had the most amazing group of intellectuals you can imagine – lots of broad interests – and they were single-mindedly pursuing highly dangerous, maybe potentially lethal activities, not just for the victims, but even beyond, without thinking about it. Well that can happen too, and the question about what a university can be or what academic life or a free intellectual life can be, these questions always arise. You can get caught up in what's called 'the sweetness of the problem'.[33] It's a sweet problem, you really want to solve it. You can easily get caught up in that, or you can ask what am I doing? What's the purpose of it? What's the right way to distribute your energies in the world and in life? There's a lot to say about that, so I don't think there's a simple answer to your question.

---

33 American Institute of Physics, *Interview with Joel Bengston by Finn Aaserud*, Center for History of Physics, Niels Bohr Library and Archives, 1 July 1986.

Interview with Richard Glover

This interview with Richard Glover was broadcast on ABC Radio's *Drive* program on 2 November 2011 and is reproduced here courtesy of the ABC.

People use various terms to describe your politics. Can we be really simple about it and have you describe the society you'd like to see. What would you like America and Australia to look like in a perfect world?

Well, I'm not ambitious enough to talk about perfect worlds, but let's talk about a better world. A better world would be one in which informed popular opinion – based on interaction, discussion, free access to information and so on – influences policy, decisively in fact. It would be a society in which you eliminate, to the extent possible, illegitimate structures of authority. By 'illegitimate' I mean the kind that can't justify themselves: they're just there for power reasons, or historical reasons and so on. That can be true at every level, from family to international affairs, and we can spell out many examples of them. I would also want to see a society where the institutions of the society make it possible to deal seriously with problems of extreme importance to the survival of the species. Take, say, the United States and Australia: Australia has a pretty well functioning economy. A lot of it is based on mining, which happens to have consequences that are very harmful to the decent survival of our grandchildren.

In the United States, if you take a look at this morning's *Financial Times* – the main business daily in the world – you'll see that there's euphoria about new fossil fuel discoveries in North America.[1] They'll give the United States energy independence for a hundred years; it can be a hegemonic power, and so on and so forth. The real headline ought to read 'Discoveries in North America, unless controlled, will undermine the possibilities for decent existence for our grandchildren'.

You're talking about coal-seam power, are you?

---

1   Ed Crooks, 'The Pendulum swings', *Financial Times*, 1 November 2011, p. 6.

I'm talking about the gas and oil discoveries through fracking; you know, fancy techniques of extraction. Yeah, you can get more fossil fuels that way; you can also get more greenhouse gases. You can undermine the development of the kind of sustainable economy that's going to be necessary if we're going to survive. Well, all of this is understandable within the kind of state capitalist structures that we have. In these systems the goals are to try to attain short term gain, whatever the consequences for other people, including our own descendants. But that's pathological, and I'd like to see a society where the institutions are not pathological.

Can we talk about 'illegitimate sources of power'. Your phrase. Do you see that as companies or governments or courts? What's included in that for you?

Anything that is not selected by the population and responsive to them. You can duplicate this anywhere but take, say, the United States; in Washington there is a policy spectrum that's focused narrowly on dealing with the deficit. What does the population want? The population regards the deficit as a minor problem.[2] They want policy focused on joblessness, and they're right. Joblessness is a very serious problem. The deficit is a minor problem. But both political parties are so deep in the pockets of financial corporations that they do what they want.

I mean, maybe you'll accuse me of conventional economic thinking here, but once the deficit gets to a certain level, you know past eighty per cent, 100 per cent of GDP, the interest payments then become self-perpetuating and the economy collapses under the weight of them, creating more joblessness, rather than less.

It's possible that a deficit might be a problem, but we're talking about today. Today the deficit is a minor problem. It can be dealt with in the longer term by stimulating economic growth; that's what the population wants and I think that's the right decision. There are plenty of Nobel laureates in economics who think the same thing.[3] But the point is this isn't even discussable in Washington. Financial institutions say the deficit is a problem, so we have a Deficit Commission – not a Joblessness Commission. Now, take a look at the deficit: suppose we say, okay that's a problem, let's deal with it. Well,

---

2   Ruy Teixeira, Public Opinion Snapshot: The Public's Priorities: Jobs vs. the Deficit. http://www.americanprogress.org/issues/2010/01/snapshot010410.html.
3   Paul Krugman, 'Nobody Understands Debt', *New York Times*, 1 January 2012.

again, take a look at the polls. The public says overwhelmingly that the way to deal with the deficit is by rescinding the radical tax cuts for the super rich; rescind those and let's go back to the days when we had high economic growth, but also protected the benefits system. The policies that are coming out are the opposite. There actually is a very straightforward answer to the US deficit problem, but it's not discussable.

Which is the military?

That's part of it. It's one of the two answers. One answer is the huge military budget, which is roughly the same as the rest of the world combined – and it's not for security. But there's an even simpler answer: the US health system is an absolute international scandal. If the United States had the same kind of health system as, say, Australia or France or Canada and other industrialised societies, there wouldn't be any deficit. But the privatised – virtually unregulated – system has about twice the per capita costs of other countries. It doesn't have very good outcomes. It leaves tens of millions uninsured altogether. It's very expensive, and …

I think a lot of Australians will agree with you about that, but can we talk about capitalism generally and whether it's provided – I think a lot of people would say that despite all of its problems, and it needs to be ameliorated constantly in order to rip out its unfairness – it still is a very efficient model for increasing the size of the pie; for providing wealth and good living standards for people.

First of all, it's so far from true; there's no society that functions by the principles of capitalism. I mean, take the stuff that's on the table here. The computer you're using, the internet and so on: where'd that come from? That's mostly developed in the United States, and it developed substantially in the state sector of the economy. For decades, in fact, right at the place where I work: MIT. It was funded by the Pentagon for decades, and that's true of high technology generally.[4] Furthermore, it goes way back: any successful, developed society has had a very substantial state component that carries

---

4 N. Chomsky, *Rogue States: The Rule of Force in World Affairs*, Pluto Press, London, 2000, pp. 192–8; Kenneth Flamm, *Targeting the Computer: Government Support and International Competition*, Brookings Institution, Washington, 1987; David F. Noble, *Forces of Production: A Social History of Industrial Automation*, Knopf, New York, 1984; Winfried Ruigrok and Rob Van Tulder, *The Logic of International Restructuring*, Routledge, New York, 1995.

out research initiatives, and does the costly parts of development.[5] That goes back to the beginnings of British industrialisation.[6]

But I mean few people are defending a pure capitalism that doesn't have state R&D, and doesn't have welfare components to it; I guess my question is whether a properly ameliorated capitalism can't be a rather good thing for ordinary people in the West?

It depends how it's ameliorated, and how good it can become. So let's take something concrete. Two years ago President Obama essentially bought the US auto industry; it was publicly owned. He had a couple of options. One option was to reconstruct it: give it back to its former owners and managers or others rather like them, and have it pursue its traditional path. Another option was to hand it over to the workforce: subsidise, produce and develop things that the country badly needs, like say high-speed rail and so on. Well that would be a worker-owned, and in fact worker- and community-managed form of enterprise based on production for human needs. Is that capitalism? Well, it depends how you want to define the term. But I think it would be a much better system. Bits and pieces of it are in fact developing, and it would be a cooperative, democratic system which extends freedom, democracy and choice into the economic institutions. I think that could be an even better system. Now, you can't just say, 'that's what I think it ought to be;' you have to try, and you have to experiment. You have to see what works and what doesn't work.

There are indications that this would work very well. It would be much more free and democratic, and would also be free of some of the pathological aspects – and I stress 'pathological' – of systems in which decisions have to be made to maximise short term profit, whatever the consequences for others. Take a careful look at market systems and you see that's basically what they are. In fact that's called a 'market inefficiency' which people study in undergraduate economics. Well that market inefficiency may destroy the species. It means you don't pay attention to the consequences for your grandchildren when making choices to maximise profit today. That shouldn't be tolerated.

---

5   W. Lazonick, *Business Organization and the Myth of the Market Economy*, Cambridge University Press, Cambridge, 1991; Ha-Joon Chang, *Kicking Away The Ladder, Development Strategy in Historical Perspective*, Anthem Press, London, 2005.
6   F. Clairmonte, *Economic Liberalism and Underdevelopment: Studies in the Disintegration of an Idea*, Asia Publishing House, New York, 1960; A. Gerschenkron, *Economic Backwardness in Historical Perspective*, Harvard University Press, Cambridge, 1962.

Can we talk about peace? Because you I know grew up in a neighbourhood in Philadelphia where there was a great mix of Jews on one side and Catholics on the other, and they often didn't get on. Some people say the great enemy of peace is this innate tribalism of people.

Well, actually where I lived, the balance was simpler than that: there was one Jewish family, and they were my parents. And the Irish Catholic kids down the street, whom we were terrified of. But you know every city that I know of anywhere has conflicts, ethnic problems, other kinds of class problems and so on. And they don't have to be like it was when I grew up. When I grew up it was severe enough so that there was actually a curfew on teenagers, a 7 o'clock curfew, just because there was too much violence.

On both sides, on all sides?

Well, it wasn't all sides but it was enough. And that can be overcome, and has been overcome. And in fact, sometimes dramatically overcome. So, take say Northern Ireland: it's a very interesting case. It tells us a lot about how to deal with terror, violence and conflict. IRA terror was pretty serious. It was no joke and it was getting worse. The British for years responded to it by more violence and more repression. And that just created a kind of a cycle of escalating violence and tension. I was in Belfast in 1993, and it was a war zone. You couldn't park in places without police inspection. People were afraid to go from, you know, the suburbs into west Belfast. Well, finally the British with US initiative – Clinton had a good role here – moved at last towards dealing with and paying attention to the sources of the violence. It turned out that the sources of the violence, as is usually the case, were based on authentic grievances.

Job security among the Catholics was very low, and wage rates were much lower than the Protestants.

A lot of things: the repression, and so on. When they began to pay attention to the grievances – which they should have done independently of violence, but when they began to do that – the violence subsided. When I was there in 1993, I met people in hiding who were IRA hit men on the run from the government. A couple of years later they were on the negotiating committees. Now one of them is in the government. The violence was reduced. I was in Belfast about a year ago, and there are tensions but it's like any city. Well, that's the way to deal with problems of, in this case, pretty serious terror, but also other kinds of violence and conflict. Figure out where they're coming from. There's usually a reason, and the reason ought to be dealt with independently of the violence. If you can deal with it, that cuts down violence, it leads to interaction and to the forming of friendly relations. The areas where I grew up are not like what they were when I was a kid.

Can we stay with the areas in which you grew up; paint me a picture of this family life because your father and mother were both quite political. So I think was your uncle who ran the local newsstand. (That was New York) Paint me a picture of that scene when you were growing up, and how you became politicised.

My uncle was in New York. Well, first of all, my parents were first generation immigrants, and they lived in not a physical ghetto, but a kind of a cultural ghetto. All their friends and associates, their work, the synagogue and the schools were all part of an immigrant society of a particular kind: one that was trying to revive the Hebrew language, to sustain Jewish culture and to break from the East European diaspora tradition, the Yiddish language and so on. That's the community they were in; they happened to be scattered in different parts of the city, but that was the community. I was partly in that, but I was partly in other communities. You mentioned my uncle. That happened to be in New York, not Philadelphia; but he was disabled and as a disabled person he was able to run a newsstand under New Deal programs – there were some advantages. So he was about the only person in the family who had a job; almost everybody was unemployed working class. So a lot of people worked in the newsstand; I did too, in fact. He himself had never gone past fourth grade, but he was one of the most educated people I ever met in my life. And he attracted around the newsstand a collection of people, many of whom were émigrés from Europe fleeing fascism. They were having all kind of interesting lively discussions about all sorts of things.

That's the late 1930s and early 1940s. I don't know if you know New York but below Union Square there was a row of bookshops – now it's all gentrified with office buildings, and so on – small bookstores, often run by European exiles, many of them exiles from the Spanish Civil War: interesting people, many of them anarchists, driven out of Spain. By the time I was about twelve and was old enough to go to New York by myself, I gravitated to and kind of hung around those stores. I went to the anarchist offices, picked up lots of pamphlets and just became immersed in the achievements of the 1936 anarchist revolution.

Well I love the image of you as a young boy, I think you were ten years old when you wrote an essay about the Spanish civil war.

That's right after the fall of Barcelona, so I can date it perfectly, right at February 1939.

So, a ten year old or an eleven year old obsessed with the rise of fascism.

I was concerned about the rise of fascism. I'm sure it wasn't a great article, although I can remember parts of it.

And so it's continued throughout your life. One thing I don't understand: you're famous for two sets of things, if you like: One is being the father of linguistics. There are not many people who have kind of invented a whole discipline. The other thing you're famous for is your role as a dissident and activist: what are the connections between those two things?

Very little, actually. There are some pretty abstract connections, which I've written about when asked about it.[7] But there are no logical connections; I mean, I could be an algebraic topologist and do the same things in the political sphere and so on. But at its roots there is a connection – which goes back to the Enlightenment, actually, and it was discussed and written about – between a sort of radical politics and a concern for the nature of the human mind. It goes back to Enlightenment ideas and even earlier ones: about creativity being a kind of core component of human nature. Now you look back at the founders of classical liberalism, like Wilhelm von Humboldt – who was a great linguist, too, one of the most important linguists – who was concerned in both his political and linguistic work with sort of a core creative element in human thought which is exhibited very dramatically in human language.[8] He and Rousseau and others argued that that should be the basis for a free society as well. In the case of language it manifests itself in what you and I are now doing. People have this remarkable capacity to produce new thoughts without being provoked by particular stimuli or even internal stimuli; which are new,

---

7   Noam Chomsky, 'Language and Freedom', in James Peck, ed., *The Chomsky Reader*, Pantheon New York, 1987.
8   See Noam Chomsky, *Cartesian Linguistics*, Cambridge University Press, Cambridge, 2009; 'Language and Freedom', 1969, reprinted in *For Reasons of State*, Pantheon, New York, 1973; *Problems of Knowledge and Freedom: The Russell Lectures*, Harper and Row, 1971; James Peck, ed., *The Chomsky Reader*, Pantheon, New York, 1987.

maybe new in the history of the world; they're certainly intelligible to others; appropriate to situations but not caused by them.

It's a kind of creative aspect, which is apparently a core part of human nature, not found elsewhere. Carrying it over to the political sphere, it led to the belief that a society should be based on people carrying out free creative activity under their own control. The way Humboldt put it, kind of nicely, is that 'freedom is undoubtedly the indispensable condition, without which even the pursuits most congenial to individual human nature can never succeed in producing such salutary influences. Whatever does not spring from a man's free choice, or is only the result of instruction and guidance, does not enter into his very being, but remains alien to his true nature; he does not perform it with truly human energies, but merely with mechanical exactness.'[9] Actually Adam Smith said very similar things, so there is that kind of weak but maybe meaningful connection at a pretty abstract level.[10]

Well there's also the kind of importance of rational thought, and as you say the Enlightenment. You don't have truck with this post-modern idea that truth is beyond us, that it's no good even striving for truth, there's just a kind of endless relativism based on where we find ourselves in life. You don't hold with that, do you?

I mean there's a kind of fragment of rationality in it. It's been understood since the seventeenth century that you cannot have certainty in empirical matters. You can have certainty in arithmetic – in fact to be technical about it, even most of mathematics involves assumptions that come from somewhere else. At most you can have conviction, more or less established, but if you're sensible you'll always have an open mind because it might be wrong; you might have to change it radically.

But it's worth striving for, I suppose is the point.

It's certainly worth striving for, that's with everything from physics to human life. So a part of postmodernism is correct, but conventional and uninteresting. To go on and add that 'everything is a social construction', or something, is just ridiculous.

---

9   J.W. Burrow, ed., Wilhelm von Humboldt, *The Limits of State Action*, Cambridge University Press, Cambridge, 1969.
10 Patricia Werhane, *Adam Smith and His Legacy for Modern Capitalism*, Oxford University Press, Oxford, 1991.

Selections from additional interviews

In 2011, Noam Chomsky gave a series of interviews while he was in Australia to accept the Sydney Peace Prize. Below are extracts from some of these interviews.

The first five questions were asked by Shraysi Tandon, Bloomberg TV. I thank Ms Tandon and Mr Derek Pascoe for providing me with the footage so quickly.

The G20 summit is to discuss this week. No doubt all eyes will be on the European debt crisis. What's your opinion of the resolution they've come to and do you think it's on its way to being resolved?

It doesn't look like it's on its way to being resolved. In fact, this morning the Dutch Labor party already withdrew its support.[1] Others may do so because of the Greek referendum. I think there are fundamental questions that ought to be faced. I'm not the only one to raise this; many economists have: should the effort to deal with the crisis in a time of recession be austerity policies or stimulus policies. Europe has opted for austerity policies, but those are almost guaranteed to increase the crisis.

There are funds available for stimulative policies. They would threaten to increase the inflation rate. And the European Central Bank has almost religiously held to a very specific figure on possible inflation – which I think is more a point of religion than of economic sanity … I think that in the short term they should be willing to accept a higher rate of inflation – stimulative policies – rather than austerity programs which are almost guaranteed to increase the damage. Also, there is this kind of odd sense on the part of the creditor countries that they're somehow virtuous, and therefore must maintain their position as net creditors, but that's an arithmetical impossibility. There's a tie between creditors and debtors that

---

1 'Dutch Opposition Warns Greek Referendum Could Unravel EU Deal', *Dow Jones International News*, 2 November 2011.

can't be cut. Martin Wolf of the *Financial Times* has put it simply. He said, 'We can't trade with Mars. Everyone's in together, creditors and debtors.'[2]

Are you optimistic or pessimistic about Obama's plan to revive the stagnating US economy with his jobs act?

It's not a bad plan. I think it should have happened earlier and much greater, but it's a plan that's moving in the right direction. Unfortunately it hasn't a chance of getting through Congress. I don't think anyone thinks it's going to be implemented. But I think it's basically the right idea, and should have been done before. There was a very small stimulus, and – contrary to a lot of propaganda – it was effective. It saved a couple of million jobs according to independent analyses, congressional research offices and so on.[3] Well that's something. But in fact there was no stimulus at all if you look closely. The federal stimulus, which was too small, just about compensated for the decline in spending on the state and local level, so the net effect was essentially no stimulus. Nevertheless, even that slight push to the economy was helpful. And if there had been a substantial stimulus, it could have gotten the country out of the recession.

Now the financial institutions don't like stimulus. They don't want inflation. Okay, that's their problem. But for the economy that doesn't make sense. The financial institutions are far too powerful, they've grown enormously since the 1970s, and their net effect on the economy is very dubious. There's a place for banks in a capitalistic economy; they take what's in your bank

---

2 'Since the world cannot trade with Mars, creditors are joined at the hip to the debtors ... We are all on the same planet. Agree to fix its messes, right now.' Martin Wolf, 'Creditors can huff and puff but they depend on debtors', *Financial Times*, 2 November 2011.

3 Jane G. Gravelle, Thomas L. Hungerford and Marc Labonte, *Economic Stimulus: Issues and Policies*, Congressional Research Service, 9 December 2009; Linda Levine, *Job Loss and Infrastructure Job Creation During the Recession*, Congressional Research Service, 17 March 2009; Christina Romer and Jared Bernstein, *The Job Impact of the American Recovery and Reinvestment Plan*, Chair, Nominee Designate Council of Economic Advisors and Office of the Vice President Elect, 9 January 2009, http://otrans.3cdn.net/45593e8ecbd339d074_l3m6bt1te.pdf; Mark Zandi, *The Economic Impact of the American Recovery and Reinvestment Act*, 21 January 2009, http://www.economy.com/mark-zandi/documents/Economic_Stimulus_House_Plan_012109.pdf; Congressional Budget Office, *Estimated Macroecnomic Impacts of the American Recovery and Reinvestment Act of 2009*, Letter to Senator Charles Grassley, 2 March 2009. http://www.cbo.gov/ftpdocs/100xx/doc10008/03-02-Macro_Effects_of_ARRA.pdf; Council of Economic Advisors, *The Economic Impact of the American Recovery and Reinvestment Act of 2009*, 10 September 2009, http://www.whitehouse.gov/assets/documents/CEA_ARRA_Report_Final.pdf

account, your unused capital, and transfer it to some productive purpose – to somebody who wants to buy a house, or whatever.' During the 1950s and 1960s, the great growth period, when the New Deal regulations and the Bretton Woods system were still in place, that's essentially what banks did. And there was rapid growth – unprecedented. It's never been equaled since. It was also pretty egalitarian; the lowest quintile did about as well as the highest quintile.[4] That all collapsed in the 1970s, for a variety of reasons, and since then there's been a sharp growth in financial institutions which are dedicated not to the role of banks in a healthy state capitalist economy, but rather to manipulations with money. It's dubious that they contribute anything to the economy; they may harm it. In fact there are finally the beginnings of studies by serious economists, like Robert Solow and others that are trying to estimate their net effect, and it's probably harmful to the economy. Solow says, 'the successes probably add little or nothing to the efficiency of the real economy, while the disasters transfer wealth from taxpayers to financiers'.[5]

It has one effect though – it leads to very high concentration of wealth. Over the last three decades, wealth has concentrated very sharply in a tiny fraction of the population. The US is very unequal, but it's largely weighted by a tenth of a per cent of the population – hedge-fund managers, CEOs with huge bonuses and so on. And with concentration of wealth goes concentration of political power. It's a truism as old as Adam Smith.[6] Concentration of political power leads to legislation that increases the concentration of wealth: fiscal policies, the rules of corporate governance, deregulation ... You get a vicious cycle. And for the majority of the population – I'm talking about the United States, although it's not that different elsewhere – since roughly the late seventies and early 1980s, there's been more or less stagnation or decline. There may have been slight increases on occasion, but mostly it's been stagnation or decline. People have been getting by, but by putting in higher working hours, much higher than in Europe.[7] There's also a growing

---

4   Lawrence Mishel, Jared Bernstein and John Schmitt, *The State of Working America, 1998–1999*, Cornell University Press, Ithaca, 1999.
5   Robert M. Solow, 'The Bigger They Are ...' *Daedalus*, Fall 2010.
6   Adam Smith, *The Wealth of Nations*, University of Chicago Press, Chicago, 1976 (original 1776): 'We rarely hear, it has been said, of the combinations of masters, though frequently of those of workmen. But whoever imagines, upon this account, that masters rarely combine, is as ignorant of the world as of the subject ...' (Book I, chapter VIII). 'It cannot be very difficult to determine who have been the contrivers of this whole mercantile system; not the consumers ... but the producers, whose interest has been so carefully attended to ...' (Book IV, Chapter VIII).
7   Juliet B. Schor, *The Overworked American: The Unexpected Decline of Leisure*, Basic Books, New York 1991.

debt, which is of course unsustainable in the long term, asset inflation bubbles and repeated crashes. As soon as the Reagan administration came in and deregulation began, there were repeated financial crises, bailouts of banks and other things that are going to happen with a system like that. It's led to the point where there's now a very serious crisis, of global scope.

I don't happen to like the whole system, but that's a separate question – just accepting the framework of the existing system, it seems to me there are remedies which have been proposed by sensible economists: Joseph Stiglitz, Paul Krugman and other Nobel laureates, namely that there should be a move towards stimulation to increase growth, and the deficit problem will be overcome by growth.[8] In the United States, the real problem is joblessness. The deficit is a very minor problem. That's what the population believes, and I think they're correct.[9] The bankers don't like it, but I think that the right decision would be a joblessness commission, rather than a deficit commission, which is coming out with probably a non-agreement in a couple of weeks.[10] That's the problem.

Speaking of the economy needing more stimulus, do you think that President Obama should turn on the printing presses again and maybe introduce a quantitative easing program?

Well that's the Fed, not Obama. Maybe that's a small fix, maybe not. But I think there really has to be a stimulus, like infrastructure spending. The record of the 1930s is at least suggestive. In the early 1930s, the early part of the Roosevelt administration, there were New Deal programs to stimulate the economy, but they were too small. Also, they came under pressure from Wall Street and other sectors. The economy went right back to recession. Then it picked up again, and started improving. Of course the Second World

---

8   Paul Krugman, 'Nobody Understands Debt', *New York Times*, 1 January 2012: '... families have to pay back their debt. Governments don't – all they need to do is ensure that debt grows more slowly than their tax base. The debt from World War II was never repaid; it just became increasingly irrelevant as the U.S. economy grew, and with it the income subject to taxation.'

9   'In a mid-December CNN poll, the public was asked what should be more important for the Obama administration – reducing the deficit even if that slowed down economic recovery or stimulating economic recovery even if that meant less deficit reduction. By 57–40, the public chose stimulating economic recovery.' Ruy Teixeira, *Public Opinion Snapshot: The Public's Priorities: Jobs vs. the Deficit*. http://www.americanprogress.org/issues/2010/01/snapshot010410.html

10 Eric Lipton, 'Lawmakers Trade Blame As Deficit Talks Crumble', *New York Times*, 21 November 2011.

War came, and that was an enormous economic stimulus. The economy just grew sky-high, and industrial production almost quadrupled.[11]

Although you can't duplicate that experience, since the circumstances are different, I think the general character of it is correct. An economy can be stimulated, for example by infrastructure spending. Now, I don't know if you've been to the United States lately, but infrastructure is in ridiculous shape. I'll just give a personal example. When I came to Australia, I left home on Saturday night without power. The power system crashed. The reason was that there had been a very light snowfall. The infrastructure is so fragile that even in relatively affluent suburbs of Boston, there's no power when it snows. It doesn't have to be that way. If you take a train from Boston to Washington, it's practically a day's trip. It's not very different from when my wife and I took that train sixty years ago. I happened to be in France recently, and I ended up giving talks in southern France. The train from Avignon to De Gaulle Airport, which is about the same distance as Boston to Washington, took I think two hours; and that's true in much of the world.

The United States has had a very serious break up of basic infrastructure. This is harmful to the economy in all sorts of ways, including the burden it imposes on individuals. Those are costs that are usually not calculated by economists as costs but they obviously are. When the auto industry was pretty much nationalised under Obama, who essentially bought it, it could have been reconstituted in such a way as to focus on these problems. It wasn't. I think that's a mistake. But it can be done, and there are options. Take green technology, for example. There's a lot of US investment in green technology, but most of it's going to China because they're setting up conditions in which it's profitable for investors to put in money. It's claimed in the United States that you can't do that because it interferes with the market, but that's total nonsense. Anyone who uses a computer and the internet ought to be aware that it's nonsense: both came basically out of the state sector economy in the 1950s and 1960s, the growth period, in fact right where I was working, M.I.T.[12] That's the kind of place where the basic technology for the I.T. revolution was developed, under Pentagon funding, in fact, and that's the

---

11   Richard DuBoff, *Accumulation and Power: An Economic History of the United States*, M.E. Sharpe, New York, 1989.
12   N. Chomsky, *Rogue States: The Rule of Force in World Affairs*, Pluto Press, London, 2000, pp. 192–8; Kenneth Flamm, *Targeting the Computer: Government Support and International Competition*, Brookings Institution, Washington, 1987; David F. Noble, *Forces of Production: A Social History of Industrial Automation*, Knopf, New York, 1984; Winfried Ruigrok and Rob Van Tulder, *The Logic of International Restructuring*, Routledge, New York, 1995.

way a large part of the advanced economy proceeds. It goes way back to the early stages of British industrialisation, but that's a core part of economic development that could be carried out now for green technology just as it was for electronics-based technology, what's called the I.T. revolution in the 1950s and the 1960s. Or pharmaceuticals, genetic engineering, the biology-based sciences today, again substantially developed within what amounts to the state sector – publicly funded. And the same can be done for other technologies, and that's good for the economy.

Obama is coming to Australia. How important do you think his visit is going to be in light of the rise of China and how Australia is regionally placed?

Well, China has certainly grown spectacularly over the past several decades, but the rise of China, I think is exaggerated. It's a very poor country. If you look at say GDP per capita: they're ninetieth in the IMF figures; they're ninety-fifth in the World Bank figures. Take a look at the UN Human Development Index: they're 101st in terms of human development conditions. China has huge internal problems that the Western developed countries don't have. In fact, China still is largely an assembly plant. So if you calculate the trade deficit between the United States and China in terms of 'value added' trade, which is what should be done, then the trade deficit with China goes down about twenty-five per cent. It you calculate it with surrounding industrial societies such as Japan, Taiwan or South Korea, it goes up by the same amount. I mean they provide parts, components and advanced technology, as do the United States and Europe, and the product is assembled in China. There are some recent studies of the actual value added to an iPod assembled in China. They've concluded that the Chinese part is barely a few per cent.[13]

Now China will move up the technology ladder, they're working hard on it; but it's hard. They also have demographic problems coming along. So they happen to have had a big bulge in the last roughly twenty years, and the workforce has been composed of people in their twenties and thirties, and so on, but that's declining. They're going to have a labour shortage.

---

13 '... trade statistics can mislead as much as inform. For every $300 iPod sold in the U.S., the politically volatile U.S. trade deficit with China increased by about $150 (the factory cost). Yet, the value added to the product through assembly in China is probably a few dollars at most. While Apple's share of value capture is high for the industry, the iPod's overall pattern of value capture is fairly representative.' Greg Linden, Kenneth L. Kraemer, Jason Dedrick, *Who Captures Value in a Global Innovation System? The case of Apple's iPod*, Personal Computing Industry Center (PCIC), University of California, Irvine, June 2007.

That's already beginning.[14] They have environmental problems, resource problems, and a tremendous amount of strife internal to the country. There are tens of thousands of labour actions a year, state repression, and many problems that the West just doesn't have. It's had them, but it doesn't have them now.

Do you think the Chinese growth story is too good to be true? And do you see China having a hard landing?

Well they're managing it pretty well, I have to say. They are cooling off the economy, growth is lowered, and the bureaucrats have done a pretty good job of keeping it going through the recession. So maybe they can manage a soft landing. But I'm really thinking of the overall character of the economy. The idea that it can move to some kind of hegemonic position, replacing the United States, is pie in the sky. There's no challenge. The US has plenty of problems, but I don't see any challenger for global hegemony. The world is definitely getting more diverse, but that was true in the 1970s. I mean, by 1970 the world was already economically kind of tri-polar: North America (largely US-based), Europe (largely German-based) and East Asia (mostly Japan-based at that time, now Japan and China and India on the side). Already in the 1970s Northeast Asia was the most dynamic economic region of the world. Now, in terms of other dimensions, like say military force, of course the United States was in a class by itself.

The United States has military bases in Australia, whereas China doesn't have any. That's multiplied around the world. Brazil, Russia, China and India have grown, and they play a bigger role, as does South America, for example. One of the most dramatic events of this millennium is the move of South America towards integration and independence. It's beginning to face its horrendous internal problems. That's a historic change after 500 years. And it's significant that they're pulling away from the US, and playing a relatively independent role. Maybe something like that is happening in the Middle East. It's too early to say, and it depends on the fate of the whole Arab Spring. These are all developments towards greater diversity in the global society, but it's still highly polarised in the hands of the rich developed societies.

---

14 Xizhe Peng, 'China's Demographic History and Future Challenges', *Science*, vol. 333, no. 6042 pp. 581–7, 29 July 2011.

> The following questions were asked by *Hack!* (JJJ radio) on 3 November 2011.

Yesterday on our show we talked about the world population hitting seven billion. Do you think that in the battle to share the world's resources – space, food, water – people can be optimistic about peace?

Well, it already is a problem. There's about a billion people who are at the edge of starvation; actually, not because of a shortage of food, but because of allocation and distribution. In fact it's been pretty well established that even terrible famines usually aren't the result of lack of food but of failure to get it to reach the right people.[15] The real problem – I think the overwhelming one, beyond access to resources – is too much use of resources that are available, like fossil fuels.

What's your feeling though, Noam Chomsky, people always are interested to know what you think. You're a man that's into your eighties now; are you hopeful that we will have a peaceful society as it grows and uses up more of the world's resources?

Well, whether you're hopeful or not is not really a very interesting question. It's a personal question. But whether you're optimistic or pessimistic you do the same things, so it has no practical consequences. I mean, you can decide that everything is hopeless and give up, in which case you're helping bring about the worst outcome; or you can decide that there's some hope – and I'll do what I can – and you may make things a little better. Between those two choices, it's not a real choice, so it comes out the same way whether you're personally hopeful or not.

We had a really interesting discussion on our show about defining greed, and we had the CEO from the Committee of Melbourne, a group that looks after business interests in the city, saying you need to define what greed is before you criticise it. And he was asking the question: is fifteen per cent return on equity greedy? Where would you draw the line on what greed is, and can it be defined in that way?

---

15 Jean Drèze and Amartya Sen, *Hunger and Public Action* (Oxford, 1989).

I don't think it makes much sense to define greed before proceeding to deal with human problems. We understand it well enough so that it can be dealt with. Now the question you ask is a very specific question: about particular institutions and how they're functioning. You can't criticise people in a competitive market system for being greedy. If they're not, they're out of the system. That's an institutional pathology. We have structures that require participants to carry out what is from a social point of view pathological behaviour. As the CEO of a corporation – and suppose it's a corporation, let's say an energy corporation that's polluting the atmosphere, you must pursue short-term profit and market share. If you don't, you're out and someone else is in. So, the proper criticism is of the institution, not the individual. Talk about greed is kind of beside the point, I think.

Noam you've spoken at length about the way that Western countries have intervened in the affairs of other countries, and especially in regards to the US interventions in Iraq and Afghanistan? Has the regime change in Libya given you hope that Western countries have learnt something from their mistakes? And maybe done things better this time?

First of all, they didn't 'intervene' in Iraq any more than Japan 'intervened' when it bombed Pearl Harbour. That was aggression, which is a major war crime. That's not 'intervention'. In Libya it's a different situation. Take a close look at Libya. It looked at first as if there might be a massacre in Benghazi. NATO did pass a resolution calling for a no-fly zone and protection of civilians. Now the three traditional imperial powers – the United States, Britain and France – observed that resolution for maybe five minutes. It's not imposing a no-fly zone when you start carrying out a bombing of the side in the civil war that you don't want to win. That's something else, and that has to be justified on different grounds. It's not justified under the UN resolution. Was that right or wrong? Well you can debate it, but it's complicated. Bear in mind that the final bombing – which turned the city of Sirte into something like Grozny – caused a big humanitarian catastrophe. NATO was actually attacking the home base of the largest tribe in Libya. Libya's a tribal society. Do they feel liberated? Nobody asks.

But right or wrong with the NATO intervention, what do you think the ramifications of it will be?

It depends what comes out of the wreckage, and it's not at all clear. The head of the transitional council made a speech a couple of days ago, which shocked a lot of people in Benghazi – a lot of the secular people. He called for the imposition of tough Islamic laws: sharia, abandonment of rights for women, and so on. Well, if that prevails there's going to be another civil war.

Yeah, that was a really interesting statement he made, and I think you're right in saying that it shocked a lot of people. If the national transitional council really does go down that path of implementing a harsh sharia law in Libya, do you think a lot of Western leaders will regret their involvement in Libya?

Not in the least. The Western countries, especially Britain, France and the United States, have traditionally tended to support the most extreme Islamic fundamentalists. It's a fact that's not too well known but it should be. What's the most extreme fundamentalist Islamic state in the world? Saudi Arabia. That's the darling of the United States and Britain. In fact they supported it strongly against secular nationalism. The West is not in favour of democracy in the Arab world, and there are good reasons for it.

Well their rhetoric would certainly suggest otherwise.

Yes, but Stalin's rhetoric was also in favour of democracy. You don't pay any attention to the rhetoric of leaders. Think for a minute about the actual circumstances in the world. So take say Egypt, the most important country. About a year ago, ninety per cent of Egyptians regarded the United States and Israel as the main threat that they faced. About eighty per cent are so opposed to US policy that they favoured Iran developing nuclear weapons as a balance to US-Israeli force. So, sure, the rhetoric is all 'we love democracy' and so on, but there's a good reason why the Western powers supported the dictatorships to the last minute.

Several questioners asked versions of the following question. Professor Chomsky responded with a core argument as well as a range of examples in different replies. Below is a composite answer that brings together his core argument as well as some of his examples.

What do you think of the Occupy Wall Street movement and of its going global?

It is unprecedented. I don't know a popular movement like it. And it makes sense because the situation's unprecedented. Take the United States. Throughout its history from the eighteenth century, it has been a developing society. With ups and downs, and not in pretty ways, the tendency has been to grow, develop and industrialise. There's also a kind of psychological aspect to that – there's always a sense that things are going to get better. Our children will live better than we do. That's been the character of American society from the eighteenth century to the 1970s.

In the 1970s it reversed; it started becoming a stagnating society. There was the financialisation of the economy, which pulled a lot of capital away from productive uses. In recent years, fiscal policy, tax policy and the rules of corporate governance have been deregulated, which is a very destructive thing for the economy. This was all tied with the religion called economics, based on theological dogmas like the 'efficient market hypothesis', and 'rational expectations'. They are a kind of closed system, which is internally maybe interesting as a branch of applied mathematics, or something, but it doesn't have much to do with the economy. But it was held with real theological passion. The Nobel Laureate, Joseph Stiglitz, even before he became the chief economist of the World Bank, warned about what he called the 'religion' that 'markets lead to efficient outcomes'. He said, 'Undermining this particular religion was the disturbing observation that countries that seemed to get the prices right – to follow all the advice of the visiting preachers of the free market – too often failed to grow.'[16]

And there was the off-shoring of production – production goes on, but in Mexico, China, Vietnam and elsewhere. These developments are profitable for investors but terrible for the society. Actually that's a kind of nightmare that Adam Smith and David Ricardo warned against.[17] It is now happening. That had the psychological effect you'd expect: a move towards a kind of hopelessness. I'm old enough to remember the Depression, and in the latter part of the 1930s my family was mostly unemployed working class. Objectively the situation was much worse than today, but it was a very hopeful period. There was labour organising, works projects and government-run cultural programs. My unemployed seamstress aunts had support from the union, and it was a generally hopeful period. We felt we'd get out of it somehow. That's not the sense now. In the manufacturing industry,

---

16 Joseph Stiglitz, 'Some Lessons from the East Asian Miracle', *The World Bank Research Observer*, vol. 11, no. 2 (August 1996), pp. 151–77.
17 Adam Smith, *Wealth of Nations*, bk. IV, chap. II; David Ricardo, Principles of Political Economy and Taxation, Dover, 2004, pp. 83–4.

particularly where real unemployment is pretty much at Depression levels, there's a general sense that those jobs aren't coming back. Maybe we'll get some kind of job, but not the real ones that enabled us to move into what's called a middle-class lifestyle. And these feelings are probably accurate, if policies continue like this. So it's basically an unprecedented situation. It should be an unprecedented response.

If the Occupy movements are the first real, large-scale public reaction to what's been happening, you can imagine it moving on to really address fundamental issues. We can't predict the way a popular movement will develop, but the Occupy movements are reflective of serious problems. It's claimed constantly that they don't have demands, but that's not quite true. If you look at the discussions and the documents that are coming out, there are plenty of proposals, most of them realisable. They are reformist, realisable proposals that could be implemented, and some are supported elsewhere.

Now take, say, *Bloomberg Businessweek* a couple of months ago. It proposed getting rid of the Security Exchange Commission (SEC), and starting over from zero, because the SEC is so corrupt, and so tied with the people in control.[18] The Occupy movement actually made a similar suggestion, though more mild than *Bloomberg Businessweek*. It's the same thing with a financial transaction tax, which was just proposed by the Vatican.[19] That's been a proposal of the Occupy movements too, and there are others that are more far-reaching. They're not unrealistic, I think. There are other interesting issues in the area of worker-owned, worker-managed industrial or other enterprises of all kinds. These have actually been developing since the 1970s. Contrary to the tendency that I've described, these have been growing and expanding. There are probably thousands of them, some pretty successful. And that could be implemented on a much larger scale. So, again, when the auto industry was quasi-nationalised, that was a conceivable option. That had been not too far from the consciousness of working people in the rust belt. In fact, they tried it every now and then, but that's a much further-

---

18 '... we now have the ammunition to do what should have been done years ago: terminate the SEC, with extreme prejudice, and in its place construct a new regulatory watchdog for Wall Street that's free of obvious conflicts of interest ... the agency is unsalvageable – and needs to be replaced.' William D. Cohan, 'Destruction at the SEC? Allegations of dumped documents at the agency point to something else that should be scrapped', *Bloomberg Businessweek*, 1 September 2011. http://www.businessweek.com/magazine/destruction-at-the-sec-09012011.html.

19 Pontifical Council for Justice and Peace, *Towards reforming the international financial and monetary systems in the context of global public authority*, Vatican City, 2011. Http://www.pcgp.it/dati/2011-11/08-999999/Towards%20Reforming%20ENG.pdf.

reaching option.[20] It's not like putting band-aids on immediate problems like the SEC. Not that there's anything wrong with them; I think those things should be fixed up, but there are much deeper problems which maybe can be addressed much more fundamentally. These problems have changed many aspects of society that are egalitarian. They've caused harm to decent growth and so on.

Actually, one major issue, which is kind of shockingly ignored, is the environmental issue. You take a look at say the *Financial Times* in the last couple of days. It's the world's best business newspaper in my opinion. They've had major article after article praising the fact that the United States now has maybe 100 years of internal energy supplies – fossil fuels, hydrocarbons.[21] And they describe the wonderful things this is going to do. Well there's another headline that could be there: that there are 100 years to act to ensure that there won't be any decent survival for our grandchildren, because that's what it amounts to. And those issues are part of the Occupy movement. Until they become part of much more general consciousness, the long-term consequences for the world are not very pretty.

Well, can it happen? That depends on whether the Occupy movements can proceed with what's beginning to happen, but go on. One of the exciting things just to watch and participate in is the way they're just forming functioning democratic communities: developing links, making associations, cooperative kitchens, all kinds of things which are like the germs of a decent society. It's kind of developing spontaneously – people are participating in it, learning and so on. Well, if those can be strengthened, sustained and maintained against the certain repression which is coming – those with power don't give it up easily – it could have a really major effect of historic significance. That's an optimistic view. I don't think it's totally unrealistic, but even if that's not reached I think it's already made a major change.

The very fact that it's taken place has already left I think a legacy of change that's going to remain. Whatever their outcome is, it's not going to be easy to go on. It's necessary to recognise that victories are not won quickly. There are short term issues where they can make a big difference. Take the United States again; you can, I'm sure, find analogies here. In the United States

---

20 Thirty years ago in Youngstown, Ohio, US Steel was about to shut down a major facility that was at the heart of the town's life. There were substantial protests by the workforce and community, then an effort led by labour lawyer and activist Staughton Lynd to bring to the courts the principle that stakeholders should have the highest priority. The effort failed that time, but with enough popular support it could succeed. Staughton Lynd, *Living Inside Our Hope*, Cornell University Press, Ithaca, 1997.

21 e.g. Ed Crooks, 'The Pendulum swings', *Financial Times*, 1 November 2011, p. 6.

there's a bipartisan deficit commission. It's due to come out with its results towards the end of this month. It'll probably be deadlocked. If you've been watching what's happened in Washington, you know why. It'll probably be deadlocked, at which point automatic procedures go into operation, which in fact are a kind of dagger aimed at the heart of the society. It's planned that way, it's a trap. There's a trap set up which will do exactly the opposite of what the population wants.[22]

What the population thinks about the deficit is very clear. The United States is a very heavily polled society with a ton of information about it. A large majority of the population thinks that the deficit is not a major problem. It's joblessness that's the major problem.[23] I think they're right, and they're the overwhelming majority. So if democracy was functioning, you'd have a joblessness commission, not a deficit commission, but the financial institutions say it's the deficit, so that's what Washington does, independent of the public. So let's just take a look at the deficit. Well, the public has opinions about that too. It says the deficit should be dealt with by restoring the proper form of taxation on the very wealthy – the form that was in place during the high growth period of the 1950s and 1960s. That's been dismantled; by now taxes on the super rich are ridiculously low. And the public wants them returned. Secondly, the people don't want the benefits systems attacked at all, they want them protected, and in fact to grow. The benefits are not very substantial in the United States – they're not like Australia – but they do exist. And the public doesn't want them attacked. Well you can be pretty sure that the bipartisan commission, if it has an outcome, will do the opposite. It will maintain the outrageous tax cuts on the rich, that the Bush administration initiated following from the Reagan years, and it will harm the limited benefits programs.

Actually there's another point, which isn't mentioned in the media because the financial institutions don't want it. There's a very straightforward way of getting rid of the US deficit – a very straightforward way.[24] Simply institute the kind of healthcare system that other industrial countries have:

---

22 'By law, the special congressional committee's inability to reach an agreement will lead to $1.2 trillion in automatic spending cuts over 10 years to the military and domestic programs, to start in 2013.' Jennifer Steinhauer and Eric Lipton, 'Deficit deal again eludes Congress as fallout looms', *International Herald Tribune*, 22 November 2011.
23 Ruy Teixeira, *Public Opinion Snapshot: The Public's Priorities: Jobs vs. the Deficit*. http://www.americanprogress.org/issues/2010/01/snapshot010410.html.
24 On a health care system of the kind in other industrial countries eliminating the deficit (actually creating a surplus), the best work is Dean Baker's many articles at www.cepr.net.

Australia or Canada or France. They differ, but there are things in common among them. They have some kind of national healthcare system. It's highly efficient – there are plenty of things wrong with it, you know that better than I do, but compared with the US system of privatised, more or less unregulated healthcare, it's quite efficient, and also much more humane. Per capita, healthcare costs in the United States are about twice as high as other industrial societies, and the outcomes are pretty poor. It means tens of millions of people just don't have healthcare. Or maybe they get it in an emergency room or something like that. It's extremely inefficient, very expensive and quite savage. In fact if the US simply adopted a healthcare system like other industrial countries – for example by expanding Medicare, the national medical insurance program for the elderly, to the whole population – that would very sharply cut the deficit. In fact it would eliminate it, and actually leave a surplus, but that can't be discussed, even though the population wants it, because the financial institutions are against it.[25] And they now have such inordinate power that they determine what happens in Washington.

Well, that's something that the Occupy movements could deal with very quickly. If they can reach a substantial enough scale, they could compel the large majority opinion in the United States to influence policy within the next few weeks. That's literally the case. I don't know if it'll happen, it probably won't, but it could happen in the very short term.

The Occupy movements are beginning to formulate and articulate the anger, frustration, and fear that the population has felt, but has not had a way to carry forward in some constructive way. And it will leave a kind of legacy. If you think about other movements, say the civil rights movements, they didn't win with a single march on Washington or Martin Luther King making a speech – that's mythology. The civil rights movement in the United States goes way back, but really hard work on it began in the 1930s and 1940s. It was beaten back and repressed violently. In the early 1960s, black students began sitting in in lunch counters; freedom riders began trying to register voters. It was pretty brutal. A lot of people were killed; there was a lot of violence. But they kept at it, and within a couple of years

---

25 Eric Kleefeld, 'Poll: Public Still Doesn't Like Health Care Bill – And Still Like Public Option, Medicare Buy-In', *Talking Points Memo*, 22 December 2009, http://tpmdc.talkingpointsmemo.com/2009/12/poll-public-still-doesnt-like-health-care-bill----and-still-like-public-option-medicare-buy-in.php; Katherine Seelye, *New York Times*, 22 December 2009; CBS News Poll, 'The President, Health Care, and Terrorism', 6–10 January, 2010, http://www.cbsnews.com/htdocs/pdf/poll_obama_011110.pdf. Research poll, January 19, 2010, commissioned by pro-Democrat organisations.

there was a large scale popular movement. Then you could get the march on Washington, Martin Luther King's 'I Have a Dream' speech and voter registration legislation – which was not an insignificant victory, though a very limited one and far short of what King had in mind, or what any of us should have in mind. But that's the way popular movements develop, that's the way society becomes more civilised.

This question was asked by Maria Tran, filmmaker, on 4 November 2011.

What are some of the simple things even kids can do for peace?

I'm amazed by how many letters I get asking that question, and there is no single answer. I mean, the first thing young people have to do is find out who they are. It's a search for who you are; you have to try a lot of things, find out what your interests are, what your commitments are, what kind of life you want to lead. There is a lot of exploration and searching that needs to be done. And as that search proceeds, you'll figure it out for yourself. I never gave advice like that to my own children and if I had given it they would have been smart enough to not listen. They've found their own ways, and they've surprised me in terrific ways, but they had to figure it out for themselves. Like we all do. Nobody can tell you.

Index

9/11 terrorist attacks
    compared to 'the first 9/11' in Chile 65
    consequences of US response 9–10, 13

abstractions in linguistic theories xv–xvii
academic institutions
    activism 125–6
    military funding 124–5
    role 124–7
Adams, John Quincy 7–8, 67
Afghanistan, US invasion of
    adverse effects 12–13
    alternatives 12–13
    extension under Obama administration 111
    reasons 11–12
Africa
    see also South Africa
    changing US interest 60–1, 110
African Americans
    civil rights actions 151–2
    repression and exploitation 24–5
al-Qaeda
    evidence of responsibility for 9/11 12
    missed opportunity to isolate 13
Amnesty International 47, 48, 51
anarchism
    Noam Chomsky's early contact 134
    principles 117–18
Anglosphere
    colonial atrocities 1, 7
    intellectual journals 8
apartheid in South Africa
    terrorism in opposition 80–1
    US role in support 49–50
April 6 Movement 52
Arab Spring 51–2, 74
    future 143
    labour movements 52, 103
assassination campaign by US
    Anwar al-Awlaki 23–4, 111
    extension to 'suspects' 111
    Osama bin Laden 9–11, 78, 110
Australia
    in Afghanistan 111
    healthcare system 131, 150–1
    hypothetical national interest 109
    media reports of human rights abuses 27
    mining industry 129
    nuclear proliferation 19–20
    response to Indonesian invasion of East Timor xi–xii, 14–15, 50
    study of Aboriginal languages 9, 98
    support for US policy in Middle East 45, 81–2, 84, 85, 113

B'Tselem human rights group 26–7, 85
bin Laden, Osama
    assassination 9–10, 11, 78, 110
    reason for Afghanistan invasion 12
    US actions assisting 13
Blair, Tony 4, 45
boycott, divestment and sanctions (BDS) 49–51
    effectiveness 51
    South Africa 49–50
    use against Israel 50–1
Britain
    deterrent to US power 66–7
    Northern Ireland 13, 133–4
    nuclear weapons 19
    opposition to democracy in Middle East 71, 74, 146
    relationship with US 52–3, 55, 59
    role in postwar Europe 68
    sympathy towards fascism 3
    terrorist state 80
Bundy, McGeorge 14, 63
Bush administrations
    compared to Obama 73, 110–11
    economic policies 150
    invasion policies 4, 11–13, 73
    Middle East peace 33, 39, 43
    NATO expansion 72
    war on terror 25–6, 110–11
    war crimes 42
Camp David peace negotiations 30, 31–2, 37
capitalism
    and anarchism 117
    disadvantages 132
    globalisation 77
    pathology 130, 132
    role of banks 138–9
    slavery 24
    supposed benefits 131–2
chemical warfare, US use in Vietnam 13–14
China
    economic development 142–3
    'loss' to US 58, 61
    potential as a global power 57, 142–3
Chomsky, Noam
    advice to children 152

economic views 129–32, 137–42
education 93–4
Jewish heritage xiii–xiv, 90–1, 134
linguistic theories xiv–xvii, 95, 97–100
political activism xi–xiv
political influences 91–3, 94, 134–6
response to criticism 11, 89
Clinton administration
   Indonesian invasion of East Timor 15, 50
   Middle East peace negotiations 34, 37, 43, 85
   Northern Ireland 133
   rhetoric of idealism 73
communism
   impact on Noam Chomsky 92
   in Cuba 67
   in Europe 68
   in Indonesia 61–3
consumerism
   fabrication of 115–16
   global warming and 116–17
Cuba
   1898 'liberation' by US 67
   attempt by US to overthrow government 64
   public opposition to US policies 67–8
   US war of terror 66

Dayan, Moshe 36–7
democracy
   see also democratic peace
   and anarchism 117
   and capitalism 132
   in Europe 68–9
   in Latin America 63–7
   in the Arab world 54, 71, 74–5, 146
   in the US 86–7, 104–7, 149–50
   and neoliberalism 119–20
   and the Occupy movement 149
   US and European opposition 39, 52, 55, 62–3, 62–7, 146
   Western concept 39
democratic peace, thesis of 2, 107

East Timor
   Australian attitude xi–xii, 14–15, 50
   Noam Chomsky's activism vi, xi–xiii
   US position on Indonesian invasion 14–16, 50
Egypt
   attitudes towards Iran 52–3, 54–5, 146
   relations with Israel 30–2, 51–3, 75
   secular nationalism 71
   threat to US control of Middle East 75
Einstein, Albert 17
environmental damage
   impact of capitalism 116–17
   Occupy movement's views 149
   oil and gas exploration 22, 149
Europe
   culture of war 1–2, 107
   debt crisis 137–8
   NATO's role in preventing independence 69
   postwar destruction of resistance movements 68

fascism
   Japanese 4
   Noam Chomsky's early fears 92–3, 135
   US and British tolerance 3–4
Fernandes, Clinton vii
fossil fuels, dangers of 129–30, 149
freedom fighters as 'terrorists' 78–81
fundamentalism
   Islamic 71, 146
   US religious 86–7, 105–6

Gaza
   Cast Lead bombing 41–2
   Israeli kidnappings 28–9
   need for welfare support 43–4
   relationship to West Bank 35–6, 53, 75, 83, 114
   siege 40–2, 85
   US-Israeli policy 33, 75, 83
   withdrawal of settlers 48–9
genocide
   denial in relation to Native Americans 8
   in East Timor xi–xii, 14–15
   of Mayans in Guatemala 64
   potential in Gaza 85
global warming 20–2
   action by indigenous communities 22
   consumerism 116–17
   rising threat 21, 106
   US failure to act 21–2, 106–7
Gorbachev, Mikhail 72
Grand Area, the 58–60
   Latin America 63–4
greed, defining 144–5
Guantanamo [Bay] 110–11

Hale, Kenneth 9, 98–9
Halle, Morris 97, 98
Hamas 38
   agreement with Fatah 53, 75
   observation of truce 40–1
   response to Roadmap to peace 38
   role in post-election coup 39–40
human rights
   see also 'unpeople'
   Al Mezan Centre 29

East Timor vi
Indigenous rights 8–9
Israeli group 26–7, 85
Human Rights Watch 47

illegitimate power 129–30
indigenous communities
see also genocide
action on global warming 22
restoration of language 8–9
Indochina
see also Southeast Asia; Vietnam
US action to protect interests 61–2
Indonesia
economic nationalism 61–3
invasion of East Timor xi–xii, 14–16, 50
US action to protect interests 61, 62–3
intellectuals
failure to speak out on East Timor xi–xii, 16
genocide denial 8
treatment as dissidents 5–6, 101–2
international law
application to Western powers 11
Israeli settlements 36–7
juveniles 25–7
Iran
British and US intervention 71
Egyptian views 52–3, 54–5, 74–5, 146
nuclear strategy 17–19, 54
US attitude 18–19, 53–4
Islamic fundamentalism
in Libya 146
US and British support 71, 146
Israel
basis of relationship with US 71–2
compared to South Africa 44, 49–50
development of Noam Chomsky's views on xiii–xiv
expansionist policies 30–1, 35–7, 42–3, 44, 83–5, 114
human rights groups 26–7, 85
imprisonment of Palestinians 28–9
kidnapping of civilians 28–9
marginalisation of Palestinians 46, 85, 114
negotiations with Egypt 29–32
nuclear war risk 17–18, 31–2
peace negotiations with Palestinians 29–46, 82–5
see also two-state solution for Middle East
pressure on US to change attitude 46–7
treatment of Bedouins 27–8, 30

Japan
fascist policies 4
role assigned in postwar US planning 61
self-defence argument for Pearl Harbor bombing 4–5

Kapeliouk, Amnon 31, 49
Kennan, George 60
Khadr, Omar 25–6
Khmer Rouge
criticised xii
US recognition 14–15
Kissinger, Henry 16, 31, 32, 65
Israeli peace negotiations 31, 32

Latin America
see also Cuba
the 'First 9/11' in 65
US role in repression in 6, 63–6
Lenneberg, Eric 97, 98
Libya
Islamic fundamentalism 145
NATO's role 145
linguistics
Cartesian 120–1
developments 96–100, 122–4
Noam Chomsky's theories xiv–xvii, 97–100, 123–4

Mandela, Nelson 50, 81
Manne, Robert xii
media
balance and objectivity 118–19
regulation 119–20
Middle East
see also Iran, Israel, Palestine, two-state solution for Middle East
causes of nuclear tension 17–18
Islamic fundamentalism 71, 146
'Nixon doctrine' for control 71–2
nuclear free zone proposal 19–20
significance of energy resources 59, 71, 74
US and Israel seen as major threats 74
US policy focus 70–2
minors, breaches of rights of
by Israel 26–7, 29
by US 25–6
Monroe Doctrine 8, 66–7
Muste, A.J. 2–3, 5

Nader, Ralph 102–3
national interest
morality of 109–10
whose interests? 109
nationalism
economic, in Indonesia 61–3
Palestinian 31–5, 42–5, 83, 112
see also two-state solution for Middle East

threat in Middle East 70–2
Native Americans
  colonial extermination 7
  protests at use of Geronimo's name 11
  significance of language 8–9
NATO
  expansion after Soviet collapse 72
  intervention in Libya 145
  postwar role in Europe of 69
nature, legislated rights for 22
neoliberalism
  and capitalism 77, 120
  distortion of democracy 119–20
  in Egypt 52, 103
  in the US 24, 86, 103, 119–20
Netanyahu, Binyamin 27, 44–5, 83–5, 112
nuclear war
  continuing threat 2, 17–20
  Iran's deterrence strategy 18–19, 53–4
  Israeli actions 17–18, 31–2
  risk from US actions in Pakistan 10–11
nuclear weapons free zones
  support in Middle East 54–5
  US and British obstruction 19–20, 55
Nuremberg trials 3, 9–10

Obama administration
  assassination strategy 11, 23, 111
  compared to previous US governments 43, 110–12
  declining popularity in Arab world 73
  economic policies 132, 138, 140, 141
  failure to oppose Israel 41–2, 43
  Noam Chomsky's opinion 110–12
  obstruction of nuclear free zones 19–20
  use of military commissions 25–6, 111
  vetoing of peace proposals 41, 42, 113
Occupied Territories *see also* Israel, Palestine
  feasibility of Israeli withdrawal 48–9
  Israeli plans 83–5
Occupy Movement vii, 103, 146–52
  compared to civil rights movement 151–2
  potential power 149, 151–2
  proposals for change 148
Operation Geronimo 11
optimism 144

pacifism
  absolute 2
  revolutionary *see* revolutionary pacifism
Palestine
  see also two-state solution for Middle East
  international acceptance 42–3
  Israeli appropriation of territory 35–7, 83–5
  kidnap of citizens 28–9
  removal of elected government 28, 39–40
  struggle for nationhood 31–5
  UNESCO membership bid 43, 44, 81, 83
peace negotiations in Middle East
  see also Israel, Palestine, two-state solution for Middle East
  current options 45–6
  Israeli preconditions 44, 82–4, 113–14
  US role 32–3, 82–4, 112–14
Peace Prize *see* Sydney Peace Prize
Pearl Harbor bombing 4–5
Peres, Shimon 33, 35, 112
presumption of innocence, doctrine of
  abandonment 24, 110
  selective application 9–10

Quadrant magazine xii

Ramos-Horta, Jose vi
Reagan administration
  attitude to terrorism 25, 79
  economic policies 119, 140, 150
  South African apartheid 49–50, 81
  South American atrocities 64, 65–6
  support for Pakistan 10–11
Republican Party, US 21, 86, 102, 104–7
Resolution 242 32–3, 34–5
revolutionary pacifism 2–16
  central tenet of 13
  proposed by A.J. Muste 2–3
Ricardo, David 76–7, 147
Rocker, Rudolf 117
Roy, Arundhati vii
Russell, Bertrand v–vi, 17

Said, Edward vi, 23
  memorial lecture by Noam Chomsky 23–55
Santa Cruz massacre 14, 16
Schlesinger, Arthur 4, 64, 66, 67
September 11 attacks *see* 9/11 terrorist attacks
Shafi, Haidar Abdel 34, 35
Shalit, Gilad 28, 40
'Sharon plan' 44, 84–5
Slavery of African Americans 24–5
Smith, Adam
  continuing relevance of economic theories 76–7
  on division of labour 122
  on neoliberalism 120
South Africa
  terrorism 50, 80–1
  US attitude 49–50
  use of sanctions 49–50
South America *see also* Latin America
  increasing independence from US of 73–4
Southeast Asia *see also* Indochina; Indonesia; Vietnam

postwar US view of 60
US action to remove threat of
  independence in 61–3
Soviet Union, collapse of 69
Sydney Peace Prize
  citation for 2011 award v
  lecture 1–16
  Noam Chomsky's acceptance speech
    17–22
  previous winners 89

Tea Party, the 103–4
technology
  academic concerns about use 125–7
  China's needs 57, 142–3
  green 141–2
  postwar development 95–6
  state role 70, 125, 131–2, 141–2
terrorist activities
  9/11 attacks 9
  African National Congress 80–1
  British response in Northern Ireland 13
  definition 25–6, 80
  freedom fighters 78–81
  US violence 10–11
two-state solution for Middle East
  1976 UN resolution 32
  1993 Declaration of Principles 34–5
  Australia's stance 45, 81–2, 84, 85
  European attitude 45, 84
  Israeli response 33, 38–9, 82–5, 112–14
  Noam Chomsky's views 82
  Oslo agreements 33–5
  US opposition 32–3, 82–4, 112–14

UNESCO application by Palestine 43, 44,
  81, 83
United Nations
  fear in US 87
  ideals 1, 7
  Indonesian invasion 16
  Palestinian relief work 42–3
  role in Middle East peace process 38, 42,
    44, 114
United States
  auto industry 132, 141, 148
  change in economic status 76–7
  civil war 78–9
  decline as global power 57–8, 69, 76–7
  economic policies 129–31, 138–42, 147,
    149–50
  effect of Second World War 58, 95, 140–1
  fear and paranoia 87–8, 106
  healthcare system 131, 150–1
  infrastructure problems 141
  military spending 69–70
  neoliberalism 24, 86, 103, 119–20

political movements 86, 103–7
reasons for interest in Middle East 70–1
religious fundamentalism 86–7, 105–6
role in Middle East peace negotiations
  32–3, 82–4, 112–14
universality, principle of 5
'unpeople', concept of 23–5, 27, 28
US Constitution
  Fifth Amendment 24
  Fourteenth Amendment 24, 25

Vietnam war
  opposition 14, 51
  protection of US interests 61–2
  use of chemical warfare 13–14
violence
  urban 133
  ways of overcoming 133–4

Wampanoag language revival 8–9
West Bank
  see also Gaza, Palestine
  removal of settlers 48–9
  separation from Gaza 35, 53, 75, 83, 114
  settlement by Israel 35, 36, 43, 46, 83–5
  status in peace negotiations 33, 112, 114
world order, changing contours of 57–88
  decline in US global power 57–8, 60, 69
  post Second World War US planning
    58–61
  Southeast Asia's assigned role 60–3

Yglesias, Matthew 11